McSWEENEY'S No. 48

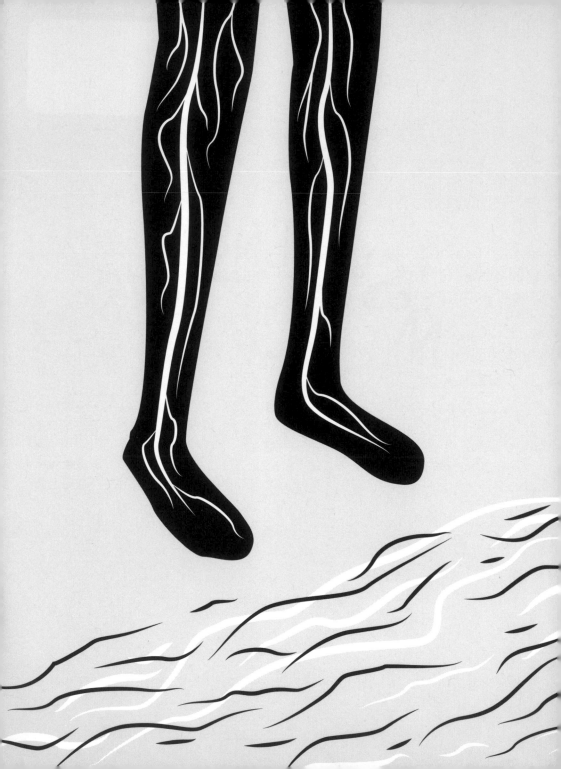

REBECCA
CURTIS

JOHN
McMANUS

BORIS
CVJETANOVIĆ

GORDAN
NUHANOVIĆ

ZORAN
FERIĆ

TÉA
OBREHT

GEORGI
GOSPODINOV

ISMET
PRCIC

DAMIR
KARAKAŠ

OLJA
SAVIČEVIĆ

DAN
KEANE

BEKIM
SEJRANOVIĆ

ETGAR
KERET

JULIA
SLAVIN

KELLY
LINK

MIRIAM
TOEWS

VALERIA
LUISELLI

TEA
TULIĆ

PAULA
WHYMAN

© 2014 McSweeney's Quarterly Concern and the contributors, San Francisco, California. INTERNS & VOLUNTEERS: Alexandra Anderson, Anna Lee, Ben Parra, Brenda Wang, Brian Tich, Chloe Farrell, Connor Greer, Hannah Gold, Jennifer Ehrlich, Joey Becker, Josephine Demme, Kenna O'Rourke, Moss Turpan, Nelson Arnous, Ratik Asokan, Rebecca Landau, Sara Fan, Seraphie Allen, Sophie Chabon, Tony Tran, Will Conley. ALSO HELPING: Andi Winnette, Annie Wyman, Ian Delaney, Casey Jarman, Sam Riley, Clara Sankey, Sunra Thompson, Brian Christian, Ruby Perez. WEBSITE: Chris Monks. SUPPORT: Jordan Karnes. ART DIRECTOR: Dan McKinley. COPY EDITOR: Will Georgantas. PUBLISHER: Laura Howard. MANAGING EDITOR: Daniel Gumbiner. EXECUTIVE EDITOR: Jordan Bass. EDITOR: Dave Eggers.

COVER AND INTERIOR ILLUSTRATIONS: Sunra Thompson.

Printed in Michigan at Thomson-Shore.

The translation of the Croatian section was supported by a grant from the Ministry of Culture of the Republic of Croatia.

ALIENATION AND ABSURDITY,
AT HOME AND ABROAD
SIX STORIES FROM CROATIA
With photos by Boris Cvjetanović

DEAR MCSWEENEY'S,

I don't know if you know the people at Gillette, but, while they might know blade technology, their people skills suck. Sorry to be blunt, but I spent a lot of time on the phone Tuesday afternoon while on my break at the urinal-cake place trying to tell them that they should have a warning label on their Fusion blades, and I just kept getting shuttled around from one department to the other. And why is their hold music "Suspicious Minds," by Elvis??

The reason I called was that I'd been using one of their four-blade Gillette Fusion Platinum Razor every day for eighteen days—at which point it turned out the razor was shot. I now think that the company should put some sort of warning on their packages, like "Change Your Blade After 18 Days, Change Your Life!"© (With or without the exclamation point.) My question to you is this: what do you think would be fair to ask for in terms of compensation for this idea?

If you know anyone in their Blade Management or Blade Marketing departments, anyway, I'd appreciate having a name to drop.

Thanks as always,

GARY RUDOREN
JERUSALEM

DEAR MCSWEENEY'S,

When you come visit us in Shanghai, here's what we'll do: we'll take you down to the river to gawk at the skyline, and we'll wave a hand across the sparkling neon towers and say, "Thirty years ago, this was all a cow pasture." That's what everyone says. I wasn't here thirty years ago but I've seen a few pictures. There were plenty of buildings back then—they were just small and forgettable. But the important thing here is the story. In Shanghai we're thirteen hours ahead of you, *McSweeney's*. History is a slippery thing when you live in the future.

My first Shanghai job, upon arriving last fall, was as a movie extra. Here in the future anyone with a Western face can be in pictures. I scrolled through dozens of online casting calls until I found one for "Office Workers in Newspaper Industry." My own personal history exactly. I e-mailed a photo, and a couple days later I signed a contract in front of a young woman working alone in a tiny office on the top floor of a drafty twenty-story building. Lizzie was her English name. Lizzie gave me a cup of warm water and we watched together as, far below us, a backhoe drove through an old house without a roof.

The movie turned out to be a music video for an aspiring Taiwanese pop star. The set was inside a warehouse deep in the city's endless gray suburbs, doubtless built on a former cow pasture. Lizzie herded us dozen or so extras to our desks in a fake office surrounded by tall windows without glass. My colleagues were from France, Poland, Uzbekistan, even Iraq. Half a dozen Chinese extras were instructed to sit in the back. The director, a former Taiwanese opera star with industrial-grade zippers on his jeans, explained in limited English that the video was for a song about having the courage to chase your dreams.

We fake-worked in silence as the pop star went about his boring day: shuffling papers, drinking a Pepsi, walking down a flight of stairs. The pop star was handsome, with the deerlike eyes and elven face of an anime hero, but he was not a natural actor. He seemed nervous, moved stiffly. "More free," the director told him. "Like you're not in China." They laughed together and the pop star tried again.

After lunch we returned to the office for the next scene. The director told us to leap up from our desks, fall to the carpet, and then scramble for the exits. "Very scared," he said, bugging his eyes in mock terror. We nodded: here was our chance to really act. The film crew sprinkled drywall dust on top of the hanging lights and then hid under our desks. Cameras rolled. Dust fell. The crew shook the desks. We stumbled and fled. Something seemed eerily familiar. "Not 9/11," the director explained. "Like 9/11, but not." We walked back to our seats, straightened our desks, and panicked again.

On an afternoon break Lizzie and I sat drinking warm water on a backstage bench. I was the only American on set, and I felt lonely and sad and a little queasy about play-acting such a terrible national memory. September 11 changed everything, I told Lizzie. We aren't the same country anymore. We're more afraid now, more divided. I don't know if this was all true, but it certainly felt true, sitting there halfway around the world with a rug-burned elbow. I apologized to Lizzie for getting so emotional. "It's all right," she said. "I never knew."

For the last shot of the day we repeated the not-9/11 scene, except with a camera on a dolly swooping in on the pop star. While we panicked and ran, the pop star rose slowly and calmly from his desk, shouldered his bag, and turned toward the empty windows with a defiant glint in his eye. His dream was to be a war photographer, the director explained, and now he had the opportunity to chase that dream.

That was months ago. The music video has yet to appear. Lizzie has since chased her own dreams to college in England; on WeChat she posts photo after photo of very old buildings. Here in Shanghai the world's second-tallest building is almost complete. At night we go down to the river to watch the welding sparks fall from the top floors and burn out in the dark.

Meanwhile, *McSweeney's*, we await the anniversary of the Tiananmen Square massacre. (That's up in Beijing; in Shanghai our largest public spaces are mostly malls.) We presume there will be no ceremony, but I hear they've ringed the square in a new heavyweight fence painted gold. And then last week they arrested a famous reporter who'd been one of the protesters twenty-five years ago. She's seventy now. The government said she'd stolen a top-secret document and published it for everyone to read.

The document is a list of prohibited Western values, particularly something called "historical nihilism." Historical nihilists are dangerous, the document says, because they refuse to believe in

the officially accepted past. The arrested reporter appeared on state TV to say yes, she had stolen the document. Or at least we think it was her. State TV blurred out her face. Whoever it was behind the blur said her actions had brought great harm to the nation, and that she was very sorry, and that she would never do such a thing again.

DAN KEANE
SHANGHAI, CHINA

DEAR MCSWEENEY'S,
I am writing to you after returning from the hospital with my ten-year-old son, Magnus.

Last night Magnus told me he had a bump on his hand.

"It's probably a callus," I said, thinking how young and pure and sweet he was, just to be getting his first callus.

"I have tons of calluses," Magnus said. "This is different. And it hurts."

I looked at the bump, which was near the base of Magnus's thumb and didn't in fact look like a callus at all. So this morning we went to the pediatrician, who examined Bump—by now I felt it had a separate identity—and asked Magnus how long it had been there.

"Since second grade," Magnus said.

"What grade are you in now?" asked the pediatrician.

"Fifth," Magnus said.

"I think he means fourth," I said quickly.

The pediatrician looked confused. "Do you know what grade you're in?" he asked Magnus.

"Yes, he does," I said. "What I mean is, I think the bump has been there since fourth grade, not second."

"I'm pretty sure it's been there since second grade," Magnus said, and I made a sort of helpless gesture meant to convey to the pediatrician that I'm really an excellent mother but certain things get past me.

The pediatrician thought that Magnus should get a CT, and sent us over to the radiology department of the hospital, where I had to explain to a further six layers of medical personnel that, yes, Bump appeared to be entering its fourth year of existence, but that fact in and of itself was really not an accurate reflection of my parenting skills.

Finally a technician whisked Magnus and Bump off for the CT and then Magnus and I met with the radiologist in his office. He had the CT scan of Magnus's hand up on a monitor on his desk.

"It's not a cyst or a tumor," the radiologist said. "It appears to be an embedded splinter."

Magnus looked at me.

"Oh, I'm sure it's not a splinter," I said.

"I'm sure it is," the radiologist said. He tapped the monitor with his pencil.

"See that little object? It's obviously been embedded in his hand for several years."

Now, *McSweeney's*, you have to understand that Magnus is an anxious person and has several phobias. The most prominent, long-standing, fear-provoking phobia is that he'll get a splinter and that the splinter will stay stuck in his body for years—something that I have assured him many times is impossible.

"I see," I said weakly.

The radiologist went on for a little while about foreign-body granuloma and soft-tissue encapsulation and protein absorption and then I said, "But you don't know for sure it's a splinter."

The radiologist stroked his beard thoughtfully. "What else could it be?"

"A thorn," I said, feeling like a balladeer. "Maybe a thistle."

"It's not organic," the radiologist said. "I'd guess it's metal."

"A staple, then," I said. I turned to Magnus. "It's probably a staple."

"It's a splinter," the radiologist said firmly, "and at this point there's nothing we can do about it and nothing to worry about." We left shortly afterward.

In the car, I talked about irony quite a bit. I talked about the definition of irony, and how rare and interesting it was to find an event that was truly ironic. I talked about verbal irony versus situational irony, and dramatic irony. I talked about irony's rich literary history, how even Shakespeare used it, even Sophocles. I talked about irony all the way to McDonald's.

Magnus ate with one hand and stretched the other open on the tabletop so he could look at Bump. "I bet I got this at Cooley Park," he said.

"I don't know why you would think that," I said, although I had thought the same thing immediately. Cooley Park is a playground where we stopped once on a road trip and I forced my sons to play even though the playground equipment was at least forty years old and the swings hung from rusty chains twenty feet long and the seesaws were made of rotting wood bristling with splinters the size of toothpicks. It was also, inexplicably, paved with crushed gravel. The boys still have nightmares about it sometimes.

Magnus closed his hand. "You only ever take us to McDonald's when you feel bad for making us do something," he said.

I pointed a French fry at him. "That is one-hundred percent not true. We also come here when I'm hungover."

A woman at the table next to us was struggling to open a ketchup packet and when I said that, she squeezed the packet so hard it flew out of her fingers and onto the floor. I gave her my good-mother look.

On the way home, Magnus was pretty quiet except for once at a stoplight, when he asked me if it was true that carpenter bees don't sting. He was clearly working his way mentally through ten years' worth of things that I'd told him and that Bump had now cast into serious doubt.

"Yes," I said, "that's true. But I may as well tell you that the car doesn't really have a backup gas tank." (One of Magnus's other phobias is the car running out of gas.)

We rode the rest of the way home in a silence as thick as a stack of towels.

Something else the radiologist told us was that the splinter would eventually work its way out, but he didn't know when. It might happen in a year, or many years, possibly even decades. The splinter may not come out of Magnus's hand until Magnus is older than I am now. Imagine that! At least I'll be free of his obviously growing skepticism, by then.

And maybe by then he'll understand something: I did the best I could.

Sincerely,

KATHERINE HEINY
BETHESDA, MARYLAND

DEAR MCSWEENEY'S,

I'm worried about our cat. He is extremely vocal, pretty much all of the time. He meows in the morning, when it's time to get up. He meows at seemingly random intervals throughout the night. He meows when I get home and put my keys in the dish in the hallway. Food, affection, playtime—these things distract him, but not for long.

We took him to the vet and she said there was nothing wrong with him. She suggested we get a device that pumps a calming pheromone into the house at all times. It is called Feliway.

Feliway.

She also said that he has a "youthful voice." That is because, when he meows, he sounds like an infant screaming.

My wife and I have been married for just over a year. The cat was our inheritance from an unrelated tragedy. Since acquiring it, we've purchased a cat tower. We've purchased Da Bird, a popular cat toy composed of a plastic rod and several feathers, with which one can tease the cat. We bought a woven wool basket, just barely the size of our cat if he were to curl into a ball and stay put, called a Cat Cave. He's never made it inside—he has no interest in climbing in, regardless of the treats we hide in there—so now we put our appliance cables in it, to keep them coiled and off the floor.

It's entirely possible that the cat is damaged. He has been through a lot. It is also entirely possible that he's after one small, simple thing, and we just can't figure it out.

He loves us. He is extremely affectionate. In fact, earlier tonight I speculated that perhaps he's meowing to make sure that we're ready for whatever it is he's about to do next. I was a little bit like this as a child.

The vet said the pheromone the device releases is the same as what the cat releases when he rubs his cheeks against our knuckles, the chair legs, the edges of my laptop, etc.—which he is always doing. The device plugs into the wall and pumps that pheromone into the house. We're supposed to put it near where he spends most of his time, but it's hard to know where that is when we're not around, because when we're around he just wants to sit on our chests and rub his cheek against us.

We feed him well, but he is still very thin.

The vet said, "Most cats are fat. He's just one of those cats that knows how much to eat."

We feed him bits of chicken from dinner sometimes, but that only makes him howl and meow more, when there's no chicken to offer.

I read a blog post that said we're not supposed to engage with him when he meows. Any response reinforces the idea that meowing will get him what he wants. And he probably doesn't know that we don't actually know what he wants.

When we brought him home from the vet, he tore his claws out, anxiously working the small holes in the walls of the carrier. He bled in the carrier, tracked blood into the house. He howled.

Most nights, he sleeps between us like a toddler. He gets under the comforter, settles it at his neck. Last night, he set his cheek against the corner of my pillow.

I should take a moment to reestablish that we are good cat owners. Or relatively good. We make a point of trying, and we care. We also have a wonderful network of supportive friends who help care for the cat while we're away for various social or professional obligations. We provide the majority of things one might think a cat would want.

And yet, he meows.

It's rarely directed at us, directly. Typically, he perches on the corner of the bed and meows out into the room. Away from us. Out into the hollows. Or he'll sit in the corner of the kitchen and meow into the hallway. He looks away from us. He stares off at what seems like nothing. He meows and meows and meows.

I put fresh food in the bowl. Clean the water dish and refill it. I whip Da Bird around like a tassel. I drag it across the comforter.

If you have any thoughts on any of this, I would truly love to hear them.

Sincerely,

COLIN WINNETTE
SAN FRANCISCO, CALIFORNIA

DEAR MCSWEENEY'S,

When I was twelve years old, my family and I moved into a new house that had a fifty-gallon fish tank embedded in a wall. One side of the tank could be seen from the hallway; the other side faced my mother's desk in the kitchen. We'd had a small freshwater fish tank at the old house, with little pebbles at the bottom and darting neon fish, but this new tank was four times as big, and would be filled with salt water.

My dad ordered "live rock"—porous rocks from the ocean floor, made up of dead coral that contained algae, microorganisms, sponges, and snails. These rocks give a tank a readymade ecosystem of plants and tiny creatures, while also stabilizing the water chemistry. My dad piled them up in the tank, creating a network of hidden paths and hiding places. I would sit in a rolly chair with a magnifying glass, examining the growing number of little tubes pressed against the glass, trying to discern if they were plants or animals.

My dad ordered fish, too, and hermit crabs, jumbo snails, clams, shrimp, and sea anemones. The clown fish fed and tended to their anemones. Cleaner shrimp swayed side to side under their rocks; one time I saw them cleaning a clown fish's teeth. There was a red-banded coral shrimp, Sylvester, with six-inch antennae, who would always hang upside down beneath a rock of his own, his razor-sharp claws outstretched, waiting.

We had two hermit crabs—Rocky and Hermie. Rocky often had flowing green algae growing from his shell, and once we saw Hermie riding on top of him, eating the algae. We were so drawn to these creatures that when, one day, my mom and I spotted Rocky's shell perched on the highest rock, the remains of his body below him, we mourned his death. It was hours before we learned that Rocky had just shed his skin, a typical phase in his growth. Every few months, the hermit crabs did this. We called Hermie's shed skin his "pajamas," because that's what it looked like— orange stripes on reddish orange.

There were always new things going on. Beautiful "feather duster" tube

worms unfurled like ornate fans. Home from school one day, I got to witness a snail give birth against the glass. My favorite creature was something we called the Green Pancake, which slowly traveled the rocks. The Green Pancake had a whitish base and a green dimpled platform top that contorted with the creature's mood. An anemone crab the size of a penny rode this Pancake around, pawing at the air with two webbed claws.

Tragedy often befell the tank. There was a fish named Hawk, who was red and sort of reptilian—his fins were separated like fingers, his eyes rotated to all angles, and he perched on particular rocks for long periods of time before scurrying off. Hawk always minded its own business, and often roosted on Dad's fingers when he fed the fish from a block of frozen shrimp. When Hawk died, my parents replaced him with another, almost identical fish, a spotted Hawk, except this Hawk was evil and killed most of the other fish. We would see Sylvester the shrimp eating their remains.

Throughout the ongoing drama of the fish tank—who was attacking who, which corals were struggling—there were brief, startling glimpses of a creature we had not purchased. The creature was a sectioned worm with hundreds of leglike protrusions and an iridescent sheen. It was as fat as my thumb, and we never saw its full body. It had six antennae and a big, smiling mouth. We called it Smiley. When it didn't react to our flashlight, we decided it was blind.

Smiley ate massive amounts of algae. Since we didn't see him eat the shrimp my dad occasionally fed the fish, we concluded that Smiley was a vegetarian. Months would go by without a Smiley spotting, and then he'd appear, extending slowly out of the rocks, taking in a mouthful of sand. He was my favorite part of the tank and the greatest mystery of my young existence. Sometimes we saw dark gray egg-shaped deposits that we guessed were Smiley's poops. These were lightweight and swayed with the water. We called them "movin' poops."

Over the years, Smiley became more brazen. By the time he began emerging while my dad fed the fish, we had seen at least ten inches of him, and had been appalled and amazed that, as I put it, Smiley "had hands in his mouth"— black, handlike jaws that grabbed things and pulled them into his mouth. The other fish were diminishing, and we suspected that Smiley was eating them.

My friend Joe did some research. The internet claimed that Smiley was a pest, and that no creature or plant could survive in a tank with him. The easiest way to catch him, according to the message boards, was to take a plastic container and cut an X in its lid. Then

you were meant to push the points of the X inward, and put food in the container. Smiley would go for the food and get speared by the plastic points of the X, after which he could be removed from the tank by gloved hands. His skin was poisonous. I liked Smiley far too much to ever tell my dad about this.

But fish kept dying. The sea anemones shrank and withered. A crazy hermit crab named Chip grew surprisingly fast and began attacking the feather dusters and anything else that moved. When my dad reached into the tank to grab Chip, the crab abandoned his shell and ran naked into the rocks. When I mentioned Smiley at a fish store, they advised me to capture him immediately.

And so we placed the trap in the tank. Smiley had stripped all the rocks of algae by then, and few fish remained. Where there had once been colorful, gleaming, spectacular creatures, there was now bare rock and this bizarre sea worm, who slunk mannerless behind the rocks and made slimy tunnels in the sand. He wouldn't go near the plastic container.

My dad grew frustrated. It was declared that after the last fish died, the rocks would be removed, the water drained, and the tank would be filled with fresh water. I was very opposed to this, but by then I was out of college and not living nearby. The only fish that remained were one damselfish—just a small blue body and yellow tail, who had lived in the tank for a least a decade and did nothing of note—and the latest Hawk fish, who had the exact characteristics of the first Hawk.

One day, on a visit home, my parents told me Smiley had died, and that the dead body was visible. I looked, and it was true. A portion of Smiley lay outside of the rocks, but as before, I still couldn't see the whole length. I stood with my flashlight, examining the scene. Glumly, I studied the remaining algae on the glass. After a moment, I saw them—teeny worms! There were colonies of them between the glass and the algae, visible only to a squinting, longing eye.

Some segmented sea worms, it turns out, reproduce asexually. They die, and from each segment of their body hatch their offspring. Our tank was full of Baby Smileys. I watched over them with my magnifying glass; my friend Noah wanted us to raise them, then travel the country selling them to aquariums. But the next day my dad cleaned the tank walls with a razor (as he had always done), and to my horror clumps of Baby Smileys were sent to choke on air in the compost pile in our yard.

There may still be young Smileys hidden in the tank, catching things with the black hands of their mouth, but I haven't been able to spot one in years. Hawk is the last fish standing, swimming around by himself, delaying the freshwater transition, while algae grows thick on the walls.

Through the years I've told this story to friends, presenting a photo I took of Smiley in the late nineties. My boyfriend is afraid of the photo, which adds to Smiley's undying power. All the narratives and beauties of the tank—the mandarin fish with its frog face, paisley-print body, and fluttery, gauzelike fins; the strange, puffy brain coral—are eclipsed by this sand monster. Every few months a news story about a weird aquarium creature is posted online, and friends of mine send me the link, always prefacing it with a question: "Smiley?"

Yours,

RACHEL B. GLASER
NORTHAMPTON, MASSACHUSETTS

DEAR MCSWEENEY'S,

Okay, hear me out. I know you think I'm crazy, but I tried reusing my eighteen-day-old Gillette Fusion blade. As a shaving scientist, I felt I should go the extra mile to confirm my results. On day twenty-four, I tried to take a selfie with the four-inch gash under my nose, but I have a new phone and I couldn't figure it out. Good news, though: I believe that Gillette will now have to believe me about their blade usefulness. Bad news: my cut is likely to look like a mustache made of scabs for a while. I'm going to choose to think positively, because that's the kind of guy I am.

"New Blade At 24 Days Or Scabby Mustache—Your Choice!"© It grows on you, right? Always thinking,

GARY RUDOREN
JERUSALEM

DEAR MCSWEENEY'S,

If you want to know what's wrong with the modern banking industry, look no further than the following sentences. Last week, my local bank refused my request for a loan based on the claim that my collateral wasn't acceptable. This would make sense if my collateral was something silly, like intangible shares of ownership in a company or jewelry that the bank would never wear, but turning down a K-type star in the highly regarded constellation of Cassiopeia proves that banks are now just clown shows without the novelty of a large tent.

I bought HD 240210 (a name I chose, since I felt the original name needed more numbers) fair and square from a legitimate celestial salesman at a mall kiosk a few years ago. I even had the holographic space deed on hand, yet Paul at the bank merely scoffed, saying they don't accept collateral from outside the solar system. I had thought that we, as a people, had advanced beyond such backward thinking. We're talking about a star with a radius thirteen times larger, and thus better, than the sun! For some reason a bank will take fifty useless acres of farmland as collateral, but not billions of acres of useful radiating energy. Four hundred sixty-six light years away or not, you get a few solar panels out by my star and I guarantee your electricity bill will drop.

It's almost as if these banks aren't even planning for the very distant future. As the years go on, the value of currency is going to plummet, but the value of stars, asteroids, and comets is going to skyrocket. (Actual skyrockets will be valuable, too.) When I mentioned this to Paul, he said I read too much science fiction. I said he didn't read enough science fiction. Then it turned out we both read the exact same amount of science fiction. We bonded over that fact, and quickly determined we should be friends. Yet when I tried to use our newfound friendship as possible collateral for the loan, Paul once again revealed his true, diabolical, and sadly close-minded nature.

The fact that banks need to know why you're requesting a loan also shows a disgusting lack of trust in their clients. Of *course* I want the loan so I can buy

more stars. And yes, I'll probably use those stars as collateral to take out additional loans, so that I can buy still more stars with the bank's money. If they didn't want to hear that, they shouldn't have asked. They should've just handed

me a briefcase filled with checks of various amounts.

It's only a matter of time before the entire banking industry crumbles due to this kind of hidebound thinking. And on that day, as those clown bankers look to the heavens seeking answers, they'll spot a particularly bright star in the constellation of Cassiopeia, and see the error of their ways shining before them.

Unless it's cloudy out. I sure hope it isn't cloudy that day.

Your pal,

KEATON PATTI
NEW YORK, NEW YORK

DEAR MCSWEENEY'S,
I'd like to tell you a story about a complicated place. It's a place I currently wander, by way of buses, boats, and hotels, stinking of sweat. It's a story about family and violence and the weight of the Past, which as far as I can tell is the Great Story of Latin America. It is about a man, the Son of the General, whom I met through Couchsurfing.

The day I arrived in Brazil, the Son of the General took me to the airport in the center of town to watch the planes land. At this point I did not know he was the Son of the General. He was just a divorced Zen Buddhist in his late fifties with a gray buzz cut and big bones who was allowing me to sleep on his futon. A yellow-and-green plane roared in over our heads.

"Must be someone important," he noted. There was a high note somewhere in his voice box that made an appearance at the end of his sentences. "A minister, or even the president." We talked corruption. "There's no word in Portuguese for 'accountability,'" he said. "I think this is very interesting. We only have a phrase: *Matar a cobra e mostrar o pau.* It means 'Kill the snake and show the stick.'"

Later, over dinner, he casually mentioned that his father had died under house arrest. "He was the Minister of the Interior under the Junta in Argentina," he explained.

"Ah, after the Junta," I said, thinking I had misheard.

"No, during the Junta," he said, and then looked at his plate of fried fish. "The presidents of the nineties wanted to revisit the problems of the past, and they put him under arrest." He did not seem ashamed or proud—it was just his life.

When we returned to his tiny, dirty apartment in Rio's nightclub district, I surreptitiously googled his surname and found a Wikipedia article on his father. A controversial man, to say the least, a general, a minister, possibly a killer. And in front of me, his son, a living contradiction: the vegetarian offspring of an alleged mass murderer, an early-rising Zen monk in the epicenter of Rio's nightlife.

I suspect this story is interesting to me only because we are fascinated by figures of power and violence. The Son of the General is not such a person. He is a good man, kind, learned, goofy, and a little crude. He laughs well and often.

DAVID GUMBINER
PARATY, BRAZIL

DEAR MCSWEENEY'S,
Granted, Day 38 was a rough one. Pun intended. I'm writing this to you with a face full of bloody tissue squares. Using the same Gillette Fusion blade for five and a half weeks in a row was a not-so-naked attempt to silence the future critics who I know will be lying in wait to discredit my blade-life findings, yes; it also took a Shylockesque toll I can't deny. If I could remember my Instagram

password I would post a picture of my face to shock the world, I swear I would.

Just wait, this isn't over yet,

GARY RUDOREN
JERUSALEM

DEAR MCSWEENEY'S,

I was given this monstrous, gorgeous piano, a 1920s Winterroth, a nice big upright piano, a vintage thing worth probably three grand. It was like a dream come true to have one of these things. And I finally had a little apartment I could just barely get it into. Sal and I had just moved into this little place at Twenty-Fifth and Bryant, and we had our son, our little boy, too.

I got a few people to help me move the piano. Chris put his back out lifting it, and one other friend doesn't call me anymore, now. But as we were getting the thing to the top of the stairs, I couldn't stop thinking RING, and how I gotta get one. Because everything was going real good, and everything was working out just right, and I needed to get a ring.

I went out into the neighborhood thinking RING, and I saw Murray Rapinski on his way to his bar. He had a bunch of flowers under his arm and he was walking to his bar, Lovers' Lane, like he did every night around six, to put some flowers in there, light candles, set the lights, and set the music.

I was walking along with him thinking about flowers and rings and candles and everything romantic and I thought about a few days before, when Sal and I were standing out front of this jewelry store. The Texis Joyeria jewelry store on Twenty-Fourth Street around Alabama, next to this Mexican doughnut shop. The kid was with us and we were just pleasantly zoning out on the rings in the window and I saw Sal's hair in the reflection of the glass and it was golden and brown and then I looked at the Mexican doughnuts and they were perfectly golden brown in the sun and I was thinking how they're the same color, and I was feeling love, I guess, or just how nice it was to be around her.

I asked the guy how much the rings were and the prices were so high I just went right into the dumps. I just felt depressed and my whole mood was blown and all of a sudden all I wanted was to get out of this thing with Sal, I wanted to set her free so she could be free to find a rich man, a very beautiful, optimistic, good-hearted and rich man.

* * *

Now, I've never made any money, I've never wanted to make money, and every job I've ever had has been solely to pay the rent. And I've taken every chance I've ever had to call in sick, take a day off, or quit so I could stay home and write.

When you're young that kind of thing is seen as heroic, to chase your dreams is seen as courageous and brave, but when you get older people don't really see it that way, they see you as selfish or foolish or lost.

When I first met Sal, she had some divorce money, she wanted to have a party that would last a whole year, so naturally I moved in. Sal could afford the rent, she could afford the booze, the food, and all I had to do was stay home and write.

Pretty soon a friend of mine came to town and he had some big dreams and some big schemes, he wanted to buy a coffee plantation down in Costa Rica. He said, Sonny, what you need is about thirty grand to get in on this, is there anybody in your family that has any money?

So I went to the only rich person I knew. He was having an art opening downtown. His art was these beautifully, expensively framed portraits of homeless people, strippers, pimps, junkies. He was there with his wife, his two kids, his dog, and his agent.

I said, I need fifty thousand dollars. Fifty grand. He just looked at me. His eyes seemed to say, Sonny, you never had any money to gamble with so you gambled with your whole life, you never developed a practical skill or a practical talent, you never went to school, you

thought you could make it on your art and you didn't.

Well, fuck you, I said. Fuck you and fuck the way this whole world works, and I walked out into the street.

I walked all night. I thought about going back to school, I thought about wearing a tie, I thought about being a carpenter, and I thought about never being poor again.

When I finally got near home I saw this big black woman getting beat up by these Latino guys. She was a prostitute I recognized and I think she'd drifted across some turf line or something. One guy had a pit bull and he was making it attack her.

I tried to call the cops and this kid came over with a cast on his hand and hit me in the head and the arm. I felt the sting of a broken bone and an ache in my head. After a while they dispersed and I crawled over to the woman, and together we limped to the hospital, just two ragged mules beat up by the night.

Dear Sal, The world is odd and senseless and I'll be home late.

* * *

After that I was having a buzzing in my head and a steady series of bad thoughts. I joined a temporary employment agency and got a job with an exterminating company run by Betty and Albert, a

Chinese couple, out of an auto garage off Bayshore.

It was very behind the times. I was given an old tin pump, something left over from the thirties. It even squeaked when you squeezed it. I was to go around the corners of a room and squirt this blue powder. Very simple.

I was having a cigarette with Albert one day outside an old Victorian. The stairs were rotting, the paint was peeling, it was old. I looked at my pump. It was old, too. Some things never change, I thought. Then I looked at my reflection. If only that would change, if only I could squirt some blue powder on that.

Weeks passed and the buzzing in my head got worse. The negative thoughts grew and grew. The blue powder was in my hair and in my fingernails. I'd sometimes find little spots of blue powder on a glass or a doorknob.

What if you got cancer? Sal said. What about the kid? She convinced me to see a doctor.

The doctor was this old Chinese man. He had this gaze. The gaze of a cow. Sunken shoulders, sunken jowls, sunken eyes. And he had this mole, and out of the mole drooped two long white hairs.

He told me to get in this motorized bed that would float me into this space-age doughnut device. I thought, Well, if you don't have cancer, this thing'll surely give it to you.

Inside the doughnut I had a panic attack, and I believe I passed out, but I was awake as well, and I witnessed some kind of divine spectrum, as if all the atoms of all matter were popping and fizzing, an electric field of stargleams, a color spectrum that was infinite. I fell into a dream.

When I was pulled out of the machine my head was throbbing and I felt tired. I saw there was a little blue stain where my head had been. I felt worse than before. Like something had been injected into me. A few days went by and I got a letter from the doctor. It said nothing bad was going down in my head, but that wasn't true.

* * *

I began to think that if it wasn't cancer or a tumor or an ulcer then it was a secret, a diabolical secret, as if I had committed a crime and buried it deep inside, and it was growing into a monster, and if I didn't exorcise it I would go insane.

I began to walk the streets aimlessly, muttering to myself. I decided I had to find someone I could confess to, whatever the confession was—but who? Surely there was some friend I could tell it all to, but I didn't really have any friends.

So I began to assess the strangers whose paths I crossed. Finally I landed on a guy by the name of Robert Bellows, a kindly person, a bit of a loner, maybe a bit simple.

I lured him to a bar with a vague business proposal. I chose a well-lit place, full of shiny copper railings and fancy trim, the kind of bar to which the young and prosperous go to exchange vapid pleasantries and the vile trivia of their daily lives.

I told him I was very unhappy. I confessed the most intimate details of my personal life. Faced with the need to make a decision concerning myself and unable to act, I'd lost control.

I explained how I'd never intended to be this person. That looking in the mirror was like seeing a stranger. I went on for about half an hour. Thirty minutes. Thirty minutes is all it took to disclose a man's entire life.

But I couldn't go on anymore after that. The look on his face was of a pinched pain. His forehead was clammy and he looked like he might have cried at one point but it was dried up by now. I told him that whatever he chose to do with this information was out of my control, but I hoped he would at least think of me sympathetically.

I made my exit in silence. As I walked home I got the sense he was following me. Several times I looked back and was pretty sure I saw him. I thought maybe he wanted to see where I lived so he could call the cops.

Or maybe he had gotten so excited he wanted to become a vigilante, taking things into his own hands. Or he had just become so obsessed with my confession that he wanted to keep studying me.

Days later I found him trailing me again. This time I confronted him. He looked horrible. There were bags under his eyes. He said, At least you should tell your son, at least your son deserves to know. And then he ran off.

So I ran after him. Right down the middle of the street. And everything was going by me so fast, and everything had eyes. Not just people, but everything— the telephone poles looked at us, the beat-up cars looked at us, even the mailboxes were looking at us, the blue one and the green one leaning together in concern. They said, Stop doing this, you might get in an accident. The houses looked at us. They said, Don't come in here. Streetlights watched us and wouldn't change, they were stubborn, they wouldn't change when we needed them to, so we had to go through traffic. And then the headlights were watching us. They would just sit there and think, Should we run them over?

And finally I was so close to him I could touch him, I was running faster than I've ever run. And he tripped and I fell on him. He was red in the face and sweaty and struggling like I was a monster. Like I was a monster about to devour him, about to rip him to shreds.

And I saw he was just a little kid. And I was a big kid. And I backed away, people were looking, people had come out of the stores, the streets were watching, the power lines were watching. I got off him and I ran away.

I decided to confess the whole thing to everybody involved. But when I got home there was a note tacked to my door. I read it slowly, like a person reads their own obituary. It wasn't signed at the bottom. I decided to leave that note tacked to the door and walk to the ocean and drown myself.

* * *

As I was walking to the beach I saw a friend of mine who asked me did I want to go to a healing ceremony where you take ayahuasca and see snakes and have visions and all that, so I said sure, but that she'd have to give me a ride to the ocean afterward, because I was gonna drown myself.

So she drove me down to Santa Cruz, along these back roads to this nice New Agey yoga-retreat-type place. I grabbed a brochure but when I looked at it, it was just blank pages, so I thought, Genius, and went in.

The room was laid out like a hexagon. And it was divided so that women were on one side and men were on the other. In the center of the hexagon were the musicians and the leader.

All the people were dressed like pilots and stewardesses, blue V-neck sweaters, slacks, and pilot shoes, and they all wore these buttons with nothing on them.

Two lines formed, one for the women and one for the men. And the leader doled out his special beverage, a stale yeasty granular beerlike substance. As he approached each person, he looked as if he were getting a divine message about how much they should get, according to their personal vibration. I do believe he gave me a large amount.

First thing to say is yes, I began seeing things. As with any trip experience I began to feel insecure about the whole thing, but I carried on anyway.

The first unfortunate thing I witnessed was that people, randomly, all around me, began to vomit. All over the place. They had these blue plastic bowls to catch the vomit but sometimes they would miss. Also the reflection of the light on the blue plastic bowls really made their vomit look blue.

After this a woman collapsed to the floor in some kind of grand mal seizure. I looked for my friend and saw her underneath a chair, looking up at the sky, her hands playing with some kind of invisible cotton candy.

Months passed, and the second drink came around. The line formed and I was given a much smaller dose this time. First there was a girl who started hopping up and down in her chair like a monkey. The leader came over, he looked like a prairie dog—he had slicked-back hair, buck teeth, and he was constantly scanning the horizon like prairie dogs do—he came over and began to slap the monkey girl. Hard. I looked over at another woman and she looked just like a mole to me. But when I looked back she was normal again.

All of a sudden I felt a snake, a huge snake, passing through my chest. As quickly as it entered it passed through my shoulder, down my arm, and out my hand, which was now pointing at the mole. The mole collapsed as soon as the snake left my hand.

I just started speaking jibber-jabber, trash can gas pedal babysitter vacuum cleaner moped NASCAR and then I was flying above the city. I was flying above this city and I could see everything. Everything was transparent, I could see the tops of buildings but I could also see the Sheetrock and what the roofs were made of, down through the plywood and insulation and the lightbulbs, through the air molecules in the top floors, through the craniums of people and through their blood vessels, through their atoms, through their computers and through the microchips and down and down and through everything. I could see it all at once.

And I said to myself, Society makes me sad. It makes me sad. Look at the people. Look at them eating. Waking and sleeping. Befriending and loving. Raising children, working hard, raising toasts, sharing sorrows, fighting for rights, marrying, birthing, adopting, chasing dreams, struggling hard, not giving up, saving money, getting hair-cuts, looking sharp, entering buildings, completing tasks. It makes me sad.

And then as I was flying I came to this factory. It was a hell factory, the conditions inside were slave conditions. It was roasting hot, people were half naked, leaning against each other, pass-ing out, dying, making things, produc-ing things, packaging things.

And the factory was producing everything. Everything that we have.

All of it. The rubber bands, the paper clips, the broom bristles, flip-flops, salt and pepper shakers, aluminum siding, tubes, pipes, clay, paint, wooden things, metal things, wax things, paper things, everything we have and all we know.

Everyone in the factory was in service to this huge vat. Out of the vat they were getting this goo, the stuff they made everything with. This bluish goo.

And then I was back in the room. Back in the ceremony. All the creatures of the forest were there, all the people in the ceremony were blinking back and forth between their normal faces and animal faces. There were moles, and raccoons, lemmings, guinea pigs, birds, all the critters of the forest. And I said to them, I found the blue powder factory!

And that's when the snake came, the snake showed up and said my name. He said, Hello, Sonny, but he had a Texas accent. He said, Do you have any money? I said, No, I don't have any money. He said, Well, get some, then. And there was a long pause as the people in the ceremony were all blinking back and forth into their animal faces and the snake said, If you can't get the money, then just balance on one leg.

* * *

I escaped the ceremony. There had been another drinking. A third drinking, but

I couldn't do it. So I walked out of there and into the road and hitchhiked back to San Francisco. But before I went home I went to Tammy Lafay's house. I talked her into buying my piano for a thousand bucks. It took me about five cups of tea listening to her talk about the bad stairwell but finally she went for it.

A thousand dollars in my pocket. I walked over to the Texis Joyeria jewelers and bought a ring. Nothing special, but something. A die-cast. Real simple. Then I walked over to the Y.C. Wong Kung Fu Academy and signed up my son.

I walked along singing a melody to myself. Some unknown thing. When I got home I took those stairs four at a time. I grabbed the note on the door and shoved it deep into my pocket. I put the package down on the table but you couldn't really see it with all the chaos so I made a quick decision to clean the table real good, Comet and 409. After I cleaned the table I decided to clean the whole apartment. I put away all of the kid's toys, organized all his books from A to Z, took all the books he didn't read anymore and put them in a bag, took all the toys and clothes he'd outgrown and put them in a box. Then I put all the books I never really read into a bag.

I took all the clothes down to the laundry. I was darting up and down the stairs every twenty minutes doing it. When I attacked the closet I resurrected an old blazer I liked to wear whenever I wanted to feel intellectual. I took it to the dry cleaner's.

I organized our bookshelves, with their random scattering of stuff. I pocketed an old Brodsky book about Venice.

When I walked out I felt glad. Nothing succeeds in which high spirits play no part. That was Nietzsche. I walked over toward the park. I didn't know what I'd find but you could rest there, I figured. That's all I needed, a little bit of rest. When I got to the park I saw some yellow flowers reaching up toward the sun. I felt just like one of them. Once I was out on the grass, I felt my body firming up against the cold and the last fumes of a burnt-up song puffing out of my ears.

SONNY SMITH
SAN FRANCISCO, CALIFORNIA

This letter is usually performed as a theatrical monologue set to music. Sonny's band, Sonny and the Sunsets, first played it live in February 2013, at The Lost Church theater in San Francisco. A recorded version of it is available on Sonny and the Sunsets' latest album, Sees All Knows All.

DEAR MCSWEENEY'S,
So like, back when I lived on this sailboat down in LA Harbor, I got this phone call from this lady who was all:

"Heyyyyy... is this the Sage Café?" No, I said, because it wasn't. It was my cell phone. "Is this 971-341562?" she said. Uh, there's too many numbers in that... number, I said. The woman apologized and hung up, and it occurred to me that, one, I would like to eat eggs for breakfast, and two, that as I was trying to explain phone numbers to her, I'd hesitated for a second as I was figuring out what I needed to say. And maybe that wasn't what I'd needed to say at all.

Maybe what I'd needed to say was that when a red light turns green, all the cars do not move forward at once—instead there's an accumulation of small hesitations between each car. You know, like, you yourself might be quick, but the farther down the line you are, the more hesitation you inherit. You may not even make the light. And this happens in other places, this happens everywhere, all the time, even in your kidney, and the grocery store twelve-items-or-less line. And so I didn't fold my clothes for three days and now they're wrinkled, and the milk went bad in the icebox, and they didn't catch the cancer early enough so my mother suffered for some time and died. I was in the room for that. Her breathing slowed, stopped, started, stopped, stayed stopped. I tried to close her clouded eyeballs and her mouth but they wouldn't stay closed, and I thought that was interesting, and then I walked upstairs to the bathroom where my brother was stepping out of the shower wrapped in a brown towel.

"Yo," I said. "She died."

"What?"

"She died."

"You're kidding?"

"No," I said, "I'm not." Then, for good measure, I added, "You fuckin' dickhead."

It's been a while since, and sometimes I think: she didn't survive that. And now I'm wondering if I didn't survive that, and now I'm wondering if I would survive if I filled my pockets with rocks and jumped in a swimming pool, and now I'm wondering how small Time is. I'd like it if, asked that question, someone answered, "As small as a microbe's microbe's microbe's microbe's microbe's microbe's front teeth. So small you could fit four billion years in the space between Elton John's front teeth." Wow, I'd say, that's a fuckin' pretty good answer.

Me, I think of Time as teeny pieces of party confetti, so small it's invisible, fluttering all over the place, all around us, even up your nose when you breathe. I also think it's carcinogenic, like burnt bacon. As for eggs, my mother liked hers hard-boiled, but I have trouble deciding between over-medium and scrambled, and waitresses make me nervous. As for hesitation, *McSweeney's*, the one that always

gets me is the smoker in bed—you figure they'd wake up, sleeping on top of fire.

MATT SUMELL
NEW ORLEANS, LOUISIANA

DEAR MCSWEENEY'S,
Day 67! I'm writing to thank you for whatever it is you did. Perhaps I've been numbed by the medical marijuana I've been co-opting from my dad's stash (he has ablutophobia, it's very sad), but I kept on shaving every day. What else was I supposed to do, right? Yesterday, though, I went into the bathroom only to find that my face was smooth—baby-butt smooth, before I even picked up the razor! I immediately had my friend Spitzy post a twitpic—it went viral, and lo and behold, I got an e-mail from some woman named Barbara, from Gillette's Blade Branding Dept., who wanted to talk to me about my experiment. Word is I may have broken through some kind of quantum shaving barrier. Gilette is now prepared to put what they call a "claimer" on their packaging: "Gil-lette Fusion—The Shave That Lasts Forever!"© or something like that. In payment, I get so many coupons you wouldn't believe.

Next up—legs! There's a market there, I think. Smoothly Yours,

GARY RUDOREN
JERUSALEM

ONLY GOOD FOR A DAY

by JULIA SLAVIN

There was a girl who had become so poor that she had to wear newspapers for clothes. Jonathan had heard of her during the first days of the demonstration but guessed she was protest lore, a tale that had woven through the crowd on nights spent warming hands over trash-can fires—a goddess who would rise from a dome tent that opened like a shell, floating over McPherson Square and the human barricades of K Street, the city of power nearly losing its breath at the sight of her. On day four, Jonathan found her.

The newsprint-covered buttons of her blouse matched meticulously with the stories around them, so there was never a break in a sentence. *A commonly held view*, he read down her back, *in both territories, is that the*

Islamist militants defeated their enemy and they did it with weapons, not words.
He squeezed between the girl and a man dressed like the Cat in the Hat,
who tried to push him back out of the line that pressed against the police.
But Jonathan dug an elbow into his ribs.

"I hope you don't mind," he asked the girl, "if I stand here."

Though unbeknown to him, Jonathan too had created a hum, through
the female half of the crowd, with his corkscrew black hair and Timberlands
instead of the requisite orange Crocs, still dusty with soil from the coffee
cooperatives and orphanages of Guatemala.

"I think anybody can stand wherever anybody wants," the girl said, and
smiled. Her front teeth were a little crooked, but they were clean. She told
him her name was Maya.

"I join you," Councilman Schaeffer said from the stage, "to get our
message to a plutocracy that has lost sight of the American vision." Jonathan held Maya's hand. The protesters' line stretched four blocks, past the
Department of the Treasury. The White House didn't look as big as he'd
thought it would. On H Street, a voice over a bullhorn instructed the
demonstrators to join arms and sit down in passive resistance, and said
that anyone who wanted to get arrested should move to the front of the
line. The crowd chanted "Ro-bin Hood! Ro-bin Hood!" over cowbells and
drumbeats. Jonathan asked Maya if she wanted to get arrested.

She shrugged. "Not today," she said.

Back at McPherson Square, groups of protesters surrounded her.

"The *LA Times* has endorsed our cause!" they shouted.

"Another protest like ours has sprung up in Chicago!"

"This op-ed says we should look to Spain!"

Jonathan, having read her already, stood back to let the others have a
chance.

"No, man. Don't do it. High parasite load," a dweller said. He was already
known as someone to avoid. The tent city was filled with dwellers who weren't

real protesters. People who would have been sleeping in the park protest or not, and who thought of the influx of pretty girls as call-in prostitutes. They grabbed at them and tore their clothes, tried to feel them up. As the days wore on and the protesters got dirtier, it would be hard to tell who was who.

"She's dirty on the inside, too," another dweller said, sucking on a cigarette filter. But Jonathan knew from genetics-politics classes that women were clean on the inside. That it was only men who made them dirty.

Another dweller, indistinguishable from the first two, said, "I'm gonna turn her every which way, and she's gonna let me." His tongue flicked out of his mouth like a rat's tail. "She going down on me without saying 'Ugh.'"

Jonathan went to the clothing tent. A hastily written sign over a table of clothes read, NO LOITER, NO LITTER, RETURN THE CLOTHES. He picked out a pink hoodie and a pair of gray leggings for Maya. The girl who worked the tent wore a wolf's-head index-finger ring and a sleeveless John & Yoko T-shirt. Her tattoo of a yellow-haired female ghost was too large for her small arm.

"Just bring them back when you're done," she said. "We take donations for cigarettes and ice cream." Jonathan handed her a twenty.

"This is too much," she said. She slipped the twenty into his shirt pocket and looked closely at his face. "I've seen you with the newspaper girl," she said. "She's the true poor. But still. You can't give her these." She took the clothes from his hands. "She would read it as an insult."

A shirtless guy in black warpaint that appeared to have bubbled up from a La Brea Tar Pit snatched the pink hoodie. The girl turned to him.

"Where's the T-shirt you borrowed?" she yelled over a shriek of air horns from the north side of the square. "You were supposed to bring it back. And the Kate Spade sunglasses." They began arguing about loans going against the heart of the protest, the painted guy saying that loans got us into this mess in the first place. Jonathan went to find Maya, who was still being read over by the food tent.

"Let's get away for a while," he said.

He pulled her from the crowd.

They held hands again as they walked up Pennsylvania Avenue. He asked if her newspaper shoes hurt her feet. She shook her head, even though at every intersection she had to take a roll of two-sided tape from her woven-newspaper messenger bag and reattach the soles. "I'd like to buy you some shoes," he said. She said no thank you.

On the M Street Bridge they kissed, Jonathan creasing her top as he pressed himself against her. They continued on, sleepy in the late-morning sun, achy from marching. She stopped in front of Intermix to sketch a dress she saw in the window.

"Do you like that?" he asked. "I'll get it for you."

"That's an eight-hundred-dollar garment," she said, and he felt ashamed for offering, but then she looked the dress over again, planning on re-creating it in newspaper, drawing a sweeping skirt with her thin white hand.

"I'd have to cut down on the fullness of the skirt. Otherwise, the hem will crumple. See how it's cut on the bias? Now imagine it in *St. Petersburg Times*."

As they continued up M Street she talked about fashion theory. Fashion's relation to global production and the female form. The intersection of fashion and cultural politics. Sweatshop labor. Industry. But he could think only of her clothes falling to the floor of his basement apartment like the papers his father let drop on Sundays when he fell asleep in a chair.

"I designed a newspaper chador for a class I took on the Role of Women in Islamic Jurisprudence. But soon everyone was making them, and with no regard for editorial content."

"So you're not really poor?" he asked.

"I'm poor," she said. "But not in the way you'd like me to be."

"What kind of poor are you?"

"The no-safety-net-but-never-wanted-for-anything kind. You?"

"Same."

"Student loans?" she asked.

"No. Fortunately. You?"

"I'm fucked," she said. "Forever."

They turned on 34th Street, then again on N, walking down some steps to the basement apartment he planned to sublet for however long the protest lasted. He told her he'd decided to take the apartment so he'd be better able to write his dispatches for his college newspaper. She remarked on the quiet, and on how nice it must be to sleep in a bed instead of on the ground in a stranger's tent. The garden is lovely, she said, looking out the back window and pointing out plants he hadn't paid any attention to. It was funny that tropical plants were all that survived the Washington heat, she said.

He didn't want to rip the weave that kept her top clasped, so she unraveled it herself. And then removed her skirt, which was held on by shredded braids of the *Baltimore Sun*.

"It's the interlining," she insisted when Jonathan saw that her naked body was covered in backward newsprint. "I'm not dirty."

"I know you're not," he said. He moved his fingers over the story about investor fraud on her collarbone, the racial shifts in the South spilling over her shoulder, a constitutional court in Egypt preparing to hear challenges running across her chest. He moved his face toward her breasts and saw an op-ed about the U.S. targeting al Qaeda operatives for assassination. His parents had always told him he'd be sent to Canada if the country reinstated the draft.

He took off his T-shirt and kicked off his pants, lowering her down onto the bed. Reciting the alphabet over and over to cleanse his mind of the soldiers' lost limbs smeared across her thighs, he was thwarted by the sight of his horoscope stamped along her stomach. He lifted his head.

"Not a good day to make financial decisions, I guess. Did you know Ahmadinejad is coming to the UN?"

She fell back on the bed. "It's not your fault," she said.

"The subject matter…"

"Boys just want to read me," she said.

"I want to go deeper," he insisted.

"Tomorrow," she assured him, "I'll wear content that's easier on the eyes."

"Please don't," he said, feeling relieved she considered their encounter more than just a protest fling—a phenomenon with which the online press was bewitched. "It's my problem, not yours."

As the light changed they lay in bed watching the glow-in-the-dark stars pasted to the stucco ceiling begin to come out.

He would never have another girlfriend he couldn't read, he decided. He would study every right-to-left language he could find, become a rabbi, write his Anthropology of Gender thesis in ancient Egyptian and finish his community-service requirements by teaching prisoners to read Urdu. Why the English language read left to right, instead of the way it did on Maya, would remain the great mystery of his life.

Qaddafi Dies in Libya, Amen.

When he awoke at 10 p.m., Maya was out of bed and getting dressed.

"Stay," he said, as she wove her skirt back on.

"It's important to sleep in the tents," she said. "And there's a committee meeting."

"Are you on the committee?" He asked.

"Everyone is on the committee," she said.

Jonathan told her he needed another hour's sleep and he would meet her that night. But he slept in his bed through morning.

* * *

Autumn in Washington. The humidity and the bugs were ferocious. When Jonathan arrived at McPherson Square, he saw the crowd united in one big itch, scores of protesters lining up at the medical tent for Cortaid. The food tent offered only greasy bags of hamburgers and cold fries in Styrofoam containers. Two guys named Austen and Charlie, infamous for such protest antics as building structures that deliberately served no purpose, stood dipping their fries into paper cups of ketchup, eating them in what looked like a race. They had become known as the Flies, a name that referred to both the way they buzzed around the square, creating mischief, and the buzz they'd created in the online press. Reporters and police chased after them for interviews and arrests. They eluded both. Jonathan looked all over for Maya, but didn't see her. A dweller asked him for a cigarette, and then a whole group of dwellers smelled blood and surrounded him.

"All the news that's printed to fit," one said.

"He got the weather report all up and down that shaft."

"Read her and weep."

Somebody hit him on the back and grabbed at his front pocket, where he kept his wallet. He ran toward 15th, where the police were angry with the food-truck owners for inciting a dweller fight. They said they would shut the trucks down if it were up to them. "You peddlers are killing all the businesses in the area," they said.

"We *are* the businesses in the area," the owner of the Indian food truck said, taping up a sign that read: FRESH OUT OF SAAG PANEER.

Jonathan broke through the scrum of police and bought a *gulab jamun.* Walking through the crowd looking for Maya, he did all he could to avoid the dwellers. From the back he couldn't tell who was who. The shirtless guy in cutoff cords scratching welts on his back could be a Georgetown University government major just as easily as the man in Nike iDs could be a dweller. Some of the protest costumes—the Cat in the Hat suits, the death masks, the balls and chains—were store-bought or handmade, but others seemed to have been pulled from the trash. Jonathan took a seat on the curb, crossing his legs in the street, and watched Austen and Charlie drag furniture out of an office and onto K Street, backing up traffic for blocks. Some drivers honked in solidarity, while others made illegal U-turns. It was lunchtime; workers from the College Republican National Committee came out onto their roof garden with their falafel to watch the protest. The Flies had skittered over to the statue of Major General James B. McPherson, where a line of young men wearing octopus hats, tentacles hanging down their faces like dreadlocks, hoisted Austen up onto the bronze horse. Once he'd mounted it, he swung his arm like he was spinning a lasso. The men threw a tarp up to him, and he began to drape it over the statue. The workers on the roof garden took iPhone pictures and then went back to their jobs.

Thanks to Maya, girls had begun wearing the clothing of the movement. Some outfits were haphazardly taped together, without a thought to design, execution, or sentence structure; others showed elements of craftsmanship, draping of op-eds, proportion, balance and fit. A few matched Maya's artistry, with their edge finishes and waist stays, and dark headlines about nuclear proliferation and arctic drilling that ran ominously across their backs.

He found her standing in the back of a tent where a panel discussion on the salient points of pressure groups was taking place. He snuck up behind her and put his arms around her waist. She laughed and put her finger to her lips, signaling for him to keep quiet during the disputation. "Our rationalization is the governing structure within the borders of the chasm," one man was saying. The uneven hem of Maya's dress was a copy of this year's Versace. People bellied up to her, reading her back.

The bodice was fitted in front with spaghetti straps that widened to a harness that was based on a Balenciaga design, he was sure. "Schaeffer is backpedaling," whispered a girl in an unbuttoned suit vest with nothing underneath. *"The councilman expressed concern about the encampment becoming a public health problem,"* she read. *"Young people are having sex in tents, and there have been arrests for indecent acts.* We're doomed."

"Bernie Sanders is coming!" another girl read.

"Fuck it," the vested girl said. "I'm going back to school."

In twenty minutes they were in his basement apartment, Jonathan making sad work of Maya's buttons. She took over and in seconds she was the beautiful backward-printed girl he had fallen in love with. He dropped to his knees and read her from bottom to top. Justice for rape victims. More on drones and double standards at the CIA. Stop-and-frisk. Steamed bass cooked in the microwave.

He lifted his head. "Hugo Chávez won't see the New Year, it says."

Some of her seams were so inconspicuous he didn't see that the lines of text had been changed until he read around her hips. TALIBAN STRONG-HOLDS TROMP VIKINGS 37-16. JUSTIN TIMBERLAKE CLASHES WITH REPUBLICANS ON DEBT LIMITS. She'd tricked his eye and it excited him. Soon they fell back on his bed, her ink running over his rocket-ship sheets, *transatlantic* forming into a bead and rolling off her. *Imperil* turning to rain. He imagined carving over her words with a filament, making them permanent.

To love Maya was to extend his tolerance for violence: the description of a child's hand found after a car bomb, a head in the trunk of a car, a recipe for veal. When he wanted to read her thoughts she gave him coupons, only good for a day. Her editorials insulted him. She left cuts on his skin. She had nightmares from which she woke sobbing, pieces of her coming off in the bed. She gave unsolicited advice and her comics weren't funny. When he asked her to stop running negative campaign ads and stories about animal experimentation, she became enraged, coming to him printed with warnings about arsenic in rice, about children locked in isolation in Belgium. And then one day a backward quote that threatened to deflate him forever. *We knew the numbers were high, but what we know now is unbelievable.* A report from the Genocide Prevention Task Force. He demanded she go and wash.

"Did you expect me to leave it out?" she said. She snatched a towel off the floor.

As she bathed, Jonathan's head throbbed with the images he'd tried to forget. Decimation and depopulation in Rwanda. He skimmed through the headlines on nytimes.com and watched a few corgi videos. She finally emerged print-free, slippery and white like squid. Even when she dried herself she looked wet, as though covered in a mucous film. She opened her messenger bag and took out the day's outfit. She'd made a pair of harem pants and a top with bell sleeves. The loose fit of the garments with her five-point Vidal Sassoon haircut made her look like a boy.

"What do you think?" she asked. He looked her over.

"A lot of panda bears," he said, still bruised. "And I'm kind of moving away from all that first-person present tense."

"It's from the *Kid's Post*," she said, making him feel stupid.

"I like a more classic silhouette," he said. "And with so much hard news, the nonproliferation treaty, curbs over gun access…" He could tell he'd hurt her. He got out of bed and put his arms around her, begging forgiveness. He said maybe they should spend more time at the protest, or even sleep there, and use the apartment only for making love. They agreed to meet by the food trucks in an hour and spend the day at the march.

At McPherson Square, Jonathan moved from tent to tent, asking if there was room for Maya and him to stay the night. No one turned him away, but he could see the tents were crowded and they'd have to curl into a corner. They could sleep outside, but there was frozen rain in the forecast. Winter was coming and a lot of kids were headed back to school. He remembered staring out the casement windows in his Poetry without Borders class when the first snow began to float across the quad.

A commotion by the food trucks caught his attention. The Indian food truck had been packed up; regular customers didn't want to let it go, so they were holding hands in the street to block its exit. Some of the demonstrators began to push against the truck, rocking it to and fro, the owners whipping off their turbans and plastic mustaches, ready for a fight. The police came to escort them out. Unable to locate Maya, Jonathan sprinted across to Au Bon Pain, where some reporters worked on stories.

A young woman who sat typing in fingerless gloves looked up at him as he took the table behind her with his coffee and cranberry muffin. She turned around in her chair and told him she was covering the march for washingtonpost.com—feature stories, tent life, food, music, nightlife in Tent City. "I've seen you with the newspaper girl," the reporter said. "Is she the real thing? Is she poor?"

Instead of answering, Jonathan separated the top of the muffin from its body and offered the rest to the reporter on his way out. She took it, she said, because she didn't want to get thrown out of the restaurant for using the table and not buying anything.

Back in the square, Jonathan ducked into a tent where a panel discussion on horizontal politics had turned into another argument. Divisions were drawn about whether the planning committee had the right to end daily marches. The protesters were burning out, one side argued—they wanted to wait for larger turnouts before heading to the streets. The HONK FOR CHANGE signs had stopped getting any response. The drivers taking the same route every day now just waved at their new friends.

Outside, the clothing-tent girl was facing off against a crowd accosting her for loaning sweatshirts made in China. The girl stood her ground, fists raised in a Thai boxing stance, ghost tattoo puffed up in a flex. Across the way the food tent was being ravaged by park dwellers; the proprietor was letting it happen, packing his messenger bag to leave. A man with a rash around his mouth sat at the base of the General McPherson statue, rocking back and forth. Jonathan went to sit beside him. "They announced tomorrow's lineup," the man wept. "It's all over. The celebrities are coming. Sarandon. Moore. Fucking Kanye and North. Now what?"

With no sign of Maya and the rain coming down now in earnest, Jonathan jogged back to his apartment. He was surprised to find her there with Austen and Charlie, who sat on either side of Maya on the bed watching corgi-dive YouTube videos on Jonathan's computer. They couldn't get enough of a corgi belly-flopping into a lake. The Flies said the word *brilliant* after virtually everything, good or bad.

"I've got all my work on there," Jonathan said.

"I saved it," Maya said, not looking up. "And I cleaned up the grammar." She slammed down the top of the computer. "I didn't like what you said about the cult of participation. That's not what the protest is about."

Jonathan snatched the computer. "You misread," Jonathan insisted.

"The country is on the brink and you're writing about the Cat in the Hat guys," Maya said.

"You haven't read the other entries," Jonathan said. They began to quarrel. Austen reached for the computer.

"I just have to show you this one dive, man. It is fucking brilliant."

Charlie hopped up from the bed and clapped his hands.

"Brilliant. We're running an errand. You're coming too." He pointed to Jonathan. "Community-service credits, let's go." Maya said she was staying at the apartment but that Jonathan should go and help. On the way to a white van outside, the Flies told him that they were going to match shoes at the thrift store.

"Nines, twelves, fives, all mixed up in big bags," Austen said. "We go in and put them in pairs."

"For the poor," Charlie said. "Though once this rich guy came in and bought a pair of Pradas for ten dollars. The prick. Fucking brilliant."

They climbed into the cab of the van and headed for the Rock Creek Parkway uptown. The van had no shocks and the brakes made grinding sounds. Untethered lawn mowers and leaf blowers bashed around in the back.

"You guys do landscaping?" Jonathan asked, stuffed into the passenger seat with Charlie, who kept rubbing his knee and singing, "Baby, baby."

"Is this even your van?" Jonathan asked.

A deer poked his head out of the woods on Oregon Avenue. Austen slammed on the brakes and then, instead of driving on, pulled over beneath some trees on the edge of the park. The three got out, stepping through the brush, and Jonathan followed the Flies onto a gravel path. A sign read CLOSED AT DARK. The air was cold and wet and Jonathan's pants were soaked up to the knees. They soon came to a victory garden, each plot surrounded by chicken wire and filled with stalks of tomatoes and pepper plants, vines with a few pumpkins, and marigolds everywhere to keep out the bugs. Charlie reached through one of the fences to snatch a tomato to eat.

"*Blech!* Gross!" He spit it out and then went about kicking in the fence, stomping on the tomato vines, and pulling up the pumpkins, smashing them on the path. "For the deer," he said, pitching cucumbers into the woods. "Here, catch." Jonathan ducked when Charlie flung a pumpkin at him so hard that it pulverized when it hit the ground. As they moved farther into the park, Jonathan suggested they get back to McPherson Square. Charlie's voice sounded like the gravel crunching under his feet.

"We gotta match shoes. Remember? This is a short cut."

Jonathan looked for an opening in the trees, somewhere he could race down to the street. But Rock Creek Park at that hour was the darkest place Jonathan had ever been. Light pollution from the city got sucked in and destroyed. He could barely make out the reflecting tape on the back of Charlie's sneakers.

"I have to get back," Jonathan said. "Someone's waiting for me."

"We know who's waiting for you," Austen said, and pushed Jonathan on the shoulder, causing him to trip. Jonathan felt a pain in his spine like a hard kick. He landed sitting on his hands, the Flies hovering above. He had a sick feeling that he was going to be raped. A headline plastered down Maya's trapezius had warned of an increase of attacks in the park.

"I have a thousand dollars in my money belt," Jonathan said.

"You think we want your money?" Austen said.

"What do you want?"

Austen knelt beside him. "We want to know what you've read. On Maya."

Jonathan looked up at Charlie, who seemed poised to hit him in the face. "Could you please, please sit down?" he asked. "I can't think."

"You gonna tell us something?" Charlie said.

"Sit down," Austen demanded. "Come on, J. Give us an article. Give us an ad or a positive review."

"Nothing political," Charlie said. "And no fucking classifieds. As if anyone ever gets a job."

"Nothing disturbing," Austen said. "Nothing from the Metro section."

"Sometimes obits are good," Charlie said. "Depending where they're placed, on the body."

"No death. Give us a feature, J. A story about someone who struggles in the first part of his life and then ends up in office."

Jonathan looked at the Flies sitting in the wet leaves as though they were at a summer camp with an Indian name in Maine. "There was a congresswoman," he began.

"Brilliant," Austen said.

"She was very poor," Jonathan continued, "homeless, in fact. Her mom was an addict. There was never any food..."

"Where was it written?" Charlie asked.

"The *Washington Post* Style section," Jonathan said.

Charlie threatened him with a stick. "Where on *her?*"

Jonathan pulled his hand out from under himself, slowly, so that Charlie wouldn't think he was making any quick moves. "It was here," he said. He pointed to his back. "And here." He slid his hand to his front.

"The flank?" Austen asked.

Jonathan felt dirty. He was betraying her, he thought.

"Tell us the whole story," Austen said, leaning back. Charlie rested his elbows on his knees. "Word for word."

But Maya didn't have rags-to-riches stories. Jonathan had to make something up about the woman having kids at seventeen and sleeping at the bus station, working as a janitor in the state house and catching the eye of Maryland's attorney general. Then he told a story about a Mexican boy who came to the States, faced brutal discrimination, and now owned a chain of hardware stores that employed the homeless.

"On her thighs?" they wanted to know.

"All 'round 'em," Jonathan replied.

He invented urban renewal without displacing the poor. Children painting cinder blocks to look like enchanted gardens. Charlie and Austen listened, tilting their heads like puppies.

"...that family never went hungry again... And what did that lady do? She married him, that's what she did... Year after year, the pileated woodpecker came back to say hello to the little boy..."

Maya's stories did not have happy endings. Maya was swastikas spray-painted on synagogues, stormed American embassies, families buried in sinkholes, mudslides across the highway. If he didn't keep coming up with the good times he'd be thrown into a ravine, eaten by animals, lost to his family and friends, reduced to a headline printed across the soles of Maya's feet.

* * *

The temperature had dropped to near freezing and the wind was gusting at thirty miles per hour by the time Jonathan and the Flies got back to the square. The tarp over General McPherson flapped manically, threatening to blow off onto Vermont Avenue.

Committee meetings were canceled. Trash cans burned with bonfires. Protesters begged those fortunate enough to have the shelter of a tent to let them in for the night.

"You gonna help us build the structure tomorrow?" Austen asked, as though he hadn't just held Jonathan hostage for three hours.

"Uh, sure," Jonathan said, and headed for the clothing tent to warm up. The girl who ran the loans had stepped outside for a cigarette.

"I've got something for you," she said. He waited for her to stamp the cigarette out in the mud, then pick up the filter and toss it into a burning trash barrel. She pulled aside the curtain that kept the wind out of the tent.

"*Après vous,*" she said.

"*Merci,*" Jonathan said.

Beckoning with her finger she led him to the back corner of the tent, where she moved aside some lawn-and-leaf bags filled with donations and pulled out a full-length black down coat, the Lands' End tags still attached.

"Take it. Your papergirl will freeze. What size shoe would you say she wears?"

Jonathan didn't know, so she pulled the shape holders and tissue paper from a new pair of size-nine black Ugg boots. Then she searched the clothing table for a wool hat, a hoodie, some leggings, and mittens, all of which she stacked up in his arms.

"Tell her to consider these a permanent loan," she said.

He left the tent with the pile of clothes. The sidewalks were covered in bumpy ice. He had to skid his way to a cab on Pennsylvania Avenue.

Maya was sitting on the end of the bed watching videos of the march when Jonathan came into the apartment.

"I keep thinking I'm going to see someone I know," she said. "But then I don't."

He dropped the clothes on a wobbly pine table. An Ugg did an ender to the floor. She stood to embrace him but he only wanted a shower and Cortaid for the welts the mosquitoes had left as a tip for his arms and ankles. He was surprised to see her in color.

"What are you wearing?" he asked.

"You don't like it?" The hang of the skirt wasn't right. The top was boxy with cheap-looking darts. She'd used the *Denver Post* and the *Wyoming Livestock Roundup*.

"Sunsets and longhorns?" he asked. "Where did you get western papers?"

"A friend brought them. He held on to the back of a train with one arm. All the way from Colorado."

Jonathan felt he'd been clawed down his back by jealousy.

"Maya," he said. "Lately, your clothes…"

"What about them?" she asked.

"Op-eds from the *Wall Street Journal*?" he said. "The *Washington Times*?"

"All sides?" she said. "Speaking of which, what exactly are you for?"

They continued quarreling until a tear fell from her eye and jumped the cliff of her cheekbone. He dropped himself into a club chair that was covered in baby-blue worn corduroy.

"I'm thinking I should sleep in the tents," he said, stunned at how cruel his words could be.

"I'll get ready," she said.

"It's cold. Put those on." He gestured toward the pile on the table. "And don't say you don't want them. I've been through a fire to get them."

She looked the table over and stood from the bed, making little rips in her skirt until it fell. When she tore her top it caught flight, then dropped diagonally to the floor. The tricolor printing technique had come off on her skin. Mountains over the Snake River looked like an irregular EKG. A piece on managing drought risk was tattooed across her lower back like a tramp stamp. The new clothes drowned her, the boots so large she had to shuffle her way to the door.

"I need to file," he said. "I'll meet you by the statue?"

She waved her hand in a mitten three sizes too big.

Jonathan couldn't sleep. He wanted to go back to school, to the food stations of the cafeteria, the weight rooms of the gym, the floor-to-ceiling casement windows in the Women's Studies department. A civil rights leader was coming for winter term to teach History of Nonviolence.

He found his ex-girlfriend online at 3:30 a.m., logging on from her semester abroad in Honduras. "What are you doing?" he asked.

"Spraying graffiti on a wall we painted when we got here," she replied.

"What for?" he asked.

"So that the next group of students will have something to paint over."

"What are you wearing?" he asked, regretting it instantly.

After they disconnected he spent hours staring at the stars on the ceiling until they faded in the morning light. He thought of stealing away, going to Union Station, getting on a train headed north. But he missed Maya. Her pulp smell. Her words. Her whimpering in her sleep from sad stories. He got dressed and went to the square to find her.

It was 65 degrees. Not unusual for Washington weather to be so changeable. Police and health department officials had mixed in with the protesters, agitation spinning through the crowd. A demonstrator had just been arrested for spray-painting FREEDOM at the base of the cherry picker the police had driven into the square. The Flies had built a new structure. Young men climbed to the top. Health department workers balled up tarps for the trash. Uncovered by the police, General McPherson gleamed in the sun, his head turned to the right, surveying the battlefield. Jonathan saw Maya sitting alone on the granite step at the base of the statue, still in her black winter outfit despite the warm day. He rushed over. But it wasn't her. What he'd thought was Maya was a pile of lawn-and-leaf bags.

"You know you've been at the carnival too long when you confuse black trash bags for your girlfriend."

It was the clothing girl. She handed him a letter. It was from Maya. She said that she and Charlie were heading to New York. A reporter had sent some pictures of her to the editor of the *Times*'s Sunday magazine. They wanted to do a spread on clothing-as-protest and designing with salvaged materials. There was also a photographer who wanted to take nude pictures, "art photos," she said, with newsprint on her skin.

"Come to New York and find us," she wrote. "We'll be there until there's change."

He followed the girl to the clothing tent, where she was packing up herself.

"We're going to Raleigh," she said. "That's the next big place. Ride with us."

Austen waved from the top of the structure. "J! J!" A cop in the cherry picker was attempting to arrest him. Austen climbed into the bucket without a fight. "I got arrested!" he yelled. "Finally!"

A white-haired policeman stepped up next to Jonathan, scanning the scene. "Boy oh boy," the policeman said. "Where's Mark Rudd when you need him?" He turned to Jonathan. "You doing okay? Do you want to get arrested?" he asked, not as a threat but as a favor.

"This business is going to shut down," he told Jonathan. "You ought to go back to school. I sure should have gone." He snapped on a pair of medical gloves and shook open a lawn-and-leaf bag. Jonathan picked up some empty Sprite cans and gave them to the officer.

The health department workers had already begun pulling up tents, the startled inhabitants waking up to homelessness, wrapping their sleeping bags around their bodies like togas. The tents the health department couldn't yank from the ground they slashed with scissors or knives. The regular park dwellers stood patiently by, waiting for their land to be returned to them, to reclaim their benches.

"Let's go, let's go," the policeman shouted to the protesters milling around them. "This park is closed."

Jonathan headed toward I Street. "You need money?" the cop called after him. Jonathan said no. At the south end of the park stood a group of women who had cut holes in the tops of brightly colored tents, wearing them as dresses. When the health department officials moved in with their knives, the women began to spin like dervishes.

THE LAZARUS CORRECTION

by DAN KEANE

Wednesday's my maid day. I'm out the door pretty early to be sure I'm gone when he arrives, so I'm the only one in the office when the report comes in: two dead girls in a cheap hotel room near the Uyuni Salt Flats.

Radio Erbol confirms only *two* and *female* and *tourists* but no nationality or cause of death. Panamericana adds *young*. I'm adding *cheap* because Uyuni the town, still a few miles from the actual Salt Flats, is famously grim and cold and backpackery, a Bolivian spaceport for wandering gringos. The police station there has no landline, so I work my contacts for a Uyuni sergeant's cell number. The sergeant says—sternly, in a whisper, as if holding up in the face of unknowable demons—that initial reports are a leaky or unventilated gas heater, and that the girls were from either Sweden or Switzerland, and to call back in half an hour. I hold off filing. Confirmed dead are a serious business. Screw up and file too soon and you have to run a Lazarus correction, and that shit the editors never forget.

Victor arrives while I wait. He hangs up his jacket and right away brings me coca tea and a cheesy roll on a flowered plate. Victor's the office man, twice my age, hair dyed black, a slight stoop. Poor things, he says. I hand him my light bill and he steps out to pay it. I message Kate: *Dead tourist alert.* But she's sleeping in and my words just sit there in the little box.

When I finally get the Uyuni sergeant back on the line he confirms *gas heater* and *Suiza*, not Suecia. The hotel owner had ducked into the girls' room at about five a.m. to shut off the heater. They were probably already dead. The windows were shut. The sergeant says the heater in question is being "closely examined." On why the women were permitted to sleep with a gas heater in an unventilated room: "It is very cold here at night." The sergeant passes off the phone to someone who dictates two chaotically mispronounced and misspelled names, probably from the hotel log. I call the Swiss embassy but their spokeswoman says she's still working on confirmation, call back in a few. I message our Geneva desk a heads-up for possible family comment. I file our first story: two Swiss women, unventilated heater, names withheld. I hold back *cheap.* I add a line about the Uyuni Salt Flats having been recently declared one of the Eight Natural Wonders of the World, but then I can't remember who did the declaring, so I cut it out.

Bolivision and TVB both lead their midday news with the Swiss girls. No footage until the next day, probably, because Uyuni's a long way out there and most likely has deathly slow internet, but they've each got a graphic with the girls' names printed in much more believable spellings, meaning the Uyuni police have found their passports: Marina Kestenholz, twenty-three, and Isabelle Bonvin, twenty-two, both listing a hometown of Bern. I call the Uyuni police sergeant to confirm the correctly spelled names but the sergeant does not pick up. I call the Swiss embassy spokeswoman and she's got the names but won't go on the record yet. The families must be notified first. I say how about I read the names to you and you tell me if I've got them right. OK, she says. I read what I've copied from TV and she says they're right, but please hold them a little longer, the Bonvins have been told but the Kestenholzes must be out to dinner or something, they're not picking up. I message Geneva and tell them to hold off on family comments. Geneva says they'll hold.

On Isabelle Bonvin's Facebook page there's a photo of three girls in bikinis under a jungle waterfall: Bonvin and Kestenholz and a third untagged girl, all with triumphant smiles and tank-top tans, hair slicked back by exotic waters, souvenir bracelets on their wrists, long legs firm from months hauling a pack. Glorious, really, though too much for a wire obit. I hunt a bit more and find two older, quieter photos from home. Bonvin, brunette, smiling in a backyard. Kestenholz, blonde, with her family at Christmas. I download the pics, e-mail them to the photo desk, then go home to eat lunch and pay the maid.

My maid, my original maid, was named Diana, a hard forty-something *cholita* with complicated teeth and a sweet, sad smile. I'd secretly hoped for someone younger and cuter, but then Diana came with the apartment somehow, and she turned out to be amazing, far better than the hapless young nieces some of the other gringos wind up with. Diana cleaned with vehement force. She would dip her broom in a mop bucket and then beat the hell out of the living room rug. Sometimes her son, Wilson, would bring her lunch, and the two of us would just stand there and watch. Drops and dust flying everywhere. The rug knapping up in choppy waves. My bedsheets, too, they're already faded because Diana washed and ironed them so vigorously. Kate and I always slept at my place Wednesday nights because peeling back those tight, crisp sheets made us feel like we were staying in a fancy hotel. Diana even ironed my underwear. I told her once not to, gently, not wanting to offend, but she kept doing it anyway. And they felt awesome, honestly. A man feels important in pressed undies. And who am I to tell her how to do her job?

But then Diana's appendix burst over Thanksgiving weekend. Kate and I had landed an invite to a dinner at the home of a USAID guy who collected rare Scotch, and we spent the rest of the holiday nursing a two-day Andean hangover and watching whole seasons of *The Wire*. Wilson never called. He just took his mom to the hospital, the doctors cut the thing out, and that was that. He told me all about it the next Wednesday when he came alone to beat the living room rug. I took him firmly by his shoulders and said: Wilson. Call me next time. That's very generous, sir, he said, but I didn't want to bother you.

The general rule among the gringos is don't overpay the maids because it messes with the market, but you help out where you can. I chip in for Wilson's college tuition. I gave him and Diana both a nice Christmas bonus. It's delicate, though. Those first few fistfuls of pink bills feel really good, but then you catch the cold breeze from the depths of the pit and realize there will never be a good place to stop. Missing the appendix mess was a relief, honestly. Wilson handled it like a man. I was proud of him. Everything was going to be OK.

Except Wilson kept coming alone on Wednesdays for the whole next month, and the month after that. This Wednesday he's here again, beating the hell out of the rug in the Nikes I gave him, sweet throwbacks that were too narrow for my feet. I guess he uses them as house-cleaning shoes. Maybe he thinks he has to wear them in front of me.

How's your mother? I ask, according to our ritual. I eat my leftover Mr. Pizza standing up, one hand out to catch the crumbs. She isn't feeling well, Wilson answers, as always. Ever since the surgery there's been something in her gut. We sigh, we nod. He sweeps. I chew. The first few weeks I would say yeah, she should just rest. Yes, Wilson would say, she wanted to rest. Then I started saying Diana should probably go back to the doctor. Wilson would give this sad little shrug and say maybe, we'll see. He does this again this week, but adds that she's in a lot of pain, she's hardly eating now, she's just drinking tea, and I say Wilson, why didn't you call me? I didn't want to bother you, sir, he says. Wilson, I say, we have to take her back to the hospital. We need to do something. And please don't call me sir.

Wilson shrugs again and says his mother doesn't want another surgery. She'd rather just stay home and rest. I tell Wilson: Staying home is not a solution here. Staying home means waiting around to die, but I can't say that to Wilson's face, not when he stops with the broom and looks down at the beaded-up rug as if it were a hopeless, dirty ocean. My mother doesn't want to be any trouble, he says, and the hospital is so expensive. The hospital is what made her sick before. She just wants to rest. I tell him forget the costs, I'll pay whatever, just call me, OK? OK, Wilson says. Thank you, sir.

I let the sir pass. We both take a breath to clear the air. Wilson resumes abusing the rug. I open a window and clap the crumbs off my hand into the street ten floors below. I ask about school. Wilson demurs. Classes are hard, he says. Lots of studying. He's a smart kid but shy and mumbly, with his mother's long bony face and glossy black hair long enough to catch on his cheap wire glasses. Wilson claims to want to be an accountant. I don't know whether this is just him aiming for a proper non-maid job, something he can support his mother on, or whether there's some kind of real passion behind the choice. I don't suppose it matters, though he'll never make it in business being so damn mumbly all the time. As a coaching tactic, I try to be supremely confident on his behalf. You'll pass, I insist. I know you will. I ask once again if he's made any friends in his classes, and he gives one of those maddening defeatist shrugs and says it's tough because he doesn't drink, his dad was an alcoholic, and he doesn't really have time anyways, with all the studying and taking care of his mom. When I hand him his month's pay I slip him an extra bill and say, Live a little! Go out and have a coffee sometime! I don't dare mention girls. Too much pressure on the poor guy already. One thing at a time. Thank you, sir, he says, stopping a moment to pocket the money. God bless you, he says.

Wilson, I say. I hardly ever set foot in here. You don't need to beat the rug so hard.

It's no problem, he says. Only way to make sure it's clean.

Lunches in La Paz are hours long, and I don't expect any confirmation from the Swiss embassy until everyone's back at their desks around three o'clock, so I grab my laptop and head to my bedroom. My underwear waits for me in loosely folded piles. I lie down on the clean but not very crisply made bed. Wilson thwacks away down the hall. I was having these thoughts at work, looking at Isabelle and Marina in that waterfall photo, so I open up my laptop and search online for something quick, anything really, blonde or brunette, whatever, and stroke myself hard and go for a quick one right there. This is not creepy, I swear. Nothing about the Swiss girls being dead. This is a life-affirming thing. I am *alive*. I wish they were alive too. Their young bodies. The water on their skin. The third girl, whoever she was—I get close to finishing and leap up, not wanting to spot the clean sheets, and I'm standing there, one hand out to catch the mess, right at the part when you feel *super* alive for a few seconds, when the door opens and Wilson walks in. He's got a trash bag in his hand. Sorry, sorry, he says, and turns around and hurries back out.

I stand there and drip on the clean floor, hot with shame. I clean up but I don't want to put the toilet paper in the trash for Wilson to see and so instead I have to flush it all down the toilet, even though the plumbing in Bolivia isn't supposed to be able to handle that. But it does, actually, if you flush one little piece at a time. On my way out I hear Wilson scrubbing

something in the kitchen, and I rattle the apartment door to let him know
I'm gone.

Back at the office Kate appears on chat: *Thanks* and then *So sad* and *You going
to this thing tonight?* Kate's freelance, she doesn't have to do the death briefs.
Features only. When an accountant from Denver rode his mountain bike off
a cliff last month she tried to call dibs on a big Growing Pains of Bolivian
Tourism feature but I said uh-uh, no dice, deaths are my beat. She offered to
trade me the Australian girl locked up for a roller bag of coke, the one whose
folks have been begging all of us for a story, and I said no deal, human interest
is *your* thing. Kate groaned. The Australian accent just kills her. Anyhow,
one really nasty run of tourist deaths and everybody's editors will holler for a
trend story, dibs be damned. And so we keep a tally, and we wait.

The thing tonight is a farewell party for a Brit photographer at a downtown expat club known for discount mojitos and sandwiches with the crusts
cut off. Someone plays the farewell card and you pretty much have to go.
Buy you a big stupid weeknight shot, I write back, which gets me a smiley face.

I call the Swiss embassy and the spokeswoman says the Kestenholzes
picked up, poor things, and we're clear to file the names. I add Bonvin's
and Kestenholz's names to the story and file an update. I message the photo
desk to go ahead and run the photos. I send Geneva the green light to call
the families. Geneva shoots back the family phone numbers and says La Paz
should do it, because La Paz "knows the details." Mexico City weighs in,
bowing to Geneva. I'm new at this and ask for tips. Mexico City says the line
is simple: We're sorry for your loss. Put that out there and see where it goes.
I take a deep breath and dial. It's a ton of numbers. The Kestenholzes are
not answering, thank god. I imagine the Kestenholzes in a restaurant, their
table overturned, wailing too loudly to hear a cell phone that's been kicked
into a puddle of wine on the floor, but it's probably just a call-waiting thing

and they're too hectic with grief to click over. I try the Bonvins. After four of those European ring-buzzes someone picks up and there's a cough and a jumble of something dropped or moved and then a low, Gallic rumble on the other end of the line: *Alo*. I introduce myself and present my token: We are sorry for your loss. Eh? the voice says. I apologize, start over, ask to speak to Monsieur Bonvin. This is him, the voice says. Does he speak English? Yes. Well then: I am calling from the Worldwide News desk in La Paz, Bolivia, sir, and we are very sorry for your loss. What loss? Bonvin says. Where are you? Who are you? I panic and hang up.

Victor asks if I want coffee and perhaps a sweet roll. No, Victor, but thank you.

I stare at the phone. Maybe that's a no comment? But the phone rings again. The caller ID shows a ton of numbers.

I take a deep breath and pick up. I'm sorry, sir, we must have been cut off. Who are you, he says.

I'm sorry, sir, there must have been some mistake. This is the Worldwide News in La Paz, Bolivia. We were looking for a Monsieur Bonvin, but I believe we—

This is me, he says. I am Bonvin, and you are sorry for my loss, but I do not know any loss. My daughter, she is in South America right now. What are you saying?

Someone should have already called, I say. I can feel the breeze from the pit but now it's a whole different pit. Bonvin presses, his voice low and steady: Called to tell me what?

About Isabelle, I say.

My computer dings. New York says that was just an intern in Geneva who didn't know protocol, you don't even speak French, don't worry about it. New York promises the intern will be given a talking to.

Isabelle is my daughter, Bonvin is saying. Is she all right? Did something happen?

Deep breath. I'm sorry, sir. There was an accident. I run through the details—the town, the Flats, the hotel, omitting its cheapness—and I'm going on about how she went in her sleep when I realize there's nothing but silence on the other end. Victor is watching, worried. Victor speaks no English but knows when an interview's gone wrong. A phone-ish thunk, and then another.

I stay on the line. Out the high-rise window clouds hang low over Illimani. I wish I could tell you it starts hailing right then, but it's just a steady, spitting mist. I tell M. Bonvin's silence that I will let him go—let him go, as if I am dangling him over the pit—and will contact him again at another time. Then I place the phone gently back on the hook and it's over.

Victor says, It's really, really sad, isn't it?

I message Kate: *BEEEER POR FAVOOOOOOOOOR*

Kate: *SI SENOOOOOOOOR*

Geneva closes up in a sulk. New York has moved on. When I leave the office at six my last update with the girls' names but no family comment sits patiently in Mexico City's editing queue behind a breaking gang-violence thing out of Honduras, a natural-gas discovery off the coast of Brazil, an update on the Colombian free-trade agreement, a cabinet shuffle in Argentina, and a feature out of Guatemala on a farm run by a French couple who claim to be growing chocolate exactly the way the Mayans did.

Kate and I meet at the farewell thing. Bronwyn, just Bron to everyone, a square, blond, and loud shooter from Manchester, has been here eighteen months. She's plowing through the nightclub's old-standby hummus plate and declaring it's been right about six months too long, though she couldn't have imagined that back in August. Bron says you have to overstay your welcome to see the actual finish line.

Around us the journos drink in slow weeknight rhythm. The band claims to be Cuban. Bron demands farewell shots. Kate and I stand her a round.

Why six months too long? Kate asks.

Because Bolivia's got a year's worth of pictures, Bron says. Riots: got it. Floods: got it. Miners throwing dynamite: bloody hell, the miners throwing dynamite! Three strikes in, what, fifteen months? Last time I'm out there like, No, no, you drunken idiot, you throw it like *this!* Bron flings an olive pit high over the dance floor and it vanishes into a far corner. You wait around for Bolivia to change, she says, but it just keeps coming round again.

I've only been in country six months. Just the one miners' strike, for those keeping score, and I'm keeping score. The rivers are already rising again out east. Kate and I are planning our own Uyuni trip this winter. I don't need to see everything. I just want to feel like I've seen *enough*.

What about the president? Kate asks. I think things are really changing here.

Tell you what, Bron says. Next riot, you ring me up, and you say Bron, we miss you, everyone hates the president and we need a drink to wash the tear-gas vomit out of our mouths, and I'll say Aha! Yes! Now you know. But seriously. Ever get to London, look me up. We'll get good and pissed.

Bron spends most of the night salsa-dancing with Tomas, one heavy British thigh up around his skinny black jeans, her last going-out dress riding up without reservation. She is flushed with the history of the moment. Tomas is grinning, but then Tomas is always grinning when he dances. Tomas calls himself a documentary filmmaker and I suppose he is. Anyone can be what they want to be. Kate and I lay odds as to whether Bron will take him home. Bron has already declared she won't sleep. No point in it, she said. Taxi's coming at four thirty. Suitcases by the door. We all nodded in recognition. The American Airlines flight to Miami keeps watch over all our Bolivian lives.

Kate says it'll be a no on Tomas. Bron will declare an uncomplicated victory on her final Bolivian dance floor and leave Tomas on the night-club steps and go home and pass out for a couple hours, all big talk aside. I say Bron's gonna go for it. You're projecting, Kate says. I say no, I just think Bron's gonna want to commemorate the night, you know, last night in Bolivia, and Kate says isn't all this commemoration enough? Never, I say. There's never enough commemoration. On the walk home I grab her and try to spin her right there next to the fountain, hey, look at us, this is the scene in the movie where we dance salsa without any music under the statue in the park, and Kate says, But *we're* not going anywhere yet.

At my apartment Kate turns down the bed and says she wishes Diana was doing better, the bed's just not the same without her, and is that a terrible thing to say? I honestly don't know. I give her the update from Wilson. I don't know what to do, I say. We go visit her, that's what we do, Kate says.

I walk naked out to the living room to turn out the lights. Back in bed I pull Kate close. Wilson told me once she used to be a cook in the mines, I say.

Just imagine, Kate murmurs.

We lie in the dark and imagine. The city lies beneath us, trapped in its canyon. The Swiss girls hold their spot on the wire until midnight in New York, when everything's wiped clean to make room for the next day's news.

Just after six the next morning my phone rings on the nightstand and it's Wilson. Sorry for waking you, sir, he says. That's OK, I say. Sir, you were right, my mother needed to go to the hospital. She was in terrible pain and so I took her, and they say they are going to operate. Can you come up and help?

Yes. Yes I can. I kiss Kate good-bye and stumble outside like a hero, blood thumping in my chest. I flag a taxi and ride uphill through the gray streets. The streetlights are still on. The hospital is the one in Diana and Wilson's neighborhood, up past the old abandoned train station. Out front of the station is a line of buses already busy with people heading out of the city. I'm not going to get poetic here, but there's a whole lot of women who look like Diana, the big skirts, the Indian faces, your classic big plastic bundles of produce and belongings. I want to see a symbol of resilience in all this but then right behind them lurks the dead train station, shuttered, graffitied, clamoring to be a symbol of its own. A few blocks higher into the bare-bricked hills we come to the hospital, which symbol-wise wins hands down. A goddamn tomb. Three stories of stained plaster once the color of flesh-tone Crayola. Narrow tile hallways cramped with sad people waiting. Wilson is standing around an upstairs hallway looking doomed. They took her in, he says. There was a twist in her intestines. Something got blocked in there and now it's infected. They said there was nothing else they could do, they had to operate. They wanted to know who was paying, and I had no choice, I had to tell them your name.

Of course, I say. Of course.

Wilson looks gaunt, skeletal with worry. We sit down on a bench and we wait.

I ask about school again, automatically, and automatically he answers: Fine. There is one semester left, one more big payment I will help him make—that I will make in its entirety, in cash, and never see a receipt for. I asked for receipts at the beginning, and he gave me one or two, handwritten receipts photocopied on one of those crappy street-stall photocopiers, ghost lines running across the page, the numbers barely legible, but then they stopped appearing. It would be cruel to press the issue. What will he do after graduation? I ask. Keep looking for a job, Wilson says. Where will he look? Everywhere, he says. Offices. Lots of offices. It's very hard, no one hires.

I go find a bathroom down the hall, and as I wash my hands I see, in the corner on the tile floor, like a mouse, like a dropped secret, a single round turd. I realize: Diana will die here. Wilson has to take her somewhere else. Back outside I sit down on the bench next to him and grab his shoulders and say: Wilson, we've got to take her somewhere else. Wilson says, If you think that's right, sir. Wilson, I say, I'm right here, I'll pay for the ambulance. Take advantage of me. Let's get Diana out of here, OK? Let's *not* accept her fate. OK, Wilson says. Thank you, sir, for everything. It really means a lot to me and my mother.

A doctor comes out of surgery—it's a curtain, not a swinging door, just a curtain on a fucking rod—holding his bloody hands up to keep them clean, and I realize it's Diana's blood, and he says through his mask he needs a family member. I don't understand at first, with the mask in the way, but Wilson does. He stands up, terrified, and nods, his hair flapping in his eyes. I'm her son, he says. He walks slowly toward the curtain and disappears behind it. Over the curtain I can hear the noises of surgery now—before they were just the noises of a hospital, but now it's surgery, specifically, the mute whispers and metallic scuffs. Morning light backs reluctantly in through the windows.

There's supposed to be a decent clinic in the suburbs, a retired American doctor. Wilson should have called me at Thanksgiving. They'd never have gone out there on their own, probably couldn't even afford the taxi, but I could have climbed out of my hangover and done something. I think about that leaky heater. I realize I never found out whether the Swiss girls died the night their bus rolled into Uyuni or the night they came back from a three-day jeep tour of the Flats. Whether they saw what they came for. Whether M. Bonvin now waits in a Swiss airport lounge to sign for a daughter with salt in her hair.

And then Wilson pops back out of the curtain in a daze, paper mask on his face and his hands at his sides, glasses down his nose, and says something I don't understand. What, I say. He tugs down his mask. Sir, can you come in here a minute? I get up and walk toward the curtain. On the other side it's not the operating room, it's just an antechamber, and Wilson hands me a robe and mask from a little metal trolley, and then we step through a second curtain into the operating room proper. There under the fluorescent lights is Diana, asleep, her face spare and bony like one of those Andean mummies in *National Geographic*, so help me god. The surgeons are standing around an open pit in her abdomen. They all wear masks. They are all shorter than me, to a man, though I know that doesn't matter. I can hear bus brakes out in the street as morning traffic begins and I wonder if there's a window open somewhere. Wilson and I stand side by side, way back from the table, and touch absolutely nothing. The surgeon speaks into his mask and suddenly I can understand every syllable: A consultation, he says. He nods at his two assistants, and the assistants reach into Diana and gently lift up a long stretch of intestines, a knotty red loop spooling up and out of her, over their gloved fingers and into the chilly hospital air. The surgeon says the plan is to cut from here (he points) to here (he points), a very delicate situation, as you can see, and we wanted to ask the son first but the son says he doesn't know, and so now we're asking you. And I look over at Wilson, who's looking at me with the light of hope in his eyes, and I say, like a man who knows: Right there. Right there is good.

I CAN SEE RIGHT
THROUGH YOU

by **KELLY LINK**

When the sex tape happened and things went south with Fawn, the demon lover did what he always did. He went to cry on Meggie's shoulder. Girls like Fawn came and went, but Meggie would always be there. Him and Meggie. It was the talisman you kept in your pocket. The one you couldn't lose.

Two monsters can kiss in a movie. One old friend can go to see another old friend and be sure of his welcome: so here is the demon lover in a rental car. An hour into the drive, he opens the window, tosses out his cell phone. There is no one he wants to talk to except for Meggie.

* * *

(1991) This is after the movie and after they are together and after they begin to understand the bargain that they have made. They are both, suddenly, very famous.

Film can be put together in any order. Scenes shot in any sequence. Take as many takes as you like. Continuity is independent of linear time. Sometimes you aren't even in the scene together. Meggie says her lines to your stand-in. They'll splice you together later on. Shuffle off to Buffalo, gals. Come out tonight.

(This is long before any of that. This was a very long time ago.)

Meggie tells the demon lover a story:

Two girls and look, they've found a Ouija board. They make a list of questions. One girl is pretty. One girl is not really a part of this story. She's lost her favorite sweater. Her fingertips on the planchette. Two girls, each touching, lightly, the planchette. Is anyone here? Where did I put my blue sweater? Will anyone ever love me? Things like that.

They ask their questions. The planchette drifts. Gives up nonsense. They start the list over again. Is anyone here? Will I be famous? Where is my blue sweater?

The planchette jerks under their fingers.

M-E

Meggie says, "Did you do that?"

The other girl says she didn't. The planchette moves again, a fidget. A stutter, a nudge, a sequence of swoops and stops.

M-E-G-G-I-E

"It's talking to you," the other girl says.

M-E-G-G-I-E H-E-L-L-O

Meggie says, "Hello?"

The planchette moves again and again. There is something animal about it.

H-E-L-L-O I A-M W-I-T-H Y-O-U I A-M W-I-T-H Y-O-U A-L-W-A-Y-S

They write it all down.

M-E-G-G-I-E O I W-I-L-L L-O-V-E Y-O-U A-L-W-A-Y-S

"Who is this?" she says. "Who are you? Do I know you?"

I S-E-E Y-O-U I K-N-O-W Y-O-U W-A-I-T A-N-D I W-I-L-L C-O-M-E

A pause. Then:

I W-I-L-L M-E-G-G-I-E O I W-I-L-L B-E W-I-T-H Y-O-U A-L-W-A-Y-S

"Are you doing this?" Meggie says to the other girl. She shakes her head. Meggie laughs. "Okay, then. So okay, whoever you are, are you cute? Is this someone I'm going to meet someday and we'll fall in love? Like my husband or something? Who is this?"

M-E-G-G-I-E W-A-I-T

The other girl says, "Can whoever this is at least tell me where I left my sweater?"

O W-A-I-T A-N-D I W-I-L-L C-O-M-E

They wait. Will there be a knock at the bedroom door? But no one comes. No one is coming.

I A-M W-I-T-H Y-O-U A-L-W-A-Y-S

No one is here with them. The sweater will never be found. The other girl grows up, lives a long and happy life. Meggie goes out to LA and meets the demon lover.

W-A-I-T

After that, the only thing the planchette says, over and over, is Meggie's name. It's all very romantic.

* * *

(1974) Twenty-two people disappear from a nudist colony in Lake Apopka. People disappear all the time. Let's be honest: the only thing interesting here is that these people were naked. And that no one ever saw them again. Funny, right?

(1990) It's one of the ten most iconic movie kisses of all time. In the top five, surely. You and Meggie, the demon lover and his monster girl; vampires sharing a kiss as the sun comes up. Both of you wearing so much makeup it still astonishes you that anyone would ever recognize you on the street.

It's hard for the demon lover to grow old.

Florida is California on a Troma budget. That's what the demon lover thinks, anyway. Special effects blew the budget on bugs and bad weather. He parks in a meadowy space, recently mowed, alongside other rental cars, the usual catering and equipment vans. There are two gateposts with a chain between them. No fence. Eternal I endure.

There is an evil smell. Does it belong to the place or to him? The demon lover sniffs under his arm.

It's an end-of-the-world sky, a snakes-and-ladders landscape: low emerald trees pulled lower by vines; chalk and apricot anthills (the demon lover imagines the bones of a nudist under every one); shallow water-filled declivities scummed with algae, lime and gold and black.

The blot of the lake. That's another theory: the lake.

A storm is coming.

He doesn't get out of his car. He rolls the window down and watches the storm come in. Let's look at him looking at it. A pretty thing admiring a pretty thing. Abandoned site of a mass disappearance, muddy violet clouds, silver veils of rain driving down the lake, the tabloid prince of darkness, Meggie's demon lover, arriving in all his splendor. The only thing to spoil it are the bugs. And the sex tape.

(2012) You have been famous for more than half your life. Both of you. You only made the one movie together, but women still stop you on the street to ask about Meggie. Is she happy? Which one? you want to ask them. The one who kissed me in a movie when we were just kids, the one who wasn't real? The one who likes to smoke a bit of weed and text me about her neighbor's pet goat? The Meggie in the tabloids who drinks fucks gets fat pregnant too skinny has a secret baby slaps a maître d' talks to Monroe's ghost Elvis's ghost ghost of a missing three-year-old boy ghost of JFK? Sometimes they don't ask about Meggie. Instead they ask if you will bite them.

Happiness! Misery! If you were one, bet on it the other was on the way. That was what everyone liked to see. It was what the whole thing was about. The demon lover has a pair of gold cuff links, those faces. Meggie gave them to him. You know the ones I mean.

(2010) Meggie and the demon lover throw a Halloween party for everyone they know. They do this every Halloween. They're famous for it.

"Year after year, on a monkey's face a monkey's face," Meggie says.

She's King Kong. The year before? Half a pantomime horse. He's the demon lover. Who else? Year after year.

Meggie says, "I've decided to give up acting. I'm going to be a poet. Nobody cares when poets get old."

Fawn says, appraisingly, "I hope I look half as good as you when I'm your age." Fawn, twenty-three. A makeup artist. This year she and the demon lover are married. Last year they met on set.

He says, "I'm thinking I could get some work done on my jawline."

You'd think they were mother and daughter. Same Viking profile, same quizzical tilt to the head as they turn to look at him. Both taller than him. Both smarter, too, no doubt about it.

Maybe Meggie wonders sometimes about the women he sleeps with. Marries. Maybe he has a type. But so does she. There's a guy at the Halloween party. A boy, really.

Meggie always has a boy and the demon lover can always pick him out. Easy enough, even if Meggie's sly. She never introduces the lover of the moment, never brings them into conversations or even acknowledges their presence. They hang out on the edge of whatever is happening, and drink or smoke or watch Meggie at the center. Sometimes they drift closer, stand near enough to Meggie that it's plain what's going on. When she leaves, they follow after.

Meggie's type? The funny thing is, Meggie's lovers all look like the demon lover. More like the demon lover, he admits it, than he does. He and Meggie are both older now, but the world is full of beautiful black-haired boys and golden girls. Really, that's the problem.

The role of the demon lover comes with certain obligations. Your hairline will not recede. Your waistline will not expand. You are not to be photographed threatening paparazzi, or in sweatpants. No sex tapes.

Your fans will: offer their necks at premieres. (Also at restaurants and at the bank. More than once when he is standing in front of a urinal.) Ask if you will bite their wives. Their daughters. They will cut themselves with a razor in front of you.

The appropriate reaction is—

There is no appropriate reaction.

The demon lover does not always live up to his obligations. There is a sex tape. There is a girl with a piercing. There is, in the middle of some athletic sex, a comical incident involving his foreskin. There is blood all over the sheets. There is a lot of blood. There is a 911 call. There is him, fainting. Falling and hitting his head on a bedside table. There is Perez Hilton, Gawker, talk radio, YouTube, Tumblr. There are GIFs.

You will always be most famous for playing the lead in a series of vampire movies. The character you play is, of course, ageless. But you get older. The first time you bite a girl's neck, Meggie's neck, you're a twenty-five-year-old actor playing a vampire who hasn't gotten a day older in three hundred years. Now you're a forty-nine-year-old actor playing the same ageless vampire. It's getting to be a little ridiculous, isn't it? But if the demon lover isn't the demon lover, then who is he? Who are you? Other projects disappoint. Your agent says take a comic role. The trouble is you're not very funny. You're not good at funny.

The other trouble is the sex tape. Sex tapes are inherently funny. Nudity is, regrettably, funny. Torn foreskins are painfully funny. You didn't know she was filming it.

Your agent says, That wasn't what I meant.

You could do what Meggie did, all those years ago. Disappear. Travel the world. Hunt down the meaning of life. Go find Meggie.

When the sex tape happens you say to Fawn, But what does this have to do with Meggie? This has nothing to do with Meggie. It was just some girl.

It's not like there haven't been other girls.

Fawn says, It has everything to do with Meggie.

I can see right through you, Fawn says, less in sorrow than in anger. She probably can.

God grant me Meggie, but not just yet. That's him by way of St. Augustine by way of Fawn the makeup artist and Bible group junkie. She explains it to the demon lover, explains him to himself. And hasn't it been in the back of your mind all this time? It was Meggie right at the start. Why couldn't it be Meggie again? And in the meantime you could get married once in a while and never worry about whether or not it worked out. He and Meggie have managed, all this time, to stay friends. His marriages, his other relationships, perhaps these have only been a series of delaying actions. Small rebellions. And here's the thing about his marriages: he's never managed to stay friends with his ex-wives, his exes. He and Fawn won't be friends.

The demon lover and Meggie have known each other for such a long time. No one knows him like Meggie.

The remains of the nudist colony at Lake Apopka promise reasonable value for ghost hunters. A dozen ruined cabins, some roofless, windows black with mildew; a crumbled stucco hall, Spanish tiles receding; the cracked lip of a slop-filled pool. Between the cabins and the lake, the homely and welcome sight of half a dozen trailers. Even better, he spots a craft tent.

Muck farms! Mutant alligators! Disappearing nudists! The demon lover, killing time in the LAX airport, read up on Lake Apopka. The past is a weird place, Florida is a weird place, no news there. A demon lover should fit right in, but the ground sucks and clots at his shoes in a way that suggests he isn't welcome. The rain is directly overhead, shouting down in spit-warm gouts. He begins to run, stumbling, in the direction of the craft tent.

* * *

Meggie's career is on the upswing. Everyone agrees. She has a ghost-hunting show, *Who's There?*

The demon lover calls Meggie after the *Titanic* episode airs, the one where *Who's There?*'s ghost-hunting crew hitches a ride with the International Ice Patrol. There's the yearly ceremony, memorial wreaths. Meggie's crew sets up a Marconi transmitter and receiver just in case a ghost or two has a thing to say.

The demon lover asks her about the dead seagulls. Forget the Marconi nonsense. The seagulls were what made the episode. Hundreds of them, little corpses fixed, as if pinned, to the water.

Meggie says, You think we have the budget for fake seagulls? Please.

Admit that *Who's There?* is entertaining whether or not you believe in ghosts. It's all about the nasty detail, the house that gives you a bad feeling even when you turn on all the lights, the awful thing that happened to someone who wasn't you a very long time ago. The camera work is moody; extraordinary. The team of ghost hunters is personable, funny, reasonably attractive. Meggie sells you on the possibility: maybe what's going on here is real. Maybe someone is out there. Maybe they have something to say.

The demon lover and Meggie don't talk for months and then suddenly something changes and they talk every day. He likes to wake up in the morning and call her. They talk about scripts, now that Meggie's getting scripts again. He can talk to Meggie about anything. It's been that way all along. They haven't talked since the sex tape. Better to have this conversation in person.

(1991) He and Meggie are lovers. Their movie is big at the box office. Everywhere they go they are famous, and they go everywhere. Their faces are everywhere. They are kissing on a thousand screens. They are in a hotel room, kissing. They can't leave their hotel room without someone scream-ing or fainting or pointing something at them. They are asked the same questions again. Over and over. He begins to do the interviews in character. Anyway, it makes Meggie laugh.

There's a night, on some continent, in some city, some hotel room, some warm night, the demon lover and Meggie leave a window open and two women creep in. They come over the balcony. They just want to tell you that they love you. Both of you. They just want to be near you.

Everyone watches you. Even when they're pretending not to. Even when they aren't watching you, you think they are. And you know what? You're right. Eyes will find you. Becoming famous, this kind of fame: it's luck indistinguishable from catastrophe. You'd be dumb not to recognize it. What you've become.

When people disappear, there's always the chance that you'll see them again. The rain comes down so hard the demon lover can barely see. He thinks he is still moving in the direction of the craft tent and not the lake. There is a noise, he picks it out of the noise of the rain. A howling. And then the rain thins and he can see something, men and women, naked. Running toward him. He slips, catches himself, and the rain comes down hard again, erases everything except the sound of what is chasing him. He collides headlong with a thing: a skin horribly clammy, cold, somehow both stiff and yielding. Bounces off and realizes that this is the tent. Not where you'd choose to make a last stand, but by the time he has fumbled his way inside he has grasped the situation. Not dead nudists, but living people, naked, cursing, laughing, dripping. They carry cameras, mikes, gear for ghost hunting. Videographers, A2s, all the other useful types and the not so useful. A crowd of men and women, and here is Meggie. Her hair is glued in strings to her face. Her breasts are wet with rain.

He says her name.

They all look at him.

How is it possible that he is the one who feels naked?

"The fuck is this guy doing here?" says someone with a little white towel positioned over his genitals. Really, it could be even littler.

"Will," Meggie says. So gently he almost starts to cry. Well, it's been a long day.

She takes him to her trailer. He has a shower, borrows her toothbrush. She puts on a robe. Doesn't ask him any questions. Talks to him while he's in the bathroom. He leaves the door open.

It's the third day on location, and the first two have been a mixed bag. They got their establishing shots, went out on the lake and saw an alligator dive down when they got too close. There are baby skunks all over the scrubby, shabby woods, the trails. They come right up to you, up to the camera, and try like hell to spray. But until they hit adolescence all they can do is quiver their tails and stamp their feet.

Except, she says, and mentions some poor A2. His skunk was an early bloomer.

Meggie interviewed the former proprietor of the nudist colony. He insisted on calling it a naturist community, spent the interview explaining the philosophy behind naturism, didn't want to talk about 1974. A harmless old crank. Whatever happened, he had nothing to do with it. You couldn't lecture people into thin air. Besides, he had an alibi.

What they didn't get on the first day or even on the second was any kind of worthwhile read on their equipment. They have the two psychics—but one of them had an emergency, went back to deal with a daughter in rehab; they have all kinds of psychometric equipment, but there is absolutely nothing going on, down, or off. Which led to some discussion.

"We decided maybe we were the problem," Meggie says. "Maybe the nudists didn't have anything to say to us while we had our clothes on. So we're shooting in the nude. Everyone nude. Cast, crew, everyone. It's been a really positive experience, Will. It's a good group of people."

"Fun," the demon lover says. Someone has dropped off a pair of pink cargo shorts and a T-shirt, because his other clothes are in his suitcase back at the airport in Orlando. It's not exactly that he forgot. More like he couldn't be bothered.

"It's good to see you, Will," Meggie says. "But why are you here, exactly? How did you know where to find me?"

He takes the easy question first. "Pike." Pike is Meggie's agent and an old friend of the demon lover. The kind of agent who likes to pull the legs off small children. The kind of friend who finds life all the sweeter when you're in the middle of screwing up your own. "I made him promise not to tell you I was coming."

He collapses on the floor in front of Meggie's chair. She runs her fingers through his hair. Pets him like you'd pet a dog.

"He told you, though. Didn't he?"

"He did," Meggie said. "He called."

The demon lover says, "Meggie, this isn't about the sex tape."

Meggie says, "I know. Fawn called too."

He tries not to imagine that phone call. His head is sore. He's dehydrated, probably. That long flight.

"She wanted me to let her know if you showed. Said she was waiting to see before she threw in the towel."

She waits for him to say something. Waits a little bit longer. Strokes his hair the whole time.

"I won't call her," she says. "You ought to go back, Will. She's a good person."

"I don't love her," the demon lover says.

"Well," Meggie says. She takes that hand away.

There's a knock on the door, some girl. "Sun's out again, Meggie." She gives the demon lover a particularly melting smile. Was probably twelve when she first saw him on-screen. Baby ducks, these girls. Imprint on the first vampire they ever see. Then she's down the stairs again, bare bottom bouncing.

Meggie drops the robe, begins to apply sunblock to her arms and face. He notes the ways in which her body has changed. Thinks he might love her all the more for it, and hopes that this is true.

"Let me," he says, and takes the bottle from her. Begins to rub lotion into her back.

She doesn't flinch away. Why would she? They are friends.

She says, "Here's the thing about Florida, Will. You get these storms, practically every day. But then they go away again."

Her hands catch at his, slippery with the lotion. She says, "You must be tired. Take a nap. There's herbal tea in the cupboards, pot and Ambien in the bedroom. We're shooting all afternoon, straight through evening. And then a barbecue—we're filming that too. You're welcome to come out. It would be great publicity for us, of course. Our viewers would love it. But you'd have to do it naked like the rest of us. No clothes. No exceptions, Will. Not even for you."

He rubs the rest of the sunblock into her shoulders. Would like nothing more than to rest his head there.

"I love you, Meggie," he says. "You know that, right?"

"I know. I love you too, Will," she says. The way she says it tells him everything.

The demon lover goes to lie down on Meggie's bed, feeling a hundred years old. Dozes. Dreams about a bungalow in Venice Beach and Meggie and a girl. That was a long time ago.

* * *

There was a review of a play Meggie was in. Maybe ten years ago? It wasn't a kind review, or even particularly intelligent, and yet the critic said something that still seems right to the demon lover. He said no matter what was happening in the play, Meggie's performance suggested she was waiting for a bus. The demon lover thinks the critic got at something true there. Only, the demon lover has always thought that if Meggie was waiting for a bus, you had to wonder where that bus was going. If she was planning to throw herself under it.

When they first got together, the demon lover was pretty sure he was what Meggie had been waiting for. Maybe she thought so too. They bought a house, a bungalow in Venice Beach. He wonders who lives there now.

When the demon lover wakes up, he takes off the T-shirt and cargo shorts. Leaves them folded neatly on the bed. He'll have to find somewhere to sleep tonight. And soon. Day is becoming night.

Meat is cooking on a barbecue. The demon lover isn't sure when he last ate. There's bug spray beside the door. Ticklish on his balls. He feels just a little bit ridiculous. Surely this is a terrible idea. The latest in a long series of terrible ideas. Only this time he knows there's a camera.

The moment he steps outside Meggie's trailer, a PA appears as if by magic. It's what they do. Has him sign a pile of releases. Odd to stand here in the nude signing releases, but what the fuck. He thinks, I'll go home tomorrow.

The PA is in her fifties. Unusual. There's probably a story there, but who cares? He doesn't. Of course she's seen the fucking sex tape—it's probably going to be the most popular movie he ever makes—but her expression suggests this is the very first time she's ever seen the demon lover naked or rather that neither of them is naked at all.

While the demon lover signs—doesn't bother to read anything, what does it matter now anyway?—the PA talks about someone who hasn't done something. Who isn't where she ought to be. Some other gopher named Juliet. Where is she and what has she gone for? The PA is full of complaints.

The demon lover suggests the gopher may have been carried off by ghosts. The PA gives him an unfriendly look and continues to talk about people the demon lover doesn't know, has no interest in.

"What's spooky about you?" the demon lover asks. Because of course that's the gimmick, producer down to best boy. Every woman and man uncanny.

"I had a near-death experience," the PA says. She wiggles her arm. Shows off a long ropy burn. "Accidentally electrocuted myself. Got the whole tunnel-and-light thing. And I guess I scored okay with those cards when they auditioned me. The Zener cards?"

"So tell me," the demon lover says. "What's so fucking great about a tunnel and a light? That really the best they can do?"

"Yeah, well," the PA says, a bite in her voice. "People like you probably get the red carpet and the limo."

The demon lover has nothing to say to that.

"You seen anything here?" he tries instead. "Heard anything?"

"Meggie tell you about the skunks?" the PA says. Having snapped, now she will soothe. "Those babies. Tail up, the works, but nothing doing. Which about sums up this place. No ghosts. No read on the equipment. No hanky-panky, fiddle-faddle, or woo-woo. Not even a cold spot."

She says doubtfully, "But it'll come together. You at this séance barbecue shindig will help. Naked vampire trumps nudist ghosts any day. Okay on your own? You go on down to the lake, I'll call, let them know you're on your way."

Or he could just head for the car.

"Thanks," the demon lover says.

But before he knows what he wants to do, here's another someone. It's a regular *Pilgrim's Progress*. One of Fawn's favorite books. This is a kid in his twenties. Good-looking in a familiar way. (Although is it okay to think this about another guy when you're both naked? Not to mention: who looks a lot like you did once upon a time. Why not? We're all naked here.)

"I know you," the kid says.

The demon lover says, "Of course you do. You are?"

"Ray," says the kid. He's *maybe* twenty-five. His look says: you know who I am. "Meggie's told me all about you."

As if he doesn't already know, the demon lover says, "So what do you do?"

The kid smiles an unlovely smile. Scratches at his groin luxuriously, maybe not on purpose. "Whatever needs to be done. That's what I do."

So he deals. There's that pot in Meggie's dresser.

Down at the lake people are playing volleyball in a pit with no net. Barbecuing. Someone talks to a camera, gestures at someone else. Someone somewhere is smoking a joint. At this distance, not too close, not too near, twilight coming down, the demon lover takes in all of the breasts, asses, comical cocks, knobby knees, everything hidden now made plain. He notes with an experienced eye which breasts are real, which aren't. Only a few of the women sport pubic hair. He's never understood what that's about. Some of the men are bare, too. *O tempora, o mores.*

"You like jokes?" Ray says, stopping to light a cigarette.

The demon lover could leave; he lingers. "Depends on the joke." Really, he doesn't. Especially the kind of jokes the ones who ask if you like jokes tell.

Ray says, "You'll like this one. So there are these four guys. A kleptomaniac, a pyromaniac, um, a zoophile, and a masochist. This cat walks by and the klepto says he'd like to steal it. The pyro says he wants to set it on fire. The zoophile wants to fuck it. So the masochist, he looks at everybody, and he says, 'Meow?'"

It's a moderately funny joke. It might be a come-on.

The demon lover flicks a look at him from under his lashes. Suppresses the not-quite-queasy feeling he's somehow traveled back in time to flirt with himself. Or the other way round.

He'd like to think he was even prettier than this kid. People used to stop and stare when he walked into a room. That was long before anyone knew who he was. He's always been someone you look at longer than you should. He says, smiling, "I'll bite. Which one are you?"

"Pardon?" Ray says. Blows smoke.

"Which one are you? The klepto, the pyro, the cat-fucker, the masochist?"

"I'm the guy who tells the joke," Ray says. He drops his cigarette, grinds it under a heel black with dirt. Lights another. "Don't know if anyone's told you, but don't drink out of any of the taps. Or go swimming. The water's toxic. Phosphorous, other stuff. They shut down the muck farms, they're building up the marshlands again, but it's still not what I'd call potable. You staying out here or in town?"

The demon lover says, "Don't know if I'm staying at all."

"Well," Ray says. "They've rigged up some of the less wrecked bungalows on a generator. There are camp beds, sleeping bags. Depends on whether you like it rough." That last with, yes, a leer.

The demon lover feels his own lip lifting. They are both wearing masks. They look out of them at each other. This was what you knew when you were an actor. The face, the whole body, the way you moved in it, just a guise. You put it on, you put it off again. What was underneath belonged to you, just you, as long as you kept it hidden.

He says, "You think you know something about me?"

"I've seen all your movies," Ray says. The mask shifts, becomes the one the demon lover calls "I'm your biggest fan." Oh, he knows what's under that one.

He prepares himself for whatever this strange kid is going to say next and then suddenly Meggie is there. As if things weren't awkward enough without Meggie, naked, suddenly standing there. Everybody naked, nobody happy. It's Scandinavian art porn.

Meggie ignores the kid entirely. Just like always. These guys are inter-changeable, really. There's probably some website where she finds them. She may not want him, but she doesn't want anyone else either.

Meggie says, touching his arm, "You look a lot better."

"I got a few hours," he says.

"I know," she says. "I checked in on you. Wanted to make sure you hadn't run off."

"Nowhere to go," he says.

"Come on," Meggie says. "Let's get you something to eat."

Ray doesn't follow; lingers with his cigarette. Probably staring at their yoga-toned, well-enough-preserved celebrity butts.

Here's the problem with this kid, the demon lover thinks. He sat in a theater when he was fifteen and watched me and Meggie done up in vampire makeup pretend-fucking on a New York subway car. The A train. Me biting Meggie's breast, some suburban movie screen, her breast ten times bigger than his head. He probably masturbated a hundred times watching me bite you, Meggie. He watched us kiss. Felt something ache when we did. And that leaves out all the rest of this, whatever it is that you're doing here with him and me. Imagine what this kid must feel now. The demon lover feels it too. *Love,* he thinks. Because love isn't just love. It's all the other stuff too.

He meets Irene, the fat, pretty medium who plays the straight man to Meggie. People named Sidra, Tom, Euan, who seem to be in charge of the weird ghost gear. A videographer, Pilar. He's almost positive he's met her before. Maybe during his AA period? Really, why is that period more of a blur than all the years he's spent drunk or high? She's in her thirties, has a sly smile, terrific legs, and a very big camera.

They demonstrate some of the equipment for the demon lover, let him try out something called a Trifield Meter. No ghosts here. Even ghosts have better places to be.

He assumes everyone he meets has seen his sex tape. Almost wishes someone would mention it. No one does.

There's a rank breeze off the lake. Muck and death.

People eat and discuss the missing PA—the gopher—some Juliet person. Meggie says, "She's a nice kid. Makes Whore-igami in her spare time and sells it on eBay."

"She makes what?" the demon lover says.

"Whore-igami. Origami porn tableaux. Custom-order stuff."

"Of course," the demon lover says. "Big money in that."

She may have some kind of habit. Meggie mentions this. She may be in the habit of disappearing now and then.

Or she may be wherever all those nudists went. Imagine the ratings then. He doesn't say this to Meggie.

Meggie says, "I'm happy to see you, Will. Even under the circumstances."

"Are you?" says the demon lover, smiling, because he's always smiling. They're far enough away from the mikes and the cameras that he feels okay about saying this. Pilar, the videographer, is recording Irene, the medium, who is toasting marshmallows. Ray is watching too. Is always somewhere nearby.

Something bites the demon lover's thigh and he slaps at it.

He could reach out and touch Meggie's face right now. Through the camera it would be a different story from the one he and Meggie are telling each other. Or she would turn away and it would all be the same story again. He thinks he should have remembered this, all the ways they didn't work when they were together. Like the joke about the two skunks. When Out is in, In is out. Like the wrong ends of two magnets.

"Of course I'm happy," Meggie says. "And your timing is eerily good, because I have to talk to you about something."

"Shoot," he says.

"It's complicated," she says. "How about later? After we're done here?"

It's almost full dark now. No moon. Someone has built up a very large fire. The blackened bungalows and the roofless hall melt into obscure and tidy shapes. Now you can imagine yourself back when it was all new, a long time ago. Back in the seventies when nobody cared what you did. When love was free. When you could just disappear if you felt like it, and that was fine and good too.

"So where do I stay tonight?" the demon lover says. Again fights the impulse to touch Meggie's face. There's a strand of hair against her lip. Which is he? The pyromaniac or the masochist? In or Out? Well, he's an actor, isn't he? He can be anything she wants him to be.

"I'm sure you'll find somewhere," Meggie says, a glint in her eye. "Or someone. Pilar has told me more than once you're the only man she's ever wanted to fuck."

"If I had a dollar," the demon lover says. He still wants to touch her. Wants her to want him to touch her. He remembers now, how this goes.

Meggie says, "If you had a dollar, seventy cents would go to your exes."

Which is gospel truth. He says, "Fawn signed a prenup."

"One of the thousand reasons you should go home and fix things," Meggie says. "She's a good person. There aren't so many of those."

"She's better off without me," the demon lover says, trying it out. He's a little hurt when Meggie doesn't disagree.

Irene the medium comes over with Pilar and the other videographer. The demon lover can tell Irene doesn't like him. Sometimes women don't like him. Rare enough that he always wonders why.

"Shall we get started?" Irene says. "Let's see if any of our friends are up for a quick chat. Then I don't know about you, but I'm going to go put on something a little less comfortable."

Meggie addresses the video camera next. "This will be our final attempt," she says, "our last chance to contact anyone who is still lingering here, who has unfinished business."

"You'd think nudists wouldn't be so shy," Irene says.

Meggie says, "But even if we don't reach anyone, today hasn't been a total loss. All of us have taken a risk. Some of us are sunburned, some of us have bug bites in interesting places, but all of us are a little more comfortable in our own skin. We've experienced openness and humanity in a way that these colonists imagined and hoped would lead to a better world. And maybe, for them, it did. We've had a good day. And even if the particular souls we came here in search of didn't show up, someone else did."

The A2 nods at Will.

Pilar points the camera at him.

He's been thinking about how to play this. "I'm Will Gald," he says. "You probably recognize me from previous naked film roles such as the guy rolling around on a hotel room floor clutching his genitals and bleeding profusely."

He smiles his most lovely smile. "I just happened to be in the area."

"We persuaded him to stay for a bite," Meggie says.

"They've hidden my clothes," Will says. "Admittedly, I haven't been trying that hard to find them. I mean, what's the worst thing that can happen when you get naked on camera?"

Irene says, "Meggie, one of the things that's been most important about *Who's There?* right from the beginning is that we've all had something happen to us that we can't explain away. We're all believers. I've been meaning to ask, does Will here have a ghost story?"

"I don't—" the demon lover says. Then pauses. Looks at Meggie.

"I do," he says. "But surely Meggie's already told it."

"I have," Meggie says. "But I've never heard you tell it."

Oh, there are stories the demon lover could tell.

He says, "I'm here to please."

"Fantastic," Irene says. "As you know, every episode we make time for a ghost story or two. Tonight we even have a campfire." She hesitates. "And of course as our viewers also know, we're still waiting for Juliet Adeyemi to turn up. She left just before lunch to run errands. We're not worried yet, but we'll all be a lot happier when she's with us again."

Meggie says, "Juliet, if you've met a nice boy and gone off to ride the teacups at Disney World, so help me, I'm going to ask for all the details. Now. Shall we, Irene?"

All around them, people have been clearing away plates of half-eaten barbecue, assembling in a half circle around the campfire. Any minute now they'll be singing "Kumbaya." They sit on their little towels. Irene and Meggie take their place in front of the fire. They clasp hands.

The demon lover moves a little farther away, into darkness. He is not interested in séances or ghosts. Here is the line of the shore. Sharp things underfoot. Someone joins him. Ray. Of course.

It is worse, somehow, to be naked in the dark. The world is so big and he is not. Ray is young and he is not. He is pretty sure that Pilar will sleep with him; Meggie will not.

"I know you," the demon lover says to Ray. "I've met you before. Well, not you, the previous you. Yous. You never last. *We* never last. She moves on. You disappear."

Ray says nothing. Looks out at the lake.

"I *was* you," the demon lover says.

Ray says, "And now? Who are you?"

"You charge by the hour?" the demon lover says. "Why follow me around? I don't seem to have my wallet on me."

"Meggie's busy," Ray says. "And I'm curious about you. What you think you're doing here."

"I came for Meggie," the demon lover says. "We're friends. An old friend can come to see an old friend. Some other time I'll see her again and you won't be around. I'll always be around. But you, you're just some guy who got lucky because you looked like me."

Ray says, "I love her."

"Sucks, doesn't it?" the demon lover says. He goes back to the fire and the naked people waiting for other naked people. Thinks about the story he is meant to tell.

The séance has not been a success. Irene the medium keeps saying that she senses something. Someone is trying to say something.

The dead are here, but also not here. They're afraid. That's why they won't come. Something is keeping them away. There is something wrong here.

"Do you feel it?" she says to Meggie, to the others.

Meggie says, "I feel something. Something is here."

The demon lover extends himself outward into the night. Lets himself believe for a moment that life goes on. Is something here? There is a smell, the metallic stink of the muck farms. There is an oppressiveness to the air. Is there malice here? An ill wish?

Meggie says, "No one has ever solved the mystery of what happened here. But perhaps whatever happened to them is still present. Irene, could it have some hold on their spirits, whatever is left of them, even in death?"

Irene says, "I don't know. Something's wrong here. Something is here. I don't know."

But *Who's There?* picks up nothing of interest on their equipment, their air-ion counter or their barometer, their EMF detector or EVP detector, their wind chimes or thermal imaging scopes. No one is there.

And so at last it's time for ghost stories.

There's one about the men's room at a trendy Santa Monica restaurant. The demon lover has been there. Had the fries with truffle-oil mayonnaise. Never encountered the ghost. He's not somebody who sees ghosts and he's fine with that. Never really liked truffle-oil mayonnaise either. The thing in the bungalow with Meggie wasn't a ghost. It was drugs, the pressure they were under, the unbearable scrutiny; a *folie à deux*; the tax on their happiness.

Someone tells the old story about Basil Rathbone and the dinner guest who brings his dogs. Upon departure, the man and his dogs are killed in a car crash just outside Rathbone's house. Rathbone sees. Is paralyzed with shock and grief. As he stands there, his phone rings—when he picks up, an operator says, "Pardon me, Mr. Rathbone, but there is a woman on the line who says she must speak to you."

The woman, who is a medium, says that she has a message for him. She says she hopes he will understand the meaning.

"Traveling very fast. No time to say good-bye. There are no dogs here."

And now it's the demon lover's turn. He says: "A long time ago when Meggie and I were together, we bought a bungalow in Venice Beach. We weren't there very much. We were everywhere else. On junkets. At festivals. We had no furniture. Just a mattress. No dishes. When we were home we ate out of takeout containers.

"But we were happy." He lets that linger. Meggie watches. Listens. Ray stands beside her. No space between them.

It's not much fun, telling a ghost story while you're naked. Telling the parts of the ghost story that you're supposed to tell. Not telling other parts. While the woman you love stands there with the person you used to be.

"It was a good year. Maybe the best year of my life. Maybe the hardest year, too. We were young and we were stupid and people wanted things from us and we did things we shouldn't have done. Fill in the blanks however you want. We threw parties. We spent money like water. And we loved each other. Right, Meggie?"

Meggie nods.

He says, "But I should get to the ghost. I don't really believe that it was a ghost, but I don't not believe it was a ghost, either. I've never spent much time thinking about it, really. But the more time we spent in that bungalow, the worse things got."

Irene says, "Can you describe it for us? What happened?"

The demon lover says, "It was a feeling that someone was watching us. That they were somewhere very far away, but they were getting closer. That very soon they would be there with us. It was worse at night. We had bad dreams. Some nights we both woke up screaming."

Irene says, "What were the dreams about?"

He says, "Not much. Just that it was finally there in the room with us. Eventually it was always there. Eventually whatever it was was in the bed with us. We'd wake up on opposite sides of the mattress because it was there in between us."

Irene says, "What did you do?"

He says, "When one of us was alone in the bed it wasn't there. It was there when it was the two of us. Then it would be the three of us. So we got a room at the Chateau Marmont. Only it turned out it was there too. The very first night, it was there too."

Irene says, "Did you try to talk to it?"

He says, "Meggie did. I didn't. Meggie thought it was real. I thought we needed therapy. I thought whatever it was, we were doing it. So we tried therapy. That was a bust. So eventually—" he shrugs.

"Eventually what?" Irene says.

"I moved out," Meggie says.

"She moved out," he says.

The demon lover wonders if Ray knows the other part of the story, if Meggie has told him that. Of course she hasn't. Meggie isn't dumb. The other part is for the two of them, and the demon lover thinks, as he's thought many times before, that this is what will always hold them together. Not the experience of filming a movie together, of falling in love at the exact same moment that all those other people fell in love with them, that sympathetic magic made up of story and effort, repetition and editing and craft and other people's desire.

The thing that happened is the thing they can never tell anyone else. It belongs to them. No one else.

"And after that there wasn't any ghost," he concludes. "Meggie took a break from Hollywood, went to India. I went to AA meetings."

It's gotten colder. The fire has gotten lower. You could, perhaps, imagine that there is a supernatural explanation for these things, but that would be wishful thinking. The missing girl, Juliet, has not returned. The ghost-hunting equipment does not record any presence.

Meggie finds the demon lover with Pilar. She says, "Can we talk?"

"What about?" he says.

Pilar says, "I'll go get another beer. Want one, Meggie?"

Meggie shakes her head and Pilar wanders off, her hand brushing against the demon lover's hip as she goes. Flesh against flesh. He turns just a little so he's facing away from the firelight.

"It's about the pilot for next season," Meggie says. "I want to shoot it in Venice Beach, in our old bungalow."

The demon lover feels something rush over him. Pour into his ears, flood down his throat. He can't think of what to say. He has been thinking about Ray while he flirts with Pilar. He's been wondering what would happen if he asked Meggie about Ray. Really, they've never talked about this. This thing that she does.

"I'd like you to be in the episode too, of course," Meggie says.

He says, "I don't think that's a good idea. I think it's a terrible idea, actually."

"It's something I've always wanted to do," Meggie says. "I think it would be good for both of us."

"Something something closure," he says. "Yeah, yeah. Something something exposure something possible jail term. Are you *insane?*"

"Look," Meggie says. "I've already talked to the woman who lives there now. She's never experienced anything. Will, I need to do this."

"Of course she hasn't experienced anything," the demon lover says. "It wasn't the house that was haunted."

His blood is spiky with adrenaline. He looks around to see if anyone is watching. Of course they are. But everyone else is far away enough that the conversation is almost private. He's surprised Meggie didn't spring this on him on camera. Think of the drama. The conflict. The ratings.

"You believe in this stuff," he says, finally. Trying to find what will persuade her. "So why won't you leave it alone? You know what happened. We know what happened. You know what the story is. Why the fuck do you need to know more?" He's whispering now.

"Because every time we're together, she's here with us," Meggie says. "Didn't you know that? She's here now. Don't you feel her?"

Hair stands up on his legs, his arms, the back of his neck. His mouth is dry, his tongue sticks to the roof of his mouth. "No," he says. "I don't."

Meggie says, "You know I would be careful, Will. I would never do anything to hurt you. And it doesn't work like that, anyway." She leans in close, says very quietly, "It isn't about us. This is for me. I just want to talk to her. I just want her to go away."

(1992) They acquire the trappings of a life, he and Meggie. They buy dishes and mid-century modern furniture and lamps. They acquire friends who are in the business, and throw parties. On occasion things happen at their parties. For example, there is the girl. She arrives with someone. They never

find out who. She is about as pretty as you would expect a girl at one of
their parties to be, which is to say that she is really very pretty.

After all this time, the demon lover doesn't really remember what she
looked like. There were a lot of girls and a lot of parties and that was
another country.

She had long black hair. Big eyes.

He and Meggie are both wasted. And the girl is into both of them and
eventually it's the three of them, everyone else is gone, there's a party going
on somewhere else, they stay, she stays, and everyone else leaves. They
drink and there's music and they dance. Then the girl is kissing Meggie
and he is kissing the girl and they're in the bedroom. It's a lot of fun. They
do pretty much everything you can do with three people in a bed. And at
some point the girl is between them and everyone is having a good time,
they're having fun, and then the girl says to them, Bite me.

Come on, bite me.

He bites her shoulder and she says, No, really bite me. Bite harder. I want
you to really bite me. Bite me, please. And suddenly he and Meggie are
looking at each other and it isn't fun anymore. This isn't what they're into.

He finishes as quickly as he can, because he's almost there anyway. And
the girl is still begging, still asking for something they can't give her,
because it isn't real and vampires aren't real and it's a distasteful situation
and so Meggie asks the girl to leave. She does and they don't talk about it.
They just go to sleep. And they wake up just a little bit later because she's
snuck back into the house, they find out later that she's broken a window,
and she's slashed her wrists. She's holding out her bloody wrists and she's
saying, Please, here's my blood, please drink it. I want you to drink my
blood. Please.

They get her bandaged up. The cuts aren't too deep. Meggie calls her
agent, Pike, and Pike arranges for someone to take the girl to a private
clinic. He tells them not to worry about any of it. It turns out that the girl

is fifteen. Of course she is. Pike calls them again, after this girl gets out of the clinic, when she commits suicide. She has a history of attempts. Try, try, succeed.

The demon lover does not talk to Meggie again, because Pilar—who is naked—they are both naked, everyone is naked of course—but Pilar is really quite lovely and fun to talk to and the camera work on this show is really quite exquisite and she likes the demon lover a lot. Keeps touching him. She says she has a bottle of Maker's Mark back in one of the cabins and he's already drunker than he's been in a while. Turns out they did meet once, in an AA meeting in Silverlake.

They have a good time. Really, sex is a lot of fun. The demon lover suspects that there's some obvious psychological diagnosis for why he's having sex with Pilar, some need to reenact recent history and make sure it comes out better this time. The last girl with a camera didn't turn out so well for him. When exactly, he wonders, have things turned out well?

Afterward they lie on their backs on the dirty cement floor. Pilar says, "My girlfriend is never going to believe this."

He wonders if she's going to ask for an autograph.

Pilar's been sharing the cabin with the missing girl, Juliet. There's Whore-igami all over the cabin. Men and women and men and men and women and women in every possible combination, doing things that ought to be erotic. But they aren't; they're menacing instead. Maybe it's the straight lines.

The demon lover and Pilar get dressed in case Juliet shows up.

"Well," Pilar says from her bunk bed, "good night."

He takes Juliet's bunk. Lies there in the dark until he's sure Pilar's asleep. He is thinking about Fawn for some reason. He can't stop thinking about her. If he stops thinking about her, he will have to think about the conversation with Meggie. He will have to think about Meggie. Pilar's iPhone is on the floor beside her bunk bed. He picks it up. No password. He types in Fawn's number. Sends her a text. Hardly knows what he is typing.

I HOPE, he writes.

He writes the most awful things. Doesn't know why he is doing this. Perhaps she will assume that it is a wrong number. He types in details, specific things, so she will know it's not.

Eventually she texts back.

WHO IS THIS? WILL?

The demon lover doesn't respond to that. Just keeps texting FILTHY BITCH YOU CUNT YOU WHORE YOU SLIME etc. Etc. Etc. Until she stops asking. Surely she knows who he is. She must know who he is.

Here's the thing about acting, about a scene, about a character; about the dialogue you are given, the things your character does. None of it matters. You can take the most awful words, all the words, all the names, the acts he types into the text block. You can say these things, and the way you say them can change the meaning. You can say, "You dirty bitch. You cunt," and say them differently each time; you can make it a joke, an endearment, a cry for help, a seduction. You can kill, be a vampire, a soulless thing. The audience will love you no matter what you do. If you want them to love you. Some of them will always love you.

He needs air. He drops the phone on the floor again where Pilar will find it in the morning. Decides to walk down to the lake. He will have to go past Meggie's trailer on the way, only he doesn't. Instead he stands there watching as a shadow slips out of the door of the trailer and down the stairs and away. Going where? Almost not there at all.

Ray?

He could follow. But he doesn't.

He wonders if Meggie is awake. The door to her trailer is off the latch, and so the demon lover steps inside.

Makes his way to her bedroom, no lights, she is not awake. He will do no harm. Only wants to see her safe and sleeping. An old friend can go to see an old friend.

Meggie's a shape in the bed and he comes closer so he can see her face. There is someone in the bed with Meggie.

Ray looks at the demon lover and the demon lover looks back at Ray. Ray's right hand rests on Meggie's breast. Ray raises the other hand, beckons to the demon lover.

The next morning is what you would predict. The crew of *Who's There?* packs up to leave; Pilar discovers the text messages on her phone.

Did I do that? the demon lover says. I was drunk. I may have done that. Oh God, oh hell, oh fuck. He plays his part.

This may get messy. Oh, he knows how messy it can get. Pilar can make some real money with those texts. Fawn, if she wants, can use them against him in the divorce.

He doesn't know how he gets into these situations.

Fawn has called Meggie. So there's that as well. Meggie waits to talk to him until almost everyone else has packed up and gone; it's early afternoon now. Really, he should already have left. He has things he'll need to do. Decisions to make about flights, a new phone. He needs to call his publicist, his agent. Time for them to earn their keep. He likes to keep them busy.

Ray is off somewhere. The demon lover isn't too sorry about this.

It's not a fun conversation.

They're up in the parking lot now, and one of the crew, he doesn't recognize her with her clothes on, says to Meggie, "Need a lift?"

"I've got the thing in Tallahassee tomorrow, the morning show," Meggie says. "Got someone picking me up any minute now."

"'Kay," the woman says. "See you in San Jose." She gives the demon lover a dubious look—is Pilar already talking?—and then gets in her car and drives away.

"San Jose," the demon lover says.

"Yeah," Meggie says. "The Winchester House."

"Huh," the demon lover says. He doesn't really care. He's tired of this whole thing, Meggie, the borrowed T-shirt and cargo shorts, Lake Apopka, no-show ghosts and bad publicity.

He knows what's coming. Meggie rips into him. He lets her. There's no point trying to talk to women when they get like this. He stands there and takes it all in. When she's finally done, he doesn't bother trying to defend himself. What's the good of saying things? He's so much better at saying things when there's a script to keep him from deep water. There's no script here.

Of course he and Meggie will patch things up eventually. Old friends forgive old friends. Nothing is unforgivable. He's wondering if this is untrue when a car comes into the meadow.

"Well," Meggie says. "That's my ride."

She waits for him to speak and when he doesn't, she says, "Good-bye, Will."

"I'll call you," the demon lover says at last. "It'll be okay, Meggie."

"Sure," Meggie says. She's not really making much of an effort. "Call me."

She gets into the back of the car. The demon lover bends over, waves at the window where she is sitting. She's looking straight ahead. The driver's window is down, and okay, here's Ray again. Of course! He looks out at the demon lover. He raises an eyebrow, smiles, waves with that hand again, need a ride?

The demon lover steps away from the car. Feels a sense of overwhelming disgust and dread. A cloud of blackness and horror comes over him, something he hasn't felt in many, many years. He recognizes the feeling at once.

And that's that. The car drives away with Meggie inside it. The demon lover stands in the field for some period of time, he is never sure how long. Long enough that he is sure he will never catch up with the car with Meggie in it. And he doesn't.

There's a storm coming in.

The thing is this: Meggie never turns up for the morning show in Tallahassee. The other girl, Juliet Adeyemi, does reappear, but nobody ever sees Meggie again. She just vanishes. Her body is never found. The demon lover is a prime suspect in her disappearance. Of course he is. But there is no proof. No evidence.

No one is ever charged.

And Ray? When the demon lover explains everything to the police, to the media, on talk shows, he tells the same story over and over again. I went to see my old friend Meggie. I met her lover, Ray. They left together. He drove the car. But no one else supports this story. There is not a single person who will admit that Ray exists. There is not a frame of video with Ray in it. Ray was never there at all, no matter how many times the demon lover explains what happened. They say, What did he look like? Can you describe him? And the demon lover says, He looked like me.

As he is waiting for the third or maybe the fourth time to be questioned by the police, the demon lover thinks about how one day they will make a movie about all of this. About Meggie. But of course he will be too old to play the demon lover.

WATERLOO!

by REBECCA CURTIS

WASHINGTON—A Congressional Budget Office analysis released Tuesday predicted that the Affordable Care Act would shrink the work force by the equivalent of more than two million full-time positions… Congressional Republican leaders called the findings "devastating," "terrible," and proof that the health care law was a job killer.

"No matter how you calculate this number or how the administration tries to explain it away, it's about two and a half times as high as the number was when they looked at it the first time," Senator Roy Blunt of Missouri said. "They can say anything they want, but this number is a lot worse than anybody thought."

The budget office analysis found that the law, in effect, nudges workers to work less. The insurance expansion reduces the need for a person to take a full-time job just to get coverage. The premium subsidies effectively bolster household income. Higher taxes for richer households also reduce the incentive to work.

Senator Joe Manchin III, Democrat of West Virginia, who has embraced a number of bills to tweak the health care law, called disappointing enrollment figures and work-force declines the law's "Waterloo."

—the *New York Times*, February 5, 2014

An extraordinarily strange thing happened in Manhattan on March 5. I, Rebecca Curtis III, a holistic nutritionist with a medium-size client list and three good Yelp reviews, awoke early to prepare for meetings with two clients—one, an industrialist who had gallstones, the other, a rock star with a goiter—and a date with a handsome doctor that had been arranged by my sister. I noticed that my alarm-clock radio sounded fuzzy. Even though I'd bought it for seven dollars in 1995, it has excellent reception. Today all I heard was *fuzz fuzz fuzz*... "Ow!" "Devastating!"... *fuzz fuzz*... "Don't bite me!" "Waterloo!"... *fuzz*.

I'd been holed up for weeks with the flu, trapped in my apartment, so I couldn't let a fuzzy radio slow me down. I donned a navy dress and my white lab coat, dabbed some pheromone sex-attractant perfume on my neck so that I might be attractive to my date, and hurried to THINK Coffee, which was completely empty.

"One whole-milk misto, please," I said, positioning myself before the counter.

The barista had her back to me. I noticed that the glass case, usually stocked with cream puffs, croissants, and pastries, today held just one scone coated with moldy icing.

The woman turned around.

"Closed," she said. "No coffee. Go."

I checked my watch: quarter to ten. Prime time for THINK Coffee, which should have been filled with Manhattanites! I suddenly craved their hot, bittersweet liquid. I even wanted a roll, though gluten gave me hives.

The woman—a pixie-cut brunette—glared at me.

"Is there any chance, if I pay double…" I said, "that you could make coffee? Old, leftover coffee is also okay. And do you have any low-sugar, gluten-free scones?"

"I'm the owner," the woman said. "Not a barista. I've no workers, so I'm closed." She pointed toward the door. "Scram."

I hesitated.

"No workers?" I said.

"That's right," she said. "Why would they work here, if they didn't *have* to?"

I shrugged. "Maybe because they love coffee?" I said.

She shoved a broom across the floor.

"So they *claimed*. They claimed to care about roasting methods… heirloom beans… they said they wanted to prepare for indie films that require actors to have years of experience working in coffee shops… but now that they've realized that the Affordable Care Act lets them buy cheap health insurance sans full-time jobs, they all quit."

I paused in the doorway, still hoping for coffee.

"That's terrible," I said. "Say, couldn't you hire part-timers?"

She pushed the broom. "Ha! Who wants to be part-time? Do you want to be *partly* satisfied, or *partly* happy?" Her eyes narrowed. "No offense," she added. "But you're partly good-looking… you've got okay lips, but a big wide nose. So you *would* think that. Now scat! Everything's disastrous! I'm going to Whole Foods before it's sacked!"

I hurried to my workplace, a windowless room with a massage bed and two cabinets full of supplements inside a health plaza on Broadway. My first client was due at 10 a.m. He was late. I got a cloth and dusted my cabinets. Hmm, I thought. What could be taking him?

At 10:30, he strode in. "Sorry I'm late," he said. "My train stopped in the middle of the Manhattan Bridge and I had to walk."

"What?" I said. "How is that possible? By the way," I added, "how's your sleep at night and how many bowel movements are you having each day? Any pain on your right side? We're late, we need to get started."

"Dunno," my client said. He was a handsome, seven-foot-three white-haired industrialist who'd started a world-famous aluminum-manufacturing company. "I guess the driver went crazy. We all heard him say on the intercom, 'I'm not doing this no more… No way, José! Yippee!' Then the train stopped."

He leaned forward.

"Maybe it was aliens? The trains aren't running—there's a food shortage, panic, inhumanity, looting… a lot of workers quit their jobs. To be frank, I'm quitting my own job as CEO of my company. Now that I can buy cheap health insurance on my own, I don't need it!"

"But…" I peered at his face. It looked rosy—good circulation. "You *love* manufacturing aluminum, you're a famous entrepreneur and businessman! You've got a multibillion-dollar firm!"

He shrugged. "Manufacturing aluminum, shmanufacturing shmaluminum," he said. "Do you know what it's like to work for forty years? Besides, now that taxes are high, I have no incentive to be rich. I have cheap health insurance now. I'm free!"

He leaned forward. I smelled his cologne. I swooned. I'd always had a crush on the industrialist.

"Say," he said. "I passed a hundred stones when I did my last flush. Thanks! I just came in to get more of that great gallstone-shrinking supplement you gave me, then I gotta go."

I handed him the herbs.

"Ten bottles," he said. "I'm stocking up."

I gave him ten.

He handed me a thousand-dollar bill and told me to keep the change.

"Say," I said. "Why does everyone *want* health care? I mean, your doctor didn't help you dissolve your gallstones. And whenever my other clients see their doctors, they don't *heal* my clients' thyroids. They just tell them to take toxic synthetic thyroid hormone!"

The industrialist patted my knee. "So what? If I feel sick, I see you or my chiropractor. But if I get run over by a cab, I want a surgeon." The industrialist frowned sadly. "Anyway, I *had* to quit my job. All my workers quit."

I said, "What?"

He stood up. "They quit! Now that they've gotten cheap, subsidized health insurance, they don't want to work for me! But listen, I've gotta go catch the big sale at Whole Foods. If you were smart, you would too!" He paused. "On the other hand... maybe you'd better stay here. It's wild out there right now, and you're a girl... big nose, rather short... not that strong..."

He ran out.

My second client never showed. The building was quiet—no one in the Vegan Buddhist Café or the acupuncturists' offices. From outside, by the square, I heard shouts, explosions, and screams.

I checked my watch. Quarter to twelve. Time for my date at Starbucks. The doctor was a Virgo, so I guessed he'd be punctilious.

I took the stairs down, since the elevator was out. Union Square was deserted. No old men played chess. No fat ladies hawked kittens, jewelry, or tube socks. I wandered into Whole Foods, but every shelf was bare. As I exited, a girl in a tattered, dirty dress ran past me, a look of fear on her face, clutching a moldy potato. "What's wrong?" I asked. But she just stared at me with huge, dark eyes, clutched the potato tighter, and dashed down the block toward Trader Joe's. Nonplussed, I walked toward Starbucks. The streets were full of dropped purses, some with very enticing logos. It was a pleasant, sunny fifty-five degrees.

Starbucks looked dark. But an aromatic, stewlike smell emanated from it.

I entered.

It was deserted, and just as in THINK, the snack case was empty. But mid-room, by the creamer and Splenda counter, sat a cast-iron cauldron the size of all four of my grandparents. It was perched atop a battery-operated space heater. Its broth bubbled. The fumes smelled of cumin, saffron, and something indescribably good. Cheese?

"Hello?" I said.

"Hey!" a pleasant French accent said. The doctor! He sat at a corner table. He had baby cheeks, hazel eyes, and a friendly smile. My sister had been right, I knew then—much better to date a kind, dedicated doctor who does things like charity work in Uganda than to date evil, polyamorous bankers!

"Sorry it's closed," the doctor, whose name was Yoni, said. "I wasn't sure what to do... Or"—he pointed at the cauldron—"what that stewpot is doing here."

I apologized in turn, for being late, and introduced myself, hoping he could smell my sex-attractant pheromone perfume.

"Thank you so much for meeting me even though the trains aren't running and Union Square is deserted!" I said. "I really appreciate it." I batted my eyes. "I know how busy you must be, as a doctor."

Yoni shrugged. He wore nice J.Crew khakis and a blue J.Crew button-down.

"Well," he said, "I'm not actually a doctor anymore... I just found out that now, thanks to the Affordable Care Act, you can buy health insurance, without working, for cheap! So I quit my job."

I cringed. Of course, like all women, I'd hoped to marry a rich man, so that he could support me and I could drink mistos, read paperbacks, do yoga, and get facelifts all day. But I didn't want to reveal this to him.

"That's a great idea," I said. "But... what about fixing poor Ugandan children's cleft lips? I thought you LOVED doing that!"

His muscled forearms spread on the table. "But now *they* can get cheap health care!" he said.

"Really?" I said. "But they're *Ugandan!*"

He frowned. My sister had warned me he wasn't the brightest.

"Well," he said, "if they come *here* they can." He bit his lip. "That is... if some of the really hardworking ones go to school and learn how to be doctors, and decide to do surgery for the lazy ones who just sailed here to get the free health care."

Our conversation was interrupted by a banging noise from within the restroom. Someone had wedged a crowbar through the door handle, I observed, so that the door could not be opened from inside.

The space heater crackled. The stew in the pot bubbled. I saw that a hammock had been hung in the corner, next to several easy chairs.

"AHHHHH!" something yelled from inside the bathroom. "My arm! AHHHHHHGH!"

Dr. Yoni frowned. "Say," he said. "There's a *reason* someone put a crowbar through that door handle!"

"Hmm," I replied. I tried to fathom the reason. But suddenly my caffeine craving returned.

"I'm so thirsty," I said. "Would you mind?" I blushed. "There's no barista..."

"Of course!" Dr. Yoni said. "Odd the place is closed... I mean, I understand everyone quit working, farms are defunct, and there's a food shortage, but STILL... it's *Starbucks!* Anyway, being a barista can't be that hard. After all, I'm a doctor!" He went behind the counter, flipped a few switches on the machines, and began opening cupboards.

I heard bumping inside the bathroom, another "Ahhhh!" and a gurgle.

Then the doctor started yelling, too.

He held up a croissant.

"It's a roll!"

He walked it toward me. The roll was moldy, like everything else, one of those 320-calorie croissant-ham sandwiches.

"So what?" I asked, feeling hungry. "It's a roll!"

"I know," Dr. Yoni said. "But inside it's…" He opened it. "This!"

Inside was a whitish, lumpy, ungainly object: an appendage with two hair-filled holes. A nose!

"Impossible," I said. "Who would put a nose inside a roll?"

Dr. Yoni turned pale. "I don't know," he said.

He added that no one good in Union Square even did cosmetic surgery.

"Well," I said, "let's not eat it."

"Hahaha," he said. "Even though I'm French, I agree!"

While he brewed coffee, I wandered outside to observe the trees in the square. A whistly breeze blew through the benches, and abruptly I heard the sound of pounding feet. Then a dozen extremely thin people sprinted past, pursued by what looked to be fifty-three strapping men and women hefting spears. Or spade-tipped broom handles, to be precise. I watched in horror as the fifty-three beefy assailants, who had AK-47s across their backs and wore J.Crew khakis (or perhaps khakis from American Eagle, or Urban Outfitters, it was hard to tell), chased the dozen screaming, skinny people—or rather *herded them*—into the public park bathroom. I saw one tall, particularly handsome, boyish but gray-haired man bash a frail, delicate, and expressive-looking man on the head. Then the strong people closed the restroom door and slipped a crowbar through the handle.

I ran back into Starbucks. Thoughts flashed across my mind.

"Yoni…" I said. "How's the coffee? Wait—that stewpot… the nose you found in the 320-calorie croissant… the crowbar across the bathroom door…"

"Hold on," Dr. Yoni said. His hand was on the crowbar. "I'm about to see what's inside the bathroom!"

"No!" I screamed. "Don't open it!"

I peered outside the window and saw with dismay that the fifty-three strong, armed men and women were laughing, high-fiving each other, and walking toward our Starbucks.

I said, "We've got to leave!"

But Yoni had removed the crowbar. Ten skeletal naked people, one without a nose and nine without arms, hungrily pulled him into the restroom with them by hooking their legs around his head. Three bit his face.

"Ahhhhhhhhh!" he screamed. "Help!"

I knew instantly what the right thing to do was. But I also knew that if I tried to help Dr. Yoni, I too would be pulled into the bathroom and eaten.

Without thinking, I slammed the door shut and slid the crowbar through its handle.

"No!" Dr. Yoni yelled from behind the door. "Help! Ahhhh!"

But I was afraid. And also, I was aware now that he was the kind of doctor who would quit his job if given health care.

I ran outside the Starbucks, but too slowly—the fifty-three buff men and women saw me.

"Another one!" a meaty, bare-breasted brunette said. "Get her!"

They grabbed each other's hands and ran toward me.

I saw, with admiration, that all fifty-three of them were awfully handsome, and that one of them, the boyish fellow, who had a square jaw, floppy gray hair, and a weathered, reliable face, was Mitt Romney. This seemed highly improbable, since I never recognize celebrities. Nevertheless, I speculated: Mitt Romney was a responsible public servant and diplomat. Yet he was also part of a chain of strong men and women who'd linked hands and were chasing down weak people in order to trap them in bathrooms, put them in stew, and eat them. But Mitt Romney was a good person, I reasoned—surely I could gain his sympathy. But how? I couldn't claim I'd voted for him... I wasn't a Mormon... I wasn't from Massachusetts... I realized I had nothing to offer.

"I saw you bash that man's head!" I yelled desperately. "I'll tell!"

The gang was thirty feet away. Mitt paused.

"Tell who?" he said.

I hesitated.

I said, "Obama!"

Mitt's eyes rolled. "Please," he said. "Obama got us into this mess. He screwed up the Affordable Care Act, and as a result, everybody's gotten health care too cheap, too fast, and quit their jobs! Now it's chaos! Thanks to Obama's leadership, it's dog eat dog! Red dog eat blue dog! Look, if you give me a choice between eating nothing and starving to death, or eating other people, I'll eat! I'm Mitt!"

The line jogged toward me again.

I ran.

"Anyway," Mitt continued, "this is Obama's Waterloo! I warned of what would happen if he returned to power—his laws are whims! His plan was to destroy the wealthy first, the entrepreneurs, the inventors, the industrial-ists... *Then* he planned to demolish the middle class, so the two groups could never form a coalition! He tried to cut the rich off at the pass, but he miscal-culated! He probably ate chicken for breakfast and had a bout of gas! Now look—our boys in the navy, the army, and the marines all left their posts as soon as they learned that they didn't have to work a job to get health care!"

The cannibals were close. I was running, but I'm a slow runner—I have Thalassemia trait, my red blood cells are small and I'm on the anemic side. I wished I'd stayed inside my office, as I surmised everyone smart was doing.

Just then, I heard a *thwap thwap thwap* sound. A large red-blue-and-silver helicopter landed in Union Square. With alacrity, out leapt Obama and the National Guard.

Or rather, what was left of them. There were six men around the presi-dent. I saw, by the special labels on their uniforms, that they were the

Special National Guard—a dyslexic unit, unable to read the Affordable Care Act communiqué.

They cocked their rifles.

"Ten hut!" Obama said.

He looked tall and handsome, and was dressed snappily in a navy uniform with gold buttons. But the six guardsmen hesitated. Mitt's fifty-three thugs spread their khaki-clad legs and casually swung their AK-47s into position.

Obama crossed his arms. He lowered his voice presidentially.

"Mitt, you can't eat people," he said.

"Frankly, Barack," Mitt said, "you are in no position to tell me what to do. The ACA is a disaster. Look at the havoc you've wreaked!"

The special national guardsmen were falling to their knees in fear. Several of Mitt's fifty-three strongmen ran over and began hitting them across their heads. Then a strange green mist rolled through the square.

In the mist was a face, that of my banker ex-boyfriend. He was actually a nice guy.

"You'll have to buy health care too, you know," the face said. "I'm *for* mandatory health insurance, so taxpayers don't have to bear the burden when uninsured people have emergencies."

"I'm *never* buying health insurance," I retorted. "I distrust Western medicine. I don't *want* toxic drugs and ignorant doctors. I claim a holistic exemption—the plans don't even cover nutritionists! It's not fair!"

My ex's handsome face grimaced. "You're complaining about the details," it said. "If you don't like what's offered, then yell and scream and change the system!"

Then I heard not just *chop chop chop*, but, all at once, from every direction,
chop chop chop
chop chop chop
chop chop chop
chop chop chop chop

The mist parted. Ten helicopters had landed. There were dozens of units—the blind unit, the deaf unit, the differently abled unit, the Down syndrome unit, the very-old unit, the one-legged unit, the diabetic, Lyme disease, and chronic-fatigue units, the Parkinson's and Lou Gehrig's disease, lupus, bipolar, multiple sclerosis, and Crohn's disease units... somehow all these men had either not heard about the Affordable Care Act, or else, for whatever reason, they just really liked their jobs. Of course, being sick, they were probably *bad* at their jobs, but so grateful to have them that they compensated via enthusiasm... this was the future of America, I thought, now that everyone would get health insurance and be put on antidepressants, statins, diuretics, antacids, and Viagra by their doctors, and made to get weight-loss surgery—they'd all think they were fine, because medicated, and so they'd keep drinking fluoridated tap water, and thus have more retarded and hermaphroditic babies, and eating hormone-stuffed meat and bioengineered super-glutenized wheat bread that would decimate their gut linings, brain function, and immune systems, and once they'd become uber-cancerous and demented, all Americans would experience a spiritual awakening about how cool it was to be alive and love their jobs!

As I watched, the soldiers poured out of the helicopters, surrounded Mitt and his compadres, and pulled them off the president.

"Bad!" a Down syndrome National Guardsman said. "Against the law! Bad!"

The guardsmen put the spear carriers in handcuffs.

In the evaporating mist, my ex yawned. "Still," he said. "He's got to lower taxes on the rich... or else there's no incentive to work!"

"You'd never quit *your* job," I said. "You *love* work!"

Then a heavy green fog rolled across the square and everything was obscured.

NIMRODS

by **ISMET PRCIC**

Hunter Lopez, my boss, he likes to talk. He likes to talk about guns and anal sex, about monster trucks, about the chances of getting away with murder by taking advantage of an antiquated California law—still in effect, according to him—that allows white men to shoot an Indian without fear of prosecution if the Indian is found to be atop a white man's wagon. Hunter dreams of the possibility of this law applying to station wagons, as well.

Today he's talking about his plans to raise his truck so high that the exhaust pipe can shoot noxious fumes right through the open windows of "nimrods" wretched enough to get stuck at a stop sign next to him. He has also admonished my immigrant sensibilities by telling me that I should stick to one brand of clothing, that no self-respecting American would ever wear a pair of Reeboks *and* a T-shirt sporting the scissor-legged silhouette of Michael Jordan suspended mid-dunk. I hate this asshole. But I need the job.

The theater lobby is empty, at the moment. Hunter has propped open the Employees Only door to the box office so he can sermonize at me—a routine. The door to *his* office, on the far side of the box office, is open behind him. He's in his managerial garb, ironed and pleated, ponytail neat, goatee hairs scarce but indispensable for furnishing his face with the appearance of a chin. From my post behind the concession stand I watch him buzzing around, holding a lit joint out through the ticket window. With his other hand he's keeping the smoke out with a generically Asian-looking fan. Every thirty seconds or so he lowers his face to the hole in the glass, takes a toke, holds the smoke in while turning to make deranged eye contact with me, then exhales out the hole again, fanning away fervently, his face agleam because, once again, he has succeeded in not activating the smoke detectors while simultaneously smoking in the splendor of an air-conditioned theater.

"These fucking nimrods," he goes on, "these so-called bank robbers who rob some branch in the burbs at noon and get caught in front of their house by five p.m., right on time for the evening fucking news, these dumb motherfuckers in wife beaters being cuffed in front of their own fucking houses, looking like somebody stepped in their breakfast burrito! How retarded can you be? If I wanted to rob a bank, I would get a sick crew and silence-shoot dead every motherfucker in there. The tellers, the guards, the managers, the… those sour-faced fuckers that process loans, whoever the fuck came in, kids, rat-faced grannies, soccer moms, I don't give a shit, man. And when my crew gets all hungry-eyed eyeing all that cash, I'd mow those sick motherfuckers down too. Set up some pipe bombs on some major beams, douse everything in gas, drive off and detonate that son of a bitch. That's how you rob a bank. No clues, no witnesses."

He goes down to the hole for another toke. He's been tweaking since we opened at noon—he smokes weed only to alleviate whatever the hell the speed does to his system. I wait until he's holding the smoke in his lungs and then, innocently, smiling my best refugee smile, ask:

"You ever saw a dead man, Hunter?"

He chokes a little, trying to keep in a cough, then doubles over to exhale through the hole, fanning twice as hard. When he looks up at me he seems capable of cutting me open—keeping me alive, taking out organ after organ, showing each one to me before squeezing them until they ooze dark liquids. Hunter's rants are monologues, soliloquies at best. My job is to be an admiring audience member, not an interlocutor.

"Here we go again," he says. "I am Bosnia. I survive war. I see dead people on the way to schoolroom. Boo-hoo. Try growing up half-whiteboy half-Mexican in Culver City, motherfucker! Shit. In war at least you know the general direction the bullets are coming from. Where I grew up you never knew when some nimrod schoolboy with his daddy's Colt would unload in your gut over a pair of fucking sneakers, man. So, no, I've never seen a dead man, but at least I never ran away from a fight like a pussy. Your own fucking family, friends—your *people*, man, are getting killed out there, and you come over here to butter popcorn and help loaded cottontops in pastel leisurewear find their fucking seats in the dark. Cry me a fuckin' river!"

Something ignites in me. It sends prickles all the way up my back, as if my T-shirt's on fire.

Hunter, still fanning, kicks the box office door shut, granting himself the last word, making sure to come out on top. The sudden silence is galling.

"I was not eighteen, man!" I yell at the door.

It's true what I say. But it's true what he says too, at least to me. To me, his truth is beefier than mine.

I take in air but my lungs can't seem to absorb it. Their bronchial receptors are apparently already occupied with something else, something you can't breathe. I stand there, leaning on the counter, the back of my neck aflame, like a spurned lover's.

Through the theater's tinted windows the plaza, its parking lot, and Vista Road beyond it look docile and cool. The only evidence of the scorching weather, the only movement at all, is the uncanny but dulcet shimmering of the SUVs parked outside.

"I can leave anytime," I say to myself, and as I do, inexorably, despite all the roadblocks I've erected against her, Halida crashes back into my mind with an audible crunch.

Two summers ago, on my annual two-month visit to the motherland, I had gotten my heart snagged on an arresting brunette with an elfin face and a mouth on her that could shame a longshoreman. Halida was her name. I had emigrated a virgin in 1994, mid-war, when I was seventeen, and it was something of a novelty, four years later, to meet a Bosnian girl who was so uncomplicated about sex. They say that libidos thrive in the presence of death, but the girls I'd known before I'd emigrated were almost asexual in their prudishness, despite the daily violence.

By the time I met Halida I'd had a few discomfited and feverish encounters with community-college girls in the U.S., generally on the flattened seats of their parents' minivans or in their childhood rooms while, just beyond the wall, their grannies napped sitting up, large-print Grisham paperbacks in their frilly laps. I had grappled in the dark, hushed and hamhanded, stress sweat abounding.

But Halida was in a league of her own. When we got introduced, on a Monday, in passing, she grabbed my ass despite our mutual friends being two feet away. On Tuesday, during a chance meeting in the park, she reprimanded me for not finding a way to get in touch with her, and demanded my number. On Wednesday, when she called, we went out to a café overlooking some tennis courts, where, as I leaned sideways in my seat trying to get my jacket off, she leaned into me and stuck her tongue down my throat,

her slight hand burning on my inner thigh. "Cradle of Love" by Billy Idol
was on the radio. That same night, in a different park, as I was still trying
to figure out who I was and what world I was in, she said something like:

"Now we have a cock to play with."

I had no clue what to do with her.

I kissed her like I'd seen men kiss girls in the movies, dramatically
attacking her mouth from the right, then from the left, then from the right
again, then from the left again, all in a span of two and a half seconds. Her
hands clasped at my shoulders and squeezed, slid down my arms and, finding no discernable musculature, climbed back up to my neck, to my hair.
She arched her back and my right hand slid to her ass, flew somewhere else,
fluttered back to the ass. I tugged hard at the back of her T-shirt, making
the shape of her breasts more visible in the front even though my eyes were
shut tight. She took my hand and put it on her crotch and then grunted like
she meant it, grunted like I'd never heard anybody grunt. It was the grunt
of someone who had, miraculously, been reunited with a long-lost limb.

It scared the shit out of me.

I kept my eyes closed as if love, passion, and performance depended on
it. I felt stupid, and outside of myself. It was obvious that I was faking the
passion, that I had no idea what it was or how to use it. I had created an aura
of vehement urgency, hoping to lose myself in it, hoping that something
inside me would tell me what to do next.

Halida figured out pretty quickly where I was at. She led, and I followed until we were both sodden and grimy and bushed, until my arms
were not my arms and my breath was the cool of the night and my heart
was dancing a tarantella.

"Yo, nimrod!"

Hunter has the entrance door propped open for me now. He's smoking a
cigarette, of all things. I snap out of my trance, start to wipe the concession
counter with a rag. It's nighttime already.

"I don't pay you to scratch your balls. Go change the motherfuckin' marquee while I'm still here."

Red-faced, I take a box of letters and a rubber-tipped stick from one of the cabinets.

"You're cutting into my pussy-eating time," Hunter says, and chortles, as I walk by him and out.

We do a midnight movie every Friday. A manager is supposed to stick around, but Hunter routinely leaves me to close up the joint in his stead. It's always me, because he "doesn't trust that Gabe nimrod with Gabe nimrod's own dick." It feels slightly comforting that I'm not the lowest of the low.

Our only marquee is in the back, positioned to greet people as they exit the freeway on Vista.

Behind the building, semi-hidden by some dense low-maintenance thicket, I find the flimsy aluminum ladder I risk my life on every Friday. I secure it against the slapdash wall—as secure as that death trap can be— find the letters for the next week's movie, put them in order and in my pocket, put the stick in my mouth, and, mutely praying, start my climb. The cheapo rungs bend and creak under my weight. I stop two rungs from the top and, using the stick, slide the old letters out from their slots, letting them fall into the shrubbery, my knees ready to buckle even if the ladder doesn't. Then I put the stick back into my mouth, pray again, and step on the penultimate rung so as to reach the slots with my hand. As swiftly and as carefully as I can, I slide in the new letters.

When I'm back on the ground I'm drenched with sweat. I look up and read:

FRIDAY MIDNIGHT CLASSICS

NEXT WK @ VISTA TWIN THEATERS

PILP FUCTION

I stand there for half a minute, catching my breath, feeling disgusting and dumb. Then I saunter over and clutch the ladder again, looking up at my handiwork, my right foot disobeying me, unwilling to step on that rung again.

"Yo! Hurry up!" Hunter yells from up front.

I stand there for a while longer, exhale into the night, then lay the ladder back behind the bushes, pick up the fallen letters, and put them in the box.

"I left some extra garbage bags in the box office," Hunter says with glee when I'm back inside. "You're gonna need 'em tonight."

I give him a shit-eating grin. He gets into that ridiculous truck of his, revs it over and over again in the parking lot, then peels out onto Vista Road, his bumping bass rattling everything.

For a time everything's quiet. Then the freaks in theater B start to freak out in ecstasy at something or other in the film. I walk to the doors and listen to the chanting, the laughter, the screaming the likes of which you might encounter at a professional wrestling extravaganza. The poster on the wall reads *Rocky Horror Picture Show.* I've never heard of it.

On Monday I park my joke of a car at the far end of Vista Plaza and scan the entrance to the theater, detecting no signs of calamity. This past weekend was my first whole weekend off in a while, and so I hadn't been around when Hunter found out about my Pilp Fuction bungle. I spent the whole weekend playing *Delta Force* on my roommate's computer and procrastinating on my take-home philosophy final. But Gabe—whose mother lives two doors down in my apartment complex—has told me that the coast is clear, that Hunter is convinced that some "nimrod from the *Rocky Horror* crowd thought he was being really funny" and that he, the nimrod, won't be laughing when Hunter catches up with him and collapses his trachea.

When I approach the box office Hunter is in there all lovey-dovey with Tracy, his underage girlfriend, whom he employs just to sit on her ass, sell tickets, and keep him company. He's living in her ultra-progressive parents' house nearby, a live-in boyfriend of their seventeen-year-old daughter, and I guess the job is a quid pro quo type of deal. She and I are paid the same, but she has never had to clean the popcorn machine, or sweep the outside area, or Windex the windows, or do inventory, or change the titles on the marquee. When Hunter sees me he goes:

"Yo, Commie, the upstairs bathroom is in need of your assistance."

He says this through the hole in the glass and goes back to molesting Tracy. She slaps his chest and runs into his office and out of sight. He follows her with an unhinged jaw, a smile of sorts.

I remember Halida one morning, late for school, running harum-scarum around my parents' weekend house in nothing but white panties, trying to locate her clothes. I remember grabbing her and picking her up and her slapping my chest until I put her down. We had spent a month together by then, and then I'd had to come back to the States for school and work and we'd made promises to meet up again the next summer, maybe go down to the Dalmatian coast and pretend we were natives, spearing cuttlefish and selling the catch to high-end restaurants for top dollar to finance our stay. In the meantime, we promised to write, to call.

Tracy screams playfully, pops me out of my mind.

Tracy is a loudmouth know-it-all beach bunny to whom the world is owed. Her hair is green with chlorine, her earlobes, lips, tongue, what-have-you pierced with metal rings and studs, her lower back stamped WICKED in a Gothic font, a word she claims really means a lot to her. When Hunter first gave her the job she went out and leased a brand-new black BMW to get her from A to B and sank most of her paychecks on the payments. What she didn't do is change the oil in the thing. Ever. I look at it now, still parked right there under a tarp, in what would otherwise be the Jesus spot in front of the theater, its engine cracked, still sucking up her money.

You deserve each other, I think.

Inside, I lumber up the narrow stairs to the projectionist's/popcorn-making room and catch Pamela, a grown woman with an unhealthy obsession with Xena, Warrior Princess, eating a PB&J sandwich with the crusts cut off. She swallows with gusto, then makes a face.

"It's disgusting in there," she says.

I turn on the bathroom light and swing the door open with my foot. For a second I don't see anything wrong. The tiled walls are clean, the sink... and then I look down at the rat, its body broken oddly, its innards out, like a spilled container of fatty noodles. The mop that was used to dispatch the creature is broken in half and jagged.

"Get rid of it, please," Pamela squeals.

"I don't touch this," I tell her, and walk back downstairs.

I go to the soda machine and pour myself a Mountain Dew—free soda, one of the perks of my position behind the concession stand. I gulp it down as Hunter emerges out of the box office.

"Did you see him?" he says, childishly revolted. "I got him good, didn't I?"

"I don't touch rat," I say, to my surprise, my palms signaling the end of the conversation. "Not my job."

Hunter scans me for a long time, his brow ribbed, his lips compressed. Then, lo and behold, he shrugs, smiles even.

"All right, man," he says. "I'll make Gabe do it. What time is it?"

I'm stunned. It takes me a second to look at the clock on the wall above me.

"Noon and fifteen."

Hunter sniggers at my reply and shakes his head, but somehow more respectfully. He doesn't whip me with his laser look, doesn't threaten my job. For a second it almost feels like we're on equal footing. I feel my status in the company mushroom.

"Okay, then," he says, handing me the inventory sheet clipped to a clipboard. "Let's get her ready."

Our storage area is a diminutive and abnormally shaped room domi-nated by an industrial-size ice machine and metal shelving with long stacks of soda cups and popcorn containers in a range of sizes, wrapped in plastic. On the floor are cardboard boxes full of individual packages of candy: Red Vines, Mike and Ikes, Raisinets. The staples, I'm told. There's only enough space for me to take a single step in. I count every goddamned thing in there out loud, in Bosnian, and write down the numbers.

When I come out both Hunter and Tracy are in the lobby, leaning on the concession stand, eyeing me. There's a weird energy about them, as if they were having sex and managed to get dressed just in time to not get caught. I hand him the clipboard and they walk off through the box office and into his office. I hear Tracy giggle before Hunter shushes her.

It's 12:30, and I have half an hour before the start of the first matinee. I gulp down some more of my Mountain Dew and check on the ice in the soda fountain. It's half empty, so I go to our ice machine and scoop some into a bucket. There is a twelve-pack of Sam Adams bottles sitting in the ice.

Gabe, a youth with a touch of a weasel about him, comes in. Hunter makes him spit out his gum, shows him where the heavy-duty cleaning sup-plies are, and sends him upstairs. He's stern with him, eyebrows furrowed, but as soon as Gabe turns to go up the stairs Hunter grimaces and smiles at me. I can't help but reciprocate. He extends his soda cup in salutation, and I pick mine up, too. We noiselessly chin-chin.

Zero patrons show up for the first showing of either movie. But it *is* Monday, and this *is* a tiny independent movie theater in a well-to-do bedroom community, nothing more than a tax write-off for our moneyed owners somewhere in Bel Air. Gabe descends the stairs seeming scarred, then spends forever in the restroom, water humming in the pipes in the wall. When he emerges he opts to watch one of the films, which we're allowed to do if there are no customers.

I don't touch rats, I think, my chest filling with elation and something like pride. I'm in charge of me, my body, the space I get to occupy. I'm in charge of this shit. I get the Windex and a rag and put them on top of the candy display in case Hunter comes out, so I can pretend I'm busy. Then, immediately, I think: Why the fuck do I have to worry about what Hunter thinks? I could run circles around this guy! He sucks at being a manager. He sucks at being a human being.

I feel my soles sticking to the black rubber mat and I'm surprised that I find it disgusting. It bothers me so much that I peel it off the tiled floor, the octopus suckers on its underside going *smack-smack-smackity-smack*. I have a sudden urge to see it up close. It's fairly new, but it's coated in a sticky syrup of dried soda sugar. I pick up the whole thing, take it outside, and hose it down against the side of the building until you could eat off of it.

The forceful heat and the physical effort make my heart bombinate, but I don't want to stop yet. I put the mat back, pick up the Windex, and give every window a twice over from the inside. I'm in the storage room getting a new thing of Windex when, in the lobby behind me, Hunter and Tracy burst into laughter. She slaps her forehead cartoonishly. Look at these dumb fucks, I think. What are they cackling about?

"Dude, I should do this more often," Hunter manages through his spasms. "Look at this motherfucker *work*!"

Tracy smacks herself again.

"Do what?" I ask.

Now both of them are doubled over. Hunter holds to the counter in earnest as he fights for breath. Their eyes are leaking.

"How're you feeling?" Tracy asks. "High?"

"Yeah, you want some more Mountain Dew, man?"

I finally connect the dots.

I feel it coming again, the heat: from my neck up into my face, and from my back up the back of my neck. I feel the panic crop up, and the rage. My heart is a machine-gun nest now, and the gunner is wasting all his ammo. The empty bottle of Windex is vibrating in my hand, like in the movies when ghosts take over an inanimate object. I hurl it at Hunter but it hits the doorway, ricochets off, and starts poltergeisting around the storage room, missing me every time. Right before my knees crumple in panic I take the door and bang it shut. Then I lock it, curl down in between boxes on the cold cement floor, lay my face upon said cement, and watch the shadow puppetry in the lobby through the crack under the door. A busy, urgent kind of play, by the looks of it.

The gunner ceases not.

It's Friday again and I'm on the ladder, teetering, sweating. Hunter is below and behind me, supervising, and Tracy is just out of my line of vision, sniping at him about how they're gonna be late, how she's waited so long to see this band live, how she will get him kicked out of her house if he makes her miss them. He goes on a diatribe about responsibility, about how *his* "taint" is on the line if he gets caught trying to take a seventeen-year-old to a twenty-one-and-over show, X-rated at that, not to mention leaving "Bosnia boy over here" and "that nimrod" in charge.

"I DON'T GIVE A FUCK!" she screams, and I almost fall down.

I spit out the stick and hug the wall with my outstretched arms, abrading my cheek against it. I stay like that until the ladder steadies some.

"Is this… good?" I say.

"Never move in with a girl with a tattoo on her tit," he says. "Come down."

I do, and look up.

FRIDAY MIDNIGHT CLASSICS
@ VISTA TWIN THEATERS
BUTCH CASSIDY AND SUNDANCE KID

"We should get a new ladder, huh?" Hunter says, patting me on my moist back.

Ever since Monday's "shenanigans" (this is what he calls it) he's been extra nice to me. He may be tough, but he's not tough enough not to sweat what would happen to him if I went to the cops and told them what he did, what he keeps in his office. On Tuesday I asked for a Thursday off and got it—a first. He even offered me a baggie of weed to take home, to implicate me in his criminal activities, but I declined because I have an operational cerebral cortex.

We go back to the front of the theater. Tracy honks thrice from the parking lot, each honk longer and more painful than the one before it.

"Just follow the list," Hunter says. "And don't forget to deposit the cash."

He goes leisurely down the steps, stops, and lights a cigarette.

Tracy starts to honk in a wicked, demented rhythm, like a goose being tortured with a fork. He ignores it, turns back to me, and grins. Slowly, prolonging every movement, Hunter gangsta-walks to the truck. By the time he reaches it, Tracy might as well be sitting on the horn.

Inside, Gabe greets me with a lewd gesture, his tongue out, his curled hand bobbing in front of his crotch, no doubt exaggerating his manhood.

"I'd fuck that bitch and wouldn't take a dime from her," he says.

"After Hunter?"

"Oh, that would only make it sweeter," he groans, then abandons jerking it and starts to mount the concession counter, thrusting his hips at it. "Christ, to fuck that asshole's girl!"

"You know she only has seventeen… I mean, she's only seventeen?"

"Me too, man. Me too."

He laughs like he's gotten away with something. I try the box office door and it gives.

"Listen, Gabe, you want to go home? I will do everything."

"I need the hours, dude."

"I'm not gonna say anything. Put whatever hours you want on the thing."

"For reals?" he says, and cocks his head.

"For reals."

"See ya," he says, and runs out of the place, bucking and pumping his fists.

I walk into theater B: thirty or so people watching John Travolta take a sip of a milkshake. Nobody seems antsy, no popcorn tub is empty. I walk out, peek into the bathrooms, scan the parking lot for unusual activity, then slip into the box office, walk through it, and try Hunter's door. It's locked.

Motherfucker.

I go back behind the concession stand and count all the money in the cash register, minus the hundred dollars we start the day with. Then I count the popcorn containers and the soda cups on the cabinets behind me and all the candy in the glass display and check the numbers against the day's inventory to figure out what was actually bought. Fridays are our busy days, and I see we've made over five hundred dollars. Doing calculations in my head I stroll into theater A, which I've yet to clean, and start looking for clean popcorn tubs, the ones that a customer didn't soil with our butter substitute or completely cover in salt. Luckily, our daytime clientele is made up of old folks worried about their cholesterol levels and soccer moms worried about their calorie intakes, and I find half a dozen containers that can pass as new. I take them back to the stand, wipe them off with paper towels, and put them on the bottom of the stacks. Four small popcorns for $2.50 apiece, two large ones for $4 apiece. I take $18 out of the cash register and put it in my sock.

Who's a nimrod now?

I watch the end of *Pulp Fiction*, stand up, and prop open the doors. Suburban creatures of the night emerge out of the theater in Korn T-shirts and hoodies, hugging their pink-haired girlfriends. None of them use the bathroom and I'm able to lock the doors immediately.

Having done the inventory and with the box office money already in the deposit bag, all I have to do is add the concession money and deposit it and clean theater B. I dash through the auditorium with a garbage bag, picking up the big things, then do another sweep with a sweeper, getting rid of the spilled popcorn. I throw it all in the garbage and then, propping the entrance doors open, I run across the plaza to the bank and drop the deposit bag through the slot in the wall. Then, elated, I go back into the theater.

With the box of letters in the lobby I take a piece of paper out of my back pocket and look it over.

BUTCH CASSIDY AND SUNDANCE KID

NUDE SASSY BITCH AND DICKHEAD CUNT

DYKE ASS IN THE SAND

BITCHASS NANCY

TIDYASS BITCH NANCY

Although NUDE SASSY BITCH AND DICKHEAD CUNT uses all the letters available outside, and although, English being my second language, I am most proud of that one, I find it a bit too much for the good folks of Vista Falls. I double-check my work, take the rubber-tipped stick, and go outside to do the deed.

FRIDAY MIDNIGHT CLASSICS

@ VISTA TWIN THEATERS

NASTY DANISH DICKSCAB

When I went to Bosnia last summer I did so with glee and trepidation, with all of Halida's letters in my carry-on, proud that I'd stayed true even though I'd had two occasions to do otherwise. True, I only knew this in retrospect, because I'm kind of—well, for lack of a better word let's call me a nimrod when it comes to deciphering what is a come-on and what is not. I don't speak body language.

Once, late at night at a party, a girl from my Women's History class whom I ate lunch with three days a week and who laughed at everything I said pulled me upstairs, saying she wanted to show me something. We went into a room and she locked the door, sat on the bed, and told me she'd had her nipple pierced and did I want to see it. I said sure, and she patted the bed next to her, then popped out a perfect boob with a young-moon stud through the nipple. I asked her if it hurt, and what the procedure was, and why did she pick that shape, and kept up my inquiries for another half an hour until the person whose party it was gonged for us to leave.

On the airplane I reread all of Halida's letters. She had written them in pencil, on graph paper, and I had retraced every letter of every word in ink for fear of the graphite fading or being smudged away. I zipped through pages about her university life, about her going out with friends, about her tumultuous family, and loitered on the ones about our plans to go to the coast, about how much fun we'd have and how happy she was when she received my letters. I signed off every one of mine with *Love*. She signed every one of hers *XO Halida*.

On July 15, when she was supposed to return from her aunt's house in the Netherlands and give me a call, I transferred my parents' rotary phone to my childhood room and sat there waiting for it to ring, trying to read Dostoyevsky's *The Idiot*. My childhood friends called, inviting me out for drinks, concerts, paint-thinner sniffing (like in the olden times), breaking my heart because they weren't her. I told them I was under the weather—a summer bug. I waited until midnight and gave up, figured there was a snag in her travel plans, that the promised phone call would come the next day. I reread the letters in bed, only the good parts.

The next day I started to experience chest pains. Certain segments of her letters, the non-fun parts, started to gnaw at me, certain phrasings about going out with friends and just having fun, the myriad ways one can interpret the words *friend* and *fun*. My fingers tingled, my eyes watered, and I paced the room in a square formation, tracing the outline of the design on the carpet compulsively. I felt like something was growing in me, filling me to capacity and growing still more. I wished I was able to let some of the pressure out through my nose, or my ears, like a cartoon character, or from under the cap of my cranium in the form of fire and volcanic smoke accompanied by the sound of a train horn.

On the third day I found her father's number in the phone book and called around 11 a.m. He was curt and sympathetic at the same time, said that Halida had gone to the seaside with her boyfriend. He seemed miffed by it. I thanked him in my highest voice, as if through a sphincter, and hung up.

On my childhood desk in front of me was a model of a Mack truck that I'd used to draw my first comic, a Skeletor action figure holding aloft the wartime Bosnian flag instead of a weapon, a beat-up Rolodex containing the name and number of every kid I'd met since first grade, a mug of pencils for penciling, a mug of Rapidographs and a mug of brushes for inking, a flesh-colored model of a human foot (as those are hardest to draw), a ninja star I'd bought with my own money through mail order from Gornji Milanovac and that I'd once stuck into the side of my cousin's knee, an orange lamp with a heavy base and an expandable neck that I'd gotten from my mother for my thirteenth birthday when she'd realized I was serious about drawing, a pinecone given to me by the first girl I'd ever gone out with during the war, plus all the marks of youth, the familiar nicks and scratches in the wood, moisture rings where my juice glasses used to sit without coasters, arranged like inebriated Olympic circles, and of course our red rotary phone—but none of it, not one thing, mattered to me a smidgeon. You could have burned all of it right then and I would have raised my hands and enjoyed the heat.

On July 18 I found myself on the roof of a building where I'd lived as a little kid, sitting on the knee-high wall, the metal guardrail burning my hands and my ass through my shorts, my feet on the gravel on the roof, my head leaning back over the ledge looking down onto a parking lot, hazily trying to identify car models from my bird's-eye point of view. Thinking, breathing. A thought came to me up there, a mind-voice saying: *Why don't you just go back to the States. If this shit doesn't get better, you can always kill yourself over there.*

I'm cleaning every inch of the popcorn warmer, inside and out, and doing it thoroughly, because Hunter is outside smoking a cigarette with two guys and monitoring me through the glass. He's calmer now, as opposed to earlier in the day when Tracy and him were going at it. It started out circumspect enough, behind the closed doors of his office, until she yelled that he was "fucking impossible" and stormed out into the box office, talked to herself there, banged some drawers, then went back into his office and—with the door open this time—told him to apologize. He laughed, said he didn't have anything to apologize for, she asked him to apologize again, he said "What for?" she called him an "infantile child," which I thought was a little redundant, he called her (surprise, surprise) a "nimrod," she said "Fuck you," he said "You act like your pussy is golden," she said "I quit," he said "Good luck getting your dad to throw his money at that Beemer," she said "Good luck moving in with your mom," and then he ran out of his office and she ran outside while he yelled "I gave you a fucking ride this morning, you octagon head." Then she turned around and marched back inside and used the phone in his office to arrange for a ride as he cackled and cackled, using all his energy to pretend that he was okay with this.

I finish cleaning the warmer and keep busy so he doesn't give me shit. I don't mind working for real today, because I'm sweating my little stunt from last night. I took the freeway over here on purpose and saw that the marquee had been fixed. By the time I came in Hunter was already fighting with Tracy, having bigger problems I guess. It couldn't have turned out better for me.

A model employee, I pop a new batch of popcorn upstairs, ask Pamela to monitor it for me, come downstairs, get more ice for the soda machine, rub the metal edges of the candy display with a rag until they're almost fulgent, then pop back upstairs to grab a huge garbage bag of warm popcorn for the warmer. As I come back down I hear the screech of a car braking outside. I turn and see this big black Bronco alongside where Hunter and those two guys are talking. The driver pulls out a neon green squirt rifle and opens up on all three of them, laughing and *wooooo*ing. They jump up and scream but the Bronco peels onto Vista, away from the freeway, and speeds off. The two guys bolt across the parking lot and into a sedan and go after the Bronco, with no regard for human life.

Hunter yells: "GET SOME!"

I peek outside.

"What is going on?" I say.

"That cockpolisher picked the wrong guys to squirt with piss, man. Those motherfuckers are training to be marines. If they catch up to him they'll fuck him up, piss in his mouth."

"Wow!" I say. "Shit."

"I said piss, not shit."

We stand there staring after them for a while, then watching Vista Plaza sink back into monotony. Hunter finishes his cigarette and puts it out in a dish of sand on top of the stand-up ashtray next to the door.

"She fucking kicked me out, man," he says.

I'm stunned. I have no clue what to say to him. Is he confiding in me? Did he forget I was there?

"What happened?" I manage.

"Nothing," he snorts. "She's fucking certifiable if she thinks she can manipulate my ass."

It's 9:30 when Hunter comes out with a kind of newspaper, holding it open, and walks up to the concession stand.

"We're empty, right?"

"Yes."

He swings the paper onto the counter so I can read it and, using a Sharpie, points to three girls' faces on page twenty. There's a name and a phone number under every black-and-white photograph.

"Which one?"

I look at the spread, all pouty lips and perfect hair, cat eyes and manicured hands, most of them showing a bit of tongue in the corner of their lips. One toward the bottom looks like Halida and something tugs at my lungs, tries to collapse them. I do a double take but it's not her.

"Come on, douche."

I look at his choices. They're all blondes like Tracy. I pick the one that looks nothing like her and press my finger on the girl's picture. He smiles.

"Cynthia it is."

The rest of the week passes in monotony. Hunter talks shit about Tracy, her parents, says he would marry Cynthia if only she would take care of him like she did that day and keep her mouth shut. He seems to be serious. I think of Halida, imagine seeing her on a night out in Tuzla, yapping with some girlfriends, and me, hiding behind beer mugs, acting like I don't give a shit but really wondering what's in her heart. Wondering if she would have been worth killing myself for.

On Friday I put my life in jeopardy once more to advertise our showing of *The Good, the Bad and the Ugly*. I keep waiting for Hunter to leave so I can work on jumbling the letters again when he calls me into his office. The only time I've been in there is some two years ago, when a long-departed assistant manager gave me the job. I come inside and realize that Hunter lives here now.

His desk is pushed all the way into the corner, with a TV on top and a sparse beard of cords leading to a VCR, a Nintendo console, and two or three controllers. Next to the desk is a small microwave and a toaster. There is a gargantuan open suitcase under the desk, like a head of a yawning hippo with neatly packed clothes in it. On a clothesline tied around a pipe on one end of the room and to a random rivet sticking out of the wall on the other hang three pressed outfits—his managerial clothes. Leaning in the corner is a rolled-up foam mattress.

Hunter's in his office chair, packing a huge bowl into a six-foot magenta bong. I think back and realize that I haven't had to wait for him to open the doors for me at noon since Saturday—a common occurrence, previously. I try to pretend I'm not surprised, but he can't be fooled.

"What was I gonna do? Sleep in my truck? Move in with my fucking mom?"

I look around, nod my head.

"Do owners know?"

"Are you limited? What's wrong with you? Don't ask bombastically moronic questions. Shit, man, think! Everybody is in B, right?"

"Yeah."

"Let's go. I need you to help me light this."

We go to theater A, and staying close to the wall so we cannot be seen by Pamela in the booth, I light the weed and he gets himself high. The theater's high ceilings and the ventilators take care of his exhalations in seconds.

"You wanna hit this?"

"Maybe next time."

He shrugs, then sees something on the back of one of the seats in the last row.

"Check this out," he says, giggling. "Remember Cynthia?"

I walk over and look at a white stain on the dark blue fabric, like Lewinski's dress. He moves his hand in front of his crotch, suggesting fellatio.

"Remind me not to watch movies here," I say, and he smacks my shoulder with hilarity.

"Hey, remember Isidro and Pat? The other day with the piss gun and everything? They're in jail. They caught up to that dude at a red light on the corner of Vista and Century, the busiest fucking intersection, knocked on his window, and when the motherfucker didn't open it, one of them just smashed it with a claw hammer, broke the guy's shoulder with it. And his fuckin' cheekbone, too. On the corner of Vista and Century, like, by the mall?"

I nod, smiling, thinking of what he would do to me if he knew I was behind the marquee shenanigans.

"Then the cops caught them," he adds after a pause, lamentably.

We go back into his office and he wraps the bong in a blanket. Then he produces a tab of pills of some variety and pops three or four of them.

"Hey, you wanna stay up tonight and wait for the joker?" he says, an aluminum baseball bat appearing in his hand by some kind of magic.

"I don't know, man."

"Come on. You can add it to your hours. Overtime. Come on!"

"Overtime?"

"Good, backup," he says, and punches out two more of those pills. "Take these. They'll fuck your ass up real good."

I take them. *What the fuck.*

"You think I can have one of those beers in the ice machine?" I ask.

"Shit yeah, take them all. They were Tracy's. That's the only downer she would take. But you should see her on speed, man. That girl is spinning. Ass like a jackhammer. Bongitty-bongitty-bongitty-bongitty!"

He smiles, but he's too high, and as soon as he's not talking it's just an empty grimace. He sits down, stares glassily at his hands. He doesn't move.

"You okay?" I say.

He looks at me like he doesn't even know that we just had a conversation. He nods.

It's four in the morning and I'm with Hunter on the side of the Vista underpass, in the shadows, not even watching the marquee anymore, but lying on the dirt and looking at the anemic sky and listening to the big rigs going by on the freeway. He's slurring, going on and on about how beautiful Tracy is, how they met at a fancy rehab in Arizona when she was only sixteen, how they fell in love in sobriety and how they slipped up and how it all turned to shit. He describes their first time, under a piano in her parents' living room while fancies were rubbing elbows by the pool, and every time afterward, every new place more dangerous and more risky than the next: while driving, in front of some industrial building, in her father's office, in the pool where she trains. And he sobs and the tears pool in his earlobes and he says that everything is over.

He tells me everything except why she kicked him out.

I sit up.

"Don't go yet," he says.

I show him that I'm only taking a sip of my beer. He takes his hand off my elbow. His head clonks back against the ground, like someone giving up. Lying there with his shirt unbuttoned he looks emaciated and thrown away.

"I love that fucking bitch," he says.

"Why did you break up, then?"

He looks back at the sky.

"It's stupid."

"Tell me."

"Nah."

"What did you do?"

"Nothing."

"Come on."

"You'd laugh."

"What is it?"

"It's dumb."

"What is it?"

He says nothing. I wait. He says nothing still, his eyes rolling from one part of the sky to another, searching. I realize I have to piss. I move to stand up and he goes:

"I want her to die."

"No, you don't."

"Yes, I do."

"Why?"

He points at the overpass above us, flops his arm back on the ground.

"See this goddamned street? Every gangsta-ass fucking day she has to drive down this goddamned street when she goes to school and on the weekends when she has trainings. She's a diver. Did I tell you this?"

"Yes."

"Well, I saw her with…" he says, and chokes up. I look at him and he might as well be a cadaver, with lips pulled away from bared teeth and hollow sockets with eyes closed—a gruesome mask of ancient, candid, lonely human pain. I drink until he opens his eyes again.

"Why don't you just apologize?" I ask him.

He looks at me like manager Hunter for the briefest of moments, then turns back to gushiness.

"I can't do that."

"Why?"

"Because then she wins."

"She wins what?"

He snorts, sadly.

"You wouldn't understand," he says, and turns away from me.

"Just call her and say Baby, I am sorry. Please take me back."

"She doesn't like those imbecilic terms of endearment."

"What do you call her?"

"I'm not telling."

We say nothing for a while. I think of the first time I met Tracy, how much I hated her and her stupid whiny voice, her sense of entitlement, the way she looked down on me. And right there, while thinking of her, something gets illuminated by a spotlight in my head, makes me smile.

"I have to go number two," I say, and stand up. My limbs feel heavy and full of meat but at least the world isn't spinning anymore. "You left the back door open?"

He grunts.

I go down to the theater and take a leak in the darkness. I go into the cabinets and pull out the box of letters, spend some time choosing the ones I need. Outside, right by the back door, I hide them behind the little brick wall along with the rubber-tipped stick and make my way to the overpass.

I remember the aftermath of Hurricane Halida, the ferocity of my hatred for her. Every time I was in love before and the love was lost, I was still me, miserable, broken, but still me. But there's something about betrayal that for a while turns love to hate, while the intensity of the feeling remains constant. I remember thoughts, vivid scenarios that would spring into my mind out of nowhere, as if someone else was putting them there. Someone evil. These palpable flashes that soiled me forever.

I wished Halida brokenhearted. I wished her poor. I wished her anorexic. I wished her obese, in one of those carts. I wished her broken under a car. I wished her decapitated. I wished her toothless. I wished her legs amputated. I wished her bald and blind. I wished her wrecked at the bottom of a flight of stairs. I wished her overdosed. I wished her floating face-first down a river. I wished her raped. I wished her buried up to her neck in a desert. I wished her dangling off a beam. I wished her poisoned. I wished her sorry. I wished her dead.

I wished these things against her for making me have these foreign thoughts in this foreign land when I first came back from Bosnia and for three months carried a jar of pills in my backpack just in case.

My friends say she's in a band these days.

When I get back to the shadows Hunter is dead to the world. I half wake him and then half carry him into his office, where I lay him down on the floor. I lock the back door and with my stash of letters and my trusty rubber-tipped stick I stand under the marquee.

Soon, some other asshole will drive that bitch Tracy to an early-morning diving practice. Puffed and groggy, she will look up at the marquee. Hunter will still be passed out on the floor inside, with no idea what I've done, and I myself will be long gone, but what she will read is this:

FRIDAY MIDNIGHT CLASSICS
@ VISTA TWIN THEATERS
I LOVE YOU, WICKED GIRL
I AM SORRY, TAKE ME BACK

BECAUSE NIGHT HAS FALLEN AND THE BARBARIANS HAVE NOT COME

by **VALERIA LUISELLI**

Translated by Christina MacSweeney

"Everyone has a theory but there's no explanation," says Mom, pointing at the headline of today's paper. Strewn over the table are three coffees and a large bowl full of sliced papaya. There's an ashtray, a lighter, and the newspaper—all my brother's. There's a copy of Cavafy's poems, which Mom is reading, and a Yellow Pages open to VULCANIZERS, which I'm leafing through, looking for telephone numbers.

We got a flat tire 281 kilometers before Acapulco and about a hundred kilometers after the tollbooth. We were lucky it happened near the diner— a Soviet-style establishment called Siberia Dos, with long metal tables waited on by women wearing identical hairstyles. After a quick lunch, my brother and I replaced the burst tire with the spare. But we still had to find a vulcanizer and a proper tire, because the spare turned out to be too small and the car was now unbalanced, huffing along as if it had a set of mismatched legs, one shorter than the other. "Like a crippled earwig," my mother said. I didn't really understand that.

In the crippled car, my brother driving gingerly on the undersize spare, we asked her, "Why have you got Maná's first album in the glove compartment, Ma? Why do you even own a Maná CD, Ma?"

"What's it to you?" she said from the back, and she was right: what's it to us? We made an effort and listened, strenuously, respectfully, to the first track, and the second. When the fifth track came on—to be exact, when Fher Olvera sang the ridiculous lines "Un tambor sonó muy Africano / Es el pumpin pumpin de tu corazón"—Mom doubled up with laughter. She offered to change the CD, and passed up a Leonard Cohen album the three of us have always liked well enough. I can't remember the first time Mom sat in the backseat like that, while we rode in the front—of course, I don't mean that metaphorically.

The house is perched on the edge of a cliff more than two hundred meters high. At the foot of the cliff, the sea stretches out like a tombless cemetery until it touches Japan. We've come here because Mom wants to give my brother and me some news. In fact, she gave us the news while we were changing the flat tire outside the Soviet diner, so we don't really understand why she's giving it to us again. The news is that Mom has a boyfriend. Having heard this, we could have just driven back to the city after we changed the tire.

The last time she made an announcement like this was when she told us our father was going to go live with Sara, and she was going to go live in a bungalow in Malinalco for a while, maybe a year or two, with her mute-meditation group. That was Christmas 1999, and the news was given to us, for reasons I cannot remember, on the roof of our building. That same Christmas, after dinner, my brother and I went back up to the roof to smoke a joint and tried to do mute meditations ourselves. But both of us kept getting distracted by little things, little thoughts, little bugs.

Luckily for us, Mom's mute-meditation group broke up around the New Year, before the great pilgrimage to Malinalco, and she stayed with us until we each got married and had children of our own. Then she was left alone in a house that was too big and too silent.

As soon as we arrived in Acapulco, I put my backpack in the end room—there's a narrow hallway with four bedrooms that each look out onto the garden—and went to the patio at the corner of the house, from which you could see the sea. The house belongs to my mother's sister, Celia, who married an architect and has no children. I was sure that, standing solemnly before the wide, wild sea, I'd come up with an idea. A wild idea, clever and broad, that would justify this slightly absurd journey our mother had obliged us to come along on. An idea I could say out loud during dinner to make my brother laugh and my mom feel uncomfortable.

The other part of the news was that Mom's boyfriend had become blind and then a Sufi, in that order. Blind, thirteen years ago; and Sufi, twelve years ago. Before that he was a Basque pelota player.

"He's meeting us in Acapulco tomorrow night, and will spend the weekend with the three of us," Mom said yesterday, as we were getting back in the slightly angled car.

My brother started the motor, and I rooted around for CDs in the glove compartment.

"He's coming by bus because he doesn't drive," she added, for clarification.

Neither my brother nor I knew what a Basque pelota player was. My mother must have suspected this, because she embarked on a detailed explanation of the sport. My brother didn't ask questions about pelota playing,

Sufism, or anything else. He's a polite, respectful person who almost never asks personal questions. I do, sometimes, but on this occasion I emulated him and kept my mouth shut. Deep down, though, I wanted to ask how the Basque pelota player had gone blind, and if his blindness was related to having been a pelota player or if his Sufism was related to his blindness. Instead I just sipped my coffee in silence, letting it scorch my tongue with each sip. Basque pelota can be played with a racket, a wooden bat, or with your hands, my mother said. That was when we put on the Maná CD.

For dinner we had cereal, the three of us standing, watching each other eat. No one said anything except "Pass the milk" and "Here is a bigger spoon" and, later, "Good night." Before going to bed, I walked to the patio overlooking the cliff again and tried calling my husband and the kids, but there was no answer.

Mom has a boyfriend and she's doing okay. I fell asleep embracing this one thought, the fan laboriously slicing through the heavy night air.

At breakfast the next morning—cereal again—I interrupt the silence and say, "*Vulcanizer* comes from Vulcan, the Roman god of fire." I repeat the name, "Vulcan," almost in a whisper. I say it to the window, beyond which the sea stretches out toward Japan, but really I say it to my brother. "*Vulcanizer* comes from Vulcan."

He says, "Hmm," and goes on reading the newspaper. The headline reads: FIVE DECAPITATED BODIES FOUND IN TRUNK OF CAR: HEADS NOWHERE TO BE FOUND.

Must we say so much? So directly? Say things to the window—that's what our father used to do when he was giving us an order. He'd say things to the window, never straight to us, knowing that the child to whom the command was directed would answer promptly. We never said "Hmm" to our father. We always said, "Right, okay."

Mom comes in from the kitchen carrying a tray with three cups of coffee and a bowl of papaya. She sets them down on the table and, pointing at my brother's newspaper, says, "Everyone has a theory."

My brother has three children. I've got a daughter and two stepsons who affectionately—or, rather, sometimes affectionately, sometimes not— call me Refrigerador. When the six children, my brother's and mine, get together, they form a perfect tribe. A noisy bunch, more self-confident and full of life than we two were as children—we were always a bit quiet, not melancholy but perhaps saturnine, which is almost the same thing but not exactly. We were always observing the adults around us. Now we observe the children around us. In that liminal place, I think, my brother and I learned to feel more at ease, maybe even happy. Now, without our kids here, we have no one to observe but our mother. We don't really know how to look at each other.

After breakfast, Mom washes the dishes, my brother goes to the market to buy an octopus for lunch, and I sit on the patio overlooking the sea, dialing numbers for vulcanizers. I also call my husband, to see how everyone is doing back in the city, but he doesn't answer the phone, so I leave a message. Everything fine here, missing you all. My mother has a new boyfriend. He's very nice—an athletic, spiritual man. Give the baby a kiss from me, on the nose, and give the boys a hug from Refrigerador.

Looking out at the sea beyond the cliff, a theory springs to mind: that's where they throw the heads.

Mom comes in while I'm having a bath and sits on the toilet seat, her pee cascading noisily into the water in the bowl. I think of that Pablo Neruda poem where he listens to his lover pee. She tells me that she's learning Braille. She has been reading her bilingual edition of Cavafy's poems with her boyfriend. The edition is in Braille and—she hesitates—in "normal."

I ask her to pass me a towel. I wonder if she has had a bath with her boyfriend yet.

"What's your boyfriend like, Ma? Is he good-looking?"

"Well, he looks a bit like Slavoj Žižek," she says, "but blind."

"Slavoj Žižek?"

"Yes," she says, "the one on the YouTube."

It's difficult to imagine how fathers and mothers make love, be it with each other or with someone else. There was a moment, during my first years of college, when everyone used to emulate the protagonist of *Hopscotch*, who always has sex on the floor and then smokes a cigarette. Then, a few years later, they all started emulating the protagonist in *The Savage Detectives*, who masturbates his partner by giving her little slaps on the clitoris. I wonder what my daughter will make of all that, twenty years from now, when she reads my copies of the novels I underlined here and there. Sex is always generational. From a certain point of view—especially from above—it's a bit ridiculous. My brother's generation fucked like the couple in *9½ Weeks*. I'll never know what books and films my parents' generation decided to emulate. But it horrifies me to imagine Žižek fornicating with my mother.

At lunchtime, we sit down to a meal of octopus ceviche my brother has made. Mom talks insistently about the need to change the tire before her boyfriend arrives that night, and how the two of us must make sure to check the size of the new one. Then she digresses. She explains that Sufi whirling dervishes might be emulating the movement of planets, rather than the gyration of tires. While she's digressing, I think of all the possible holiday activities that are useful for killing time with family members: poker, Risk, Monopoly, chess, Pictionary. They all require the faculty of sight. We have to find a game where no one needs to see the pieces.

While we do the dishes, my brother asks me if I feel jealous of Mom's new boyfriend. He washes, I dry. "No, I'm not the least bit jealous," I say without hesitation. But I spend the rest of the time we're shuffling dishes around thinking about it. I ask him if he knows any games we can play with Mom's boyfriend. He says he can't think of any.

"Perhaps poker dice," he says, because you can feel the dents in the dice. But as soon as we begin trying to refine the details, Mom comes into the kitchen and we both fall silent. No, I'm not jealous, I think again when we've finished the dishes. I want to say that what I feel is the exact opposite of jealousy, but I'm not sure what such a thing would be called, or whether it exists.

My brother and I leave the house to go to Variety Vulcanizers, whose owner I've spoken to in order to explain our problem. They've assured me that they have the exact size tire we need. When we get into the car and switch on the ignition, Leonard Cohen's "I'm Your Man" comes on. It sounds abnormally loud. I turn off the radio. My brother says, "You know *vulcanizer* doesn't come from Vulcan."

"Yes it does," I say, and he turns the music back on.

The city of Acapulco is like a military parade, armed forces everywhere—the army, the navy, judicial, federal, and state police. The most frightening ones are the navy: Mexican soldiers dressed like American ones.

Once we get to the vulcanizer's, the problem is quickly—but not effectively—solved. The tire they have is a bit bigger than our other three.

"It's better to have it be bigger than smaller," argues the vulcanizer. He raps out "The bigger the better, like the more the merrier." He also offers us a marijuana *tostón* as a bonus. This last part of the deal convinces my brother.

"We can gradually replace the other three tires with larger ones," he says.

"Do you still smoke pot?" I ask my brother as we walk toward the register, making our way between tires, odd bits of trash, tubes, and a bone from a chicken wing.

"No, you?"

"No."

After he has paid for the tire, the lady at the register hands my brother a business card, on which is printed a small figure. She explains to both of us that it's Vulcan, the Roman god of fire.

"See?" I say. "I told you."

"Told me what?"

"Nothing. Never mind."

Back at the house, Mom is standing at the mirror, getting ready. The sun will set soon, and she's going to drive to the bus station. The pelota-playing Sufi boyfriend must be less than fifty kilometers away. It's the first time in ten years that Mom's had a boyfriend. She looks beautiful. I tell her she looks good. She says, Well, he won't be able see me anyway.

I'm not sure whether to laugh, but she does, and then I do too, a little. I fasten her necklace for her.

We never ever forgive our parents anything, though they almost always forgive us everything. But at the same time we admire them much more than they ever manage to admire us. Perhaps admiration is just an acknowledgment we offer to those people we find unfathomable. And for all that time passes, as we become adults and raise walls and families and acquire careers, we're never unfathomable to them.

My brother and I play poker dice at the dining room table while waiting for Mom to come back. He takes out the *tostón* and I make a joint, carefully emptying a cigarette and surgically removing the filter.

"Do you think they throw all those heads into the sea?" I ask.

"Don't go having a bad trip before we smoke."

"Right, okay."

We smoke like beginners, with exaggerated gestures, emulating old expressions. Our present-day faces are much sterner than they were before.

"Four queens," he says.

I don't pick up the cup, even though I know he's lying. Then I look at the dice and see that there is, in fact, only a pair of queens. I pick them up and throw again, and lose, and lose again. Just like that.

The love we feel for older siblings—who are also in some way unfathomable—is also disproportionate. But we don't make them pay for our inability to fathom them, as we do with our parents. We adore them, full stop. Or if we don't adore them at every moment, we at least still love them a lot.

Mom comes back at around 10:30 p.m. The pelota player doesn't come in with her. We wait for a moment in silence, thinking that perhaps a blind person needs a bit more time to get out of the car, that he'll soon appear in the doorway with his white stick in hand. But no one appears, no stick peeks into sight. I know from the look on her face that no one's going to come. She puts her handbag down heavily on the table and sits with us.

"Are you guys stoned?"

"No," my brother says.

"A little," I say.

"Can I have some?"

My brother extracts the remaining half of the spliff from the box of cigarettes on the table, lights it, and passes it over to her.

She takes a long drag and, holding in the smoke, asks us, "Did you guys get the wrong kind of tire?"

"No," I reply.

"Yes, sorry," my brother says.

She lets the smoke out with a faint smile. My brother picks up the poker-dice cup and says, "Four aces and a queen." Mom intercepts the cup.

She raises it, sets the four aces aside, and then shakes the cup with its single die before slamming it down on the table. Peeking inside the cup, she says, "Okay, I win. End of the game."

She suggests another game: she will read to us in Braille, and we will listen.

"That's not a game, Ma," says my brother.

"Shut up and listen," she scolds, feigning authority, and looking not at him but toward the window to her right.

While she's taking the heavy book out of her handbag, she tells us the rules: she will read aloud, skipping words, and we will have to guess the words that are missing. That's all.

"That's all?"

"Yes, that's all."

She reads:

Waiting for the Something.

What are we waiting for, something *in the forum?*
The something *are due here today.*
Why isn't anything happening in the something?
Why do the something *sit there without* something?

She reads the entire poem this way, while we look at her, perplexed, not knowing if she has lost it, or if we just don't understand her game.

"You two have no sense of humor and no poetry culture," she says, and takes the joint from the ashtray.

"So where's the pelota player?" my brother asks.

"I'm not too sure," she answers, holding in the smoke. "What's your theory?"

"Cold feet?" I suggest.

"I think he's here in the house," she tells us. "We just can't see him."

"Don't be creepy, Ma," I tell her.

"I'm not. It's just a theory. We're all entitled to a theory."

"He probably got lost," my brother says.

"He got on the wrong bus," I add.

My mother is the only person I know who laughs with her entire body and isn't deformed by the physical effects of laughter. Most people acquire something monstrous in mid-cackle. Something monstrous and something demented. The voice expands and breaks, the eyes disappear, bodies sway like wounded piñatas. I once had a boyfriend, neither handsome nor ugly, whose face used to take on a porcine quality when he laughed—his nostrils flapping furiously, his face pink and swollen, his eyes two tiny, expression-less marbles fixed on infinity, like eyes open underwater, or like the eyes of the beheaded.

Nothing like that happens to Mom—she looks beautiful every time.

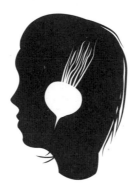

ONE, MAYBE TWO
MINUTES FROM FIRE

by TÉA OBREHT

Out of nowhere, the kid stopped in the middle of the crosswalk and put both hands on the hood of Marko's car.

That was what happened, Marko told himself. That would be the official story.

Marko had been drinking coffee. Did that matter? He had picked up a small house roast at the corner bodega before getting into his car. The cup was in his hand when he looked up and saw the kid. All of it came together so fast that he couldn't form what was going through his mind, whether he'd still been thinking about Kelly, whether he'd noticed the kid advancing toward the crosswalk, whether the kid's hat was blue or green. Only that the kid hadn't been smiling.

"Oh my God," the kid said, leaning toward the windshield. "Jesus, man!"

At first, even though he was sure he'd been stopped at the light for what must have been thirty seconds or more, Marko thought he'd hit the kid. That's what he would say. For an instant, he thought maybe his foot had slipped off the brake and that the car had drifted into the crosswalk and into the kid while he was tipping the last dregs of the coffee into his mouth. At least that hadn't happened. It could have. The instant the kid's fingertips touched the hood, Marko slammed down so hard on the brake that the rim of the coffee cup shredded his gums. But the car didn't budge. The brake was already stiff against the floor.

The light was still red. There was a gray hatchback behind Marko, its blinker flickering for the left turn down Amsterdam. Across the avenue, the tiny harridan from downstairs was shuffling her rag-doll dog toward the park. The kid, still standing there with his hands braced against Marko's car, looked like he was the only thing keeping it from sliding down the street and into the colorful onslaught of children funneling out of school in a storm of sound on Amsterdam.

"Your car, man!" the kid finally said. "Your hood's smoking."

Marko cut the wheel all the way to the right and the car slid in toward the curb. The front wheel lurched up onto the sidewalk and he heard a scrabbling thump from the backseat. He rolled down the window and peered along the flank of the car. He couldn't see smoke, smell anything— though he remembered that a garbage bag had siphoned onto the hot undercarriage last week, and the smell of it burning still drifted up to him sometimes during prolonged bumper-to-bumper standstills on the RFK bridge. He yelled "Thank you!" at the kid, whose form he could see weaving in and out between the neon-vested delivery drivers and halal carts on the avenue. That's right. That was what had happened.

Now this next part: how long did he just sit there, watching the street, letting the relief of not having hit the kid wash over him? Long enough to dab at some of the coffee that had lashed all over the dashboard. Long enough for the light to change and the gray hatchback to go by while the driver lanced Marko with stone-faced disgust. He was parked under a tree, two blocks from where he had started, just beside the little shop that sold cured meats and Italian sandwiches and that he always wished was in a different part of town, so that he wouldn't have to visit it on the sly.

What did he actually remember about the guy sitting on the pavement outside the shop? That the guy was about sixty—this was crucial, the guy's age. That the guy had a weather-beaten complexion that reminded Marko of orchardists back home, and that some kind of red-smeared sandwich rested on his knees. That he said: "Holy shit"—seriously, too, in a way that yanked down at Marko's gut, like he'd seen the whole thing and he couldn't believe his eyes. When the guy got to his feet, Marko noticed the oil stains on the knees and sleeves of his blue utility jumpsuit. He knew he remembered this.

He knew the mechanic's uniform had a handwritten nametag, but he couldn't remember what it said. PAVLE, maybe. Or PETAR. Some name remotely and reassuringly tied to Marko's neck of the woods, anyway.

"Holy shit," the mechanic said again. It stood out to Marko now, the way the guy had rested his knuckles on expansive hips. "Wow, wow, wow. That's bad, boss. Start counting your stars. What a day."

Marko had probably said, "What? What is it?" a few times. He had turned off the engine, but the mechanic made him start the car back up again and pop the hood. The latch took a moment to find, but as soon as the red bonnet went up, Marko heard it: an unmistakable, frantic clattering.

Then he had gone around the front and stood staring down into the dusty, inscrutable maw of the engine compartment. He remembered the mechanic's finger—black-nailed, he could see it now—pointing at an insanely shivering tubule that had destabilized and was now thunking furiously against the spark plugs.

"Boss," the mechanic said. "This is about to blow. You better go to church tomorrow—God is with you today."

It hadn't felt that way yesterday.

The previous morning, he'd had a quarrel with Ivana, this time about— of all things—turnips. He spotted them, between shishito peppers and garlic, on the extensive write-up of delicacies he was supposed to procure for the dinner party to honor the upstairs neighbors' engagement. In her immaculate English handwriting, Ivana had put down: *baby hakurei.*

"What's this?" he asked.

"The turnips," his wife said, carefully, in English—goading him, of course. "They are Japanese. I think they will go very nicely with the lamb."

"Japanese turnips?" he said. "Potatoes go nicely with lamb, and maybe a little tomato salad on the side. Why don't I just get some of those?"

"That does not fit the flavor profile I'm working with," she said. She was trimming the fronds off a flower arrangement she had been, for the better part of an hour, shifting from one end of the hallway table to the other. The flowers were the soft yellow of lemon cream, and the light, she insisted, better complemented them on the left side—but putting them on the right, apparently, really opened the room up. "Glazed turnips will very finely bring out the ginger marinade of the lamb."

"Turnips aren't for company, they're what my father and his brothers used to dig out of the ground to eat when they were starving in winter," he said. The air conditioner—a rattling inheritance from the apartment's last legal tenant—was off-limits for the afternoon to accommodate the electrical workload of the oven, where some sort of chamomile cake was in progress, hot-boxing the apartment and making the dog insane. Marko's sweat was running the letters of the shopping list. "This is just another one of your cooking experiments where you're trying out some exotic bullshit that nobody who's not a fag on TV actually eats, and I end up paying fifteen dollars for a pound of glorified pig feed."

The look she leveled at him was the same one reserved for the inevitable staredowns over the joint oil and curative pomade stockpiles he ordered whenever some relative from back home decided to visit.

"There is a world beyond tomato salad," she said. "It would not harm you to give the wider horizons a chance."

"Oh, turnips—turnips are going to broaden my horizons? The way to worldliness is through turnips?"

"Just get what is on the list, please, Marko."

Anyway: "You're not from around here, are you?" the mechanic said.

It sounded too accusatory for a guy who had an accent himself—Bulgarian, Marko suspected, or maybe Czech. "Not here, no," Marko said quickly. "I'm just passing through the neighborhood."

"You live in the city?"

"In Astoria." He could hear Ivana already, asking him what the hell he was thinking, telling strangers where they lived. But what did she know, the guy seemed like the kind of person who might feel allied to Astoria; maybe he had some family living out there; maybe he, too, had a wife who'd been compelled to cut her working hours to just Wednesdays and weekends so she could "manage the car during the street cleaning" because it was either that or pay for garage parking. And what was he supposed to do if the guy just left him there with his hood open and the prior-century Honda death-rattling its last, in this part of town, of all places?

"I see this all the time," the mechanic said. "See, potholes in the road, you go bumping all over them, they knock out pins in your motor. See all these moving parts? See how this is loose right here? And you don't know until: boom! God is with you today, my friend."

"This is just incredible," Marko said.

"And then—boom."

"It blows up?"

"All the fluids gone, there's no—look, there's no nothing! It's dry. You are one, maybe two minutes from fire here."

"Mother of God."

"I know, boss. It's bad."

They both crossed themselves. This was important.

"I can't believe that kid noticed it."

"And what luck for me to be taking my lunch just now?" the mechanic said. "God is with you today."

"Thank you."

What happened next, though? The mechanic told Marko to shut off the engine, and then got on the phone to his boss at the shop. He told the boss he'd be late, he was dealing with a roadside breakdown. Did he have permission to take care of it right here? No, he didn't think the man could safely drive it all the way to the shop. Marko knew he overheard this—he remembered a fizz of relief at the idea that, possibly, he would not have to call a towing service and then spend the next month intercepting that bill in the mail. He remembered, too, glancing up and down the street for the mechanic's vehicle—there was a white van parked nearby, its doors scrawled with the silhouette of a hammer. Marko stood by and watched the disconnected tube in the engine compartment palpitating. Two young black guys hoisted themselves up onto the railing outside the Italian sandwich shop. If he was honest with himself, he was pretty sure he saw them nudge each other. But Ivana didn't need to know that.

"I don't trust those kids," the mechanic said, closing his phone carefully. "What are they looking at?"

"Nothing better to do than stare at people's misfortune, I guess."

"You got some water and paper towels?"

"In the trunk."

Maybe if his knees hadn't been shaking—and he could really feel it then, that rush of relief hitting him in the legs first, the way liquor always did—he would have glanced into the backseat and remembered. Maybe he wouldn't have just handed the mechanic a water bottle and a roll of paper towels and said: "Thank God you're here."

"You got that right, boss," the mechanic said, and went to work.

At some point in the next five minutes—while the mechanic laid out one of the floor mats from the front seat and got down on his hands and knees and reached under the car, and then got up and poured water into the tank, and tightened the pins and then went back down again—they established that they both knew people at the technical university of Novi Sad. Not the same people—but still, Novi Sad. The mechanic had grand-kids in Australia: two little girls, Marko remembered, Ana and Clara, maybe. He didn't see them much, but he was saving up to visit this winter, God willing. It was hard with two jobs. Marko knew. And the best burek in town, they concurred, was at Zaha's in Brooklyn—even though it was technically run by Turks.

"You got a card?" the mechanic said.

"Sure." Marko sorted through his wallet and found one. He remembered thinking he really had to print a new set, update the old Newark address. He held it out to the mechanic. "That's my mobile there, but we're in Astoria now. If you're ever in the area, your dry cleaning's on the house."

"No—a card to pay for the service," the mechanic said. He was sitting up now, blinking at the card in Marko's outstretched hand. The wisps of hair dotted about his moist pink scalp looked like they were coming out of the top of a pillow. "You heard my boss on the phone," the mechanic said. "If it were up to me, I wouldn't charge, but you heard my boss. Three hundred dollars—that's what it would be at the shop, probably more, they'd push you to change your O_2 filter. And that's not even with labor.

That doesn't include me. But I'm on lunch—I'm not gonna count that. I was just here. God is with you today. How about two hundred and fifty instead?"

It sounded reasonable. You couldn't argue with that. It sounded like not much, a lifeline for what this little adventure would cost him in real terms. And what did they have money for—Ivana's Japanese turnips, or moments like this, situations where it really mattered, where fortune interceded and sent one of their own to eat his lunch right at the corner where Marko had almost lost his life to a latent automotive explosion?

"But I can't do card," he said. It would obliterate any of the breaks he'd caught in this incident so far. "I've got to get cash."

"You go ahead," the mechanic said. "I'll just finish up here."

It took less than five minutes to go to the bodega and back. Of this Marko was absolutely certain. The bodega had the closest ATM—even if he hadn't known, from past experience, that the address of the withdrawal would not appear on his bank statement, he would have gone there anyway. He could tell anyone—including himself—that much with a clear conscience. He didn't even pause when Ahmed greeted him from behind the counter—just smiled apologetically and waved his fistful of twenties and said "Car trouble!" and flung the door open. He heard Ahmed say: "Oh—that's bad luck!"

Down the block, the street was empty. His brain was running on so many tracks that he couldn't now remember—really couldn't—the progression of his thoughts when he reached the sandwich shop. He remembered the smear of oil and AC drip that was pooling, shifting, advancing slowly down the slope toward the crosswalk, a sun-streaked fish that reshaped itself as it went.

The black kids were still perched on the rail. "Dude," one of them said. "For fuck's sake."

* * *

He could hear Ivana's questions now: You left the car with him? A total stranger, and you just left him alone with the car? *What the fuck is wrong with you?*

But I had the keys, he thought. The keys were with me. He knows people in Novi Sad. He gets his burek at Zaha's. God was with me today.

There were ways to smooth this out. That was the important thing.

There were ways to explain, as he had explained at the police station later on, that it had all happened so quickly, that his brain had been in a vortex of confusion and relief from the instant he'd realized he hadn't, in fact, hit the kid in the crosswalk. That it hadn't actually occurred to him that he had not seen any smoke with his own eyes, because of the kid's frantic earnestness. The kid had been in on it, of course—at least according to responding officer Daley, who, in Marko's version of events, had taken down the report gravely and patiently, and without the slightest hint of amusement. Officer Daley had reassured Marko that these things happened all the time—that he shouldn't blame himself, these people were professionals working in tandem and clearly with uniforms to enhance the ruse—speaking in a voice that in no way indicated that he thought Marko was some sort of woeful pleb who'd just moved to the city from directly behind his plow.

Marko would say, too, that Officer Daley had said—or at least implied, or at the very worst allowed Marko to conclude—that many stolen cars were often retrieved within forty-eight hours of theft; that Marko's description of the mechanic fit the profile of a suspect whose case they already had on file; that Officer Daley was confident his team would find the car.

And yes, Ivana was all about the questions these days. But she wouldn't ask to speak to Officer Daley herself. And even if she did, he very much doubted that the question of which precinct the report had been filed in would come up. And in the event that it did come up, Marko didn't believe for an instant that she would have the energy to track down the precinct or look it up on the map, and furthermore piece together that she had followed him into that part of Harlem last year, when she'd first had her suspicions, about a month before she caught him outside Kelly's apartment and he swore he would break it off.

No, she had the ginger-marinated lamb and Japanese turnips to preoccupy her. And if Marko could get her to see it all in the right light, it would be a thrill, a slice of New York life, and they would recount the unfairness and temerity of it at the neighbors' engagement party that evening.

"I never would have guessed," Marko would say, "that crooks would make such an effort over a compact car."

Of course, more questions would surface by morning. But he wasn't worried yet. The folks at Penelope's Pet Spa and Salon dealt primarily with him, anyway—it wouldn't be the first time he sent a little extra their way to blur the exact hour he had brought the dog in for its weekend stay. He would tell Ivana he'd arranged an extra-long stay this time, the works, a special treat to make up for his insensitivity about the turnips. And meanwhile the absence of the car would discourage Ivana from venturing into Manhattan, at least in the coming days, while he scoured the neighborhood and put up posters:

LOST:

TEACUP POMERANIAN.

LAST SEEN CRATED IN REAR SEAT OF 1999 GREEN HONDA CIVIC.

ANSWERS TO THE NAME NIKOLA TESLA.

GAINLINESS

by JOHN McMANUS

Victor was a peculiar boy, said his parents' few friends, an assessment that irked Victor even as he suspected it was correct. Take his cage dream. Lying awake nights he fancied himself shackled to a wall beside the home-schooled boys from across the road. A hook-nosed villain would poke him and those boys with a pitchfork, naked. If he felt himself falling asleep, during this fantasy, he pressed ice to his face to sustain the scene. What was this if not peculiar? He carried needle pliers in his pocket for extracting snot without touching it. Journeys of any length had to begin on his left foot. He peed sitting down. After brushing his teeth he swallowed the toothpaste, risky as that might be, because he'd always done it that way.

In 1985, when Victor was seven, a friend of his mother's came to visit

Yazoo City. This spice-scented, easy-mannered fellow, who had the mel-
lifluous name of Micah, said to Victor, "You're trouble."

"Don't," said Victor's mother, but Micah went on: "It's true. When
you're older, Victor, you'll be a truckload of trouble."

Something stirred in Victor to hear it, but he kept quiet. Later, after
Micah had gone, Victor found his mother weeping in the kitchen. "I won't
be trouble," he said to her.

"Micah's telling people bye, is why I'm crying."

"What's wrong with that?"

"I mean he's sick."

"I'm sorry," Victor could have replied, or "Why," but instead he said,
"Micah's a name I wouldn't hate."

"You can change your name when you're grown." They'd been through
this already. To base his favor on the sound of names was another quirk of
Victor's. If he were, say, a Micah, hearing tell of a Victor, he would hate
that boy's guts—not because Victor meant *winner* but because the name's
ugly asymmetry suggested an ungainly boy. It disappointed his parents,
Mary and Raymond, for him to feel this way. But theirs were neutral names.
Victor didn't adore one or hate the other, the way he did with Albert and
Sievert Alfsson across the road.

Albert and Sievert were twins, with identically curly manes of yellow hair,
but from Victor's bedroom window perch he could distinguish them readily.
Albert was chubby, for one, but more importantly Victor's grandfather had
been an Albert. The name connoted decrepitude, unsightliness. He'd never
known a Sievert, on the other hand. Sievert—impish, lithe, fresh—was the
only twin Victor yearned to touch. If asked what sounded nice about the boy's
name, he couldn't have answered. Why were bluebirds pretty? Self-evident.
The problem was Sievert quit coming outside. For months he showed up

only in the back of the Alfssons' station wagon as Mrs. Alfsson drove out of the garage. Out his window Victor would watch roly-poly Albert bouncing alone on a pogo stick, thousands of times in a row.

"Is Micah dead yet?" he asked Mary one day, thinking that in her grief she might rename him after her late friend.

"I'm sick of your crap, Victor," she replied, upsetting him so much that he quit breathing. His skin tingled, his sight blackened, and he passed out cold. He awoke to find Mary pressing a cold cloth to his forehead.

"Thank God," she said, as if she'd solved the problem and not caused it.

Lying there under her pressed washcloth, Victor said, "Where am I?" He wanted to freak her out, because he was hurt by the betrayal of her words. It was more than their sentiment—it was that *crap*, ugly in both sound and meaning, smack at the end of a blame. A voiceless bilabial stop, as vexing as the voiceless velar plosive at the end of his father's favorite word. Although he couldn't analyze consonants that way yet, he knew what he didn't like. He breathed more quickly, aware of sucking in air, of being a breathing body. When his lungs filled up, would he remember to quit? Could he turn things around? Maybe not. His skin tingled, his sight vanished. Again he was gone.

After a dozen more spells Raymond suggested specialists, like a pediatric cardiologist, whereas Mary suggested that Victor buck up. "He needs to act like a grown-up," she said to Raymond, who went behind Mary's back to find a shrink named Dolf Pappadopolous.

"I doubt your son will ever feel a normal range of emotions," said Dr. Pappadopolous to Raymond as Victor sat between them. "This will worsen at puberty. His grasp of metaphor will be impeded, if it develops at all."

"What kind of name is your name?" said Victor, phrasing the query so as not to utter any of its horrid mishmash.

"Greek and German. You probably have not heard of a Dolf, but go to West Germany, you will meet more." Dr. Pappadopolous might as well have said, "Dunk your head in the toilet, you will eat a turd." Victor's head grew light again, his vision clouded. He put a hand out to steady himself.

"He does it again, you see? Makes himself faint? You or I could decide not to, but that is the nature of the dilemma."

If he was fainting on purpose, Victor thought, he should faint again now. If some illness was causing his problem, he should remain awake. Which action would prove this odious man wrong? He breathed sharply in and out, considering the question. Before he could choose, his lungs ballooned so full of air that he panicked again and it was too late already. He awakened on the table as Raymond pleaded a plaintive "Son?"

Victor didn't mean to reply with silence. He just didn't know what to say. It wasn't the names themselves so much as how no one, not even Raymond, perceived why Victor responded negatively. The answer wasn't as simple as a need for aesthetic bliss. In his dungeon dream the sole color was the dull gray of concrete, of cinder blocks, of skin gone sallow in lantern light. There wasn't electricity. It wasn't the 1980s above that cellar maze, but a timeless realm without paved roads or child-safety laws. The master of a lush, unspoiled land had banished each ugly thing underground, where Victor sat chained to a ball. How could he explain to his anxious father that he didn't miss the sun? In an airy meadow overhead, wisps danced in the light while Victor basked in the well-being he drew from knowing that all was neatly fenced off by the planet's curve: grandeur above, everything else below.

As time passed, the quarrels over Victor's bouts grew bigger. Raymond moved out, out of Yazoo City entirely, into an apartment in Hattiesburg. After that the house stayed messier. Alone with his mother, Victor learned to steady himself through fussy tidying. For an hour each evening he wiped down surfaces, straightened things just so. Out in the world, he and Mary would take the old highway past pawn shops, auto garages, the ball fields where several strata of asphalt merged in a chaotic pimple of broken tarmac. Victor suspected that none of the Little Leaguers hyperventilated, as he did, at the sight of Queen Anne's lace sprouting through those pavement cracks. He alone hung a wrecking ball from space to demolish every derelict building as they passed. By shutting his left eye, he crushed whatever needed it on that side, likewise with his other eye on the right. He was uncompromising. Whole cities he flattened while imagining them from a bird's-eye view, like the hideously named Hattiesburg, and then he seeded the scars with tulip bulbs, and that was how it was for years to come, until the day in ninth grade when he spotted Sievert Alfsson mowing the Alfssons' lawn, a breeze rippling his open shirt and blond curls.

Transfixed, Victor knelt at the window. He'd never seen such a compelling boy before, or a richer contrast between someone's ruddy skin and the green grass. For half an hour Sievert mowed. When he was done, he leaned on the lawnmower handle and gazed toward Victor's house until Victor raised a hand.

Sievert did the same, in a gesture that could only mean he was beckoning Victor to come say hello.

Heart fluttering, Victor ventured outside on his left foot. He crossed into the Alfssons' yard and ended in front of his neighbor on his right foot.

"Hey, Victor," said Sievert in a voice whose deep pitch stirred Victor and rendered him briefly mute.

"I'm Micah," he finally managed to reply.

"I thought you're Victor."

"That's my middle name."

"My dad says you're disturbed."

"My mom says you're a Jehovah's Witness."

"Sievert's one, but I worship the devil."

Victor's impulse was to correct this boy: "Sievert's you," he nearly said, but in fact he was speaking to ugly old Albert.

He looked the alleged Albert up and down, judging whether this newly slim kid could own such a hideous name. "You're skinny," he said, his lungs seizing a little.

"So?" said Albert, as if it had been ever thus.

"How do you worship the devil?"

"You drink," Albert said, pulling out a flask.

Albert sipped, then passed the flask to Victor, who took it, stealing a glance across the road. He'd done nothing like this before. Albert was home-schooled, ignorant of Victor's reputation as a good kid.

I'm Micah, he thought, tilting the flask to his lips to pour what tasted like medicine into his mouth. Immediately he could feel stamina spreading through him, coating his insides as he choked on the burn.

"Too hot for a shirt," said Albert, pulling his own off to toss it at his feet.

It was only about sixty degrees out, with cool gusts of wind. "Yeah," Victor said.

"Been in the woods?"

"Those?" said Victor, gesturing behind the Alfssons'.

"Know some others?" retorted Albert, so that Victor heard how moronic he'd just sounded. Did he always sound that way? He fell out of the moment and stood thinking of Albert's name, his grandpa Albert, wizened old men, until a tingling moved up his arms. Once again he would faint unless he did something. Albert was now squeezing under a barbed-wire fence toward a stand of pines. In alarm Victor drank. Right away, something flowed through him again and halted his decline. A layer of dry needles softened the pinecone crunch under his feet as Victor hurried into the dark of the woods.

"My dad works for the radio," Albert said when Victor had caught up, "so there's free trips to Gulf Shores. What's yours do?"

"He moved out of town."

"Where'd he move?"

"East of here." Victor didn't want to say *Hattiesburg*.

"My mom's on disability. She's possessed."

"Mine's a nurse."

"She wrote to Rome to ask for an exorcist, but they wouldn't send one, so she switched to Jehovah's Witness."

"Mine's nothing," said Victor, giggling, because the alcohol was in his blood now, and his body felt an unclenching fist.

"Here's the swamp."

They emerged into a meadow where willows grew by the shore of a cow pond. It wasn't a swamp. From now on, thought Victor as he drank again, if he felt like saying something dumb like "It's not a swamp," he would drink instead.

"Dad will whip me later," said Albert with a cramped smile.

"He won't find out," said Victor.

"Maybe I want it," said Albert, and suddenly it didn't matter if the blond fuzz on Albert's arm belonged to someone with an unattractive name; Victor couldn't go any longer without touching it. He reached a hand tentatively toward the boy. It felt like he was pushing through a thick morass. Then, as his finger hovered near Albert's skin, a heron's wings flapped, rippling the water.

Scared out of his reverie, Victor pulled back. "I wanted it to keep going," said Albert, as if he meant the approach of Victor's hand.

"Getting whipped?"

"Sievert and I punch each other."

Following his new protocol Victor sipped from the flask until he had a better reply than "I like Sievert's name." The better one was, "Why?"

"To see who can take more hits."

"Should I do it to you?"

"Are you gay?"

"You just said you like it."

"No, gaywad."

"Want to do it to me?"

"In the face like a girl?"

"However you like," said Victor, immediately gulping down an impulse to take it back, to run away from this strange thrall. He folded his hands across his lap. Beyond Albert the sky was ripe with white clouds that floated above the pines while Albert's cupped palm whooshed in to slap him. Right away Albert gasped as if he'd been the one hit.

"Happy now?" he asked.

"I guess," said Victor, his cheek stinging.

"Again, gaywad?" said Albert, as Victor kept unclenching. Hard not to conflate that with the stinging, so he presented his cheek. He breathed with ease. He hadn't liked the slap, but being drunk felt sublime. His lungs weren't tight anymore. His head didn't hurt. He had binocular vision, not just in the merging of his two eyes' fields but in the two halves of the earth. In this new state as he awaited Albert's palm, beauty wasn't repelling ugliness. He desired no stick for raking scum off the pond water. He didn't care about the trash strewn on the far shore.

From then on, Albert let Victor drink with him once a week when his family was at session. They did it in Albert's basement and in the woods, in an abandoned school bus there, or by the pond where it had first happened. A summer evening in the school bus could calm Victor for a week. They smoked Marlboros Albert purchased from the cousin who sold him gin. They arrived home reeking of gin and cigarettes, so Victor started stowing a toothbrush and toothpaste behind a loose house brick, brushing his teeth to mask the scent. Not that Mary noticed stuff like that. As for Albert, he didn't care what his parents smelled; he hated them for fucking up his brother's head.

"What did they do to it?" asked Victor more than once, to which Albert would say only, "Fucked it up."

Victor hadn't forgotten how he used to react to the harsh edges at the end of *fuck* and *crap*. Such a childish kid he'd been. "Is that why you worship the devil?"

"Micah, don't be a dipshit."

"What do you mean?"

"Should I hit you again?"

Victor nodded not because he liked the feeling, but because of symmetry. If Albert wished to slap him, and Victor wished to allow it, there was symmetry. Anyway it never hurt much, at least not until the day Albert watched him brush his teeth.

They had spent three hours in the bus. Afterward Victor swallowed the toothpaste like usual.

"Raise your arms," Albert said then. When Victor did, Albert punched him in the gut. He dropped his toothbrush and bowled over.

"Why'd you do that?" he howled.

"Because you're retarded."

"For swallowing toothpaste?"

"Did you swallow toothpaste?"

"I've always done it that way."

"So what?"

"Is that why you hit me?"

"You're worse than Sievert," said Albert, turning to go.

As he crossed the road home, the curtains fluttered in the Alfssons' living room. "I don't care," said Victor aloud, enjoying the words as he spoke them. He stayed put afterward, admiring their echo. Nothing was symmetrical about *I don't care*, but the phrase wasn't ungainly. He was seeing beyond its shape and sound to the deeper meaning, the notion of not caring. Who gives a fuck, he thought, feeling wise beyond his years. That night, still buzzed, he spat his toothpaste out for the first time. Thinking back to Albert's last withering glance he watched it swirl down the drain.

The next morning, sober but still wise, he did the same. "It's what I always do," he let himself whisper aloud, a workmanlike phrase striking in its plainness. After a few more days, spitting was old hat. The shift proved so strangely easy that, when Albert didn't show up the following weekend at the sermon's usual hour, Victor braved beginning a journey on his right foot, ending on the Alfssons' porch on his left.

He rang the bell. Almost immediately the door opened to reveal white-haired Mr. Alfsson, his hazel cat eyes daring Victor to ask, "Albert home?"

"Where Albert is is the Lyman Ward Military Academy," Mr. Alfsson said. "You can write to him there."

"When will he be back?"

"Sievert is inside. Would you like to play with Sievert?"

"Okay," he heard himself say, but he meant no. Suddenly Sievert appeared at the top of the stairs, as fat as his brother used to be. Their spirits had traded bodies, Victor thought, already pondering an excuse to leave. "I forgot my mother needs me," he said, backing away.

The foot switch hadn't worked out, he thought as he headed home. He should obey his own rules, heed words' sounds and keep things tidy, swallow his toothpaste every time. Except he was realizing something. He wasn't sad to lose Albert. Or he detected no sadness. What he gulped down as he crept across the road was excitement. Adrenaline. At school there were tons of better-looking boys than Albert, with names as hideous as Hugh and Horace and he didn't care, he had put that crap behind him. Names were subjective. The objective problem was obtaining alcohol.

Victor studied that problem until the day a Desert Storm veteran and addict in recovery came to speak at Magnolia High. In the gym bleachers Victor positioned himself behind two kids he'd heard speaking on the subject in biology class, the ugly-named Hugh and Hugh's neutral-named friend Clint. It seemed they drank from Clint's parents' liquor cabinet while they played Dungeons & Dragons. The fact that they were gaming nerds lowered the stakes for Victor, who waited to make his move until the assembly speaker alleged that no one ever wanted to grow up and become a drunk.

"I want to grow up and become a drunk ASAP," Victor said.

Hugh laughed and turned to see who'd spoken.

"I'll be better at it," Victor added. "I'll set high goals."

They got to talking. Victor mentioned Dungeons & Dragons admiringly. Soon enough Hugh was suggesting he hang out with them. Did he want to? "Why not," Victor answered. Within hours they were in Clint's bedroom pouring peach schnapps and rolling dice to learn what qualities his character would have in the campaign.

For six months Victor played D&D, drinking more than Hugh and Clint and their other friends. The energy he had once spent hating names like Hugh's he channeled into a crush on the boy, battling orcs until finally he acknowledged that they would never get naked together. This didn't stymie him long. Drinking had rendered him all right in the eyes of druggies, jocks, whoever. Things had changed; his old idiosyncrasies were like a logic problem he'd solved. He started going to the quarry on weekends. One moonlit Friday there, as some girls teased him about his gaming days, he thought how lucky he was that the Alfssons had banished Albert. Without outgrowing Albert, he couldn't have outgrown Hugh. Now he would also outgrow these girls, along with their friends. It was a destiny that seemed to stem from innate willpower. Night after night he drank with whoever at whatever house, whatever their names, until one day, about to check the mailbox, he heard someone saying "Micah" and gazed across at a gigantic figure in the Alfssons' downstairs window, summoning him.

Ignore, pretend, thought Victor, but in a sort of trance he walked over. There in a window that rose to the level of his neck, backward on a couch, knelt a curly-haired teenager bloated to three hundred pounds.

For a moment Victor feared there'd been yet another spirit trade, until the pale obese boy said, "I need to discuss Albert."

"You're supposed to be in high school," Victor said, hoping none of his friends would drive past and see.

"I'm in the equivalent of the twentieth grade. It's Albert who's unwell."

"Come again?" said Victor, although he'd heard clearly.

"He wonders why you abandoned him."

When Victor didn't answer, Sievert carried on. "He sends you love letters that our mom burns. He carved your name into his bed frame and everyone saw."

"I'm sorry."

"You've never asked for his address."

"What's his address?"

"If you don't love Albert back, write it. I'll send it."

Through the window Sievert offered a sheet of paper, the sight of whose untidy torn chads made Victor yearn for a drink. "Why would you want his heart broken?" he asked.

"If he falls out of love, he won't go to hell."

"Okay," said Victor, taking the paper along with a pen. Against the house siding he wrote, *Dear Albert*. About to tell a vague lie like *I miss you*, he wondered what kind of retard carved into a bed that he loved a boy.

He glanced behind him at his own house and imagined Sievert peering through a telescope, jacking off and eating hot dogs.

Fat Sievert was the one who loved him.

Now Victor knew exactly what to do. *I have a whole new life*, he wrote on the paper. *We were immature kids. You called yourself a devil worshipper, which is stupid. I don't miss you. I never loved you. —Victor (Micah)*

"Here," he said, handing it back.

"Thanks," said Sievert. "Bye."

Retreating across the Alfssons' yard, Victor doubted his reasoning. If Sievert really liked him, he'd have kept him lingering longer by the window. "Wait!" he would be calling. And what if he mailed the letter? Walking faster, Victor grew light-headed the way he used to. The idea of a lovelorn Albert reading his hateful words might have sent him regressing into a panic if not for the acceptance packet he discovered in the mailbox from Tulane.

Disrobing in his bedroom before the open blinds, Victor recalled his idea that Sievert was a hot name. It wasn't. Nor was it a fat name. Names, like most things, were far more complicated than that. He'd been correct to deem the world half beautiful and half ugly, but he'd been wrong to seek a clear dividing line. The correct line split past from future. His task as a curator of aesthetic pleasure was to locate ugliness in the future, and sequester it in the past. He'd done as much with Albert and Sievert, and now he would do it with Mississippi, too. To tidy the world in this way gratified him. Buzzing with expectancy, he knelt. As he touched himself in sight of the Alfssons' family room, he allowed himself one last image of his old friend in his defaced cot at military school, weeping poignantly for Victor, unaware of falling into the past.

Victor's cocaine habit began the night he arrived in New Orleans, when he asked an upperclassman in the dorm to point him toward the gay bars. A cab took him to Bourbon Street, where a spot called Oz swarmed with celebrants of something called Southern Decadence. Victor wound up on a balcony among men thrice his age. "Looks like trouble," said one. "Truck-load," said another, bringing Victor's rigid childhood mind clamping down on him. But before he could explore his panic's source, someone bought him a whiskey. His need to demand that these drunks be annihilated along with their gaudy city vanished like any flash of déjà vu. Where had he been all their lives? Did he want to come into the bathroom? Yes, he replied, and yes to all that was asked on every sultry evening from there on out. The flirters would muss his hair, smiling at their sly prowess as if he might ever tell anyone no. He didn't.

Years passed. He liked how New Orleans had so few unsightly buildings. The ones that did exist never had him gasping for breath. He considered structural design often enough that he wound up majoring in it, then entering the master's program. He thought too about the design of his face. Men were asking if he'd considered modeling. No, he replied coyly each time, as if he had no idea of his effect on people. He'd been drinking enough to rarely eat. Was it conceited to believe the svelte angles of his jaw derived from his state of mind? With his clutter of tics, he'd been an ugly child. These days he barely had to slouch against a bar before someone touched him.

During hangovers a memory would surface of writing *I don't miss you, I never loved you,* and he would bury his face in his hands, but mostly he was drunk and high.

In his second year of grad school he never got around to applying for internships, but it didn't matter, a partner at a prestigious firm fell for him at a bar. Victor had been staring at this silver fox's wing-tipped shoes when the man said, "Salvatore Ferragamo."

At first that seemed to be Gary's name. "I'm Victor," he replied.

"You're the sort of boy folks like to take advantage of."

"What do you mean?" he said, sensing already the pheromones Gary was exuding as he fell in love. The capture was as easy as that. A string of endless hot days followed, during which Victor seemed to have stumbled into his own dream life. Gary lived in a mansion full of mirrors and varnished wood, where old-guard fetishists whiled their dissolute days away in high abandon. Bolted to the bedroom wall was a barred-top pup cage Gary would padlock him inside of. I've arrived, thought Victor, soaking naked with the guys in a backyard pool, nursing hangovers with mint juleps. Reasoning that Gary would give him a job whenever he asked, he felt no urgency to start work. Soon a dozen coke dealers knew his name, which filled him with well-being akin to professional pride. He would emerge from blackouts inhaling powder off Gary's house key. "Boys have committed suicide over me," he told the barflies who had become his friends. "I was fourteen when I got one sent off to military school."

"You must have been a hot fourteen-year-old."

"Albert thought so," he said with a curt laugh. "When I arrived to bust him out, he'd already slit his wrists."

"Did you love him?"

"I lived to see another day."

Chuckling again, Victor wondered if his letter might really have pushed Albert over the edge. Later, alone, he searched online for his old friend. None of the Albert Alfssons he found was the one he'd known. A quest for Sievert led him to a blog about the complexity of God, with no photograph or mention of family. If he phoned home to Mississippi, his mother would inquire about his work. He'd lied and told her he had a job. Best not to call again until it became true.

One evening in January Gary kicked him out. In a near blackout Victor walked to the antique shop run by a man who winked at him in bars. His name was Ernest, and he moonlighted as a fashion photographer. "Of course I want you," he said, so Victor spent the next days modeling for Ernest under vaulted ceilings replete with the color gold. Ernest's lurid stories of the Merchant Marine took place in every port from Manila to Marseilles. Victor listened carefully, planning to retell them as if they were his own. Whenever he finished a bottle of scotch, Ernest would replace it. One humid day he overheard Ernest telling the phone, "Keep your hands off him if you know what's good," so it came as a surprise when he too banished Victor, kicking him out into the Marigny. But there were plenty of antique shops a boy like Victor could choose from.

Victor lived with James. He lived with Phillip. He lived with Ian and Timothy and Rufus. For short stints he worked as a waiter at high-end restaurants, intending to begin real work when he felt like it. He lived with Leroy, Bruce, Sebastian. Two bars banned him in one night. He developed prediabetes. The more fun he had, the more he blacked out. His cheeks grew gin blossoms. He got his own apartment. Hours after his aunt phoned to say his mother had died of pancreatic cancer, he awoke without memory of that conversation. Sure, a foreboding anxiety gripped him, but that was typical of the hours prior to a first drink. He went to the Eagle and got wasted on hurricanes. In the darkroom he met a Cajun named Thierry and rode with him out to a fishing cabin on Bayou Dupont. That was where he smoked crystal for the first time. Time increased to lightning speed under phase after phase of the moon. At some point, convinced the pelicans floating on black water were spy cameras, he left for home, and crossed into the Sprint service area to discover the voicemails.

Soaking in a hot bath, Victor steeled himself to explain that he'd been away on an architectural commission in Central America. He was already so sober that he could hardly imagine speaking at all, let alone telling and then maintaining a complex lie. He'd missed the funeral anyway. Why bother, he thought as the water grew cold. He pulled up his aunt in his phone contacts and deleted the number. Then he collected the liquor bottles from every room and poured them out in the sink.

Late on that first sober day the liquid in him began trickling into his fingers to evaporate into the stale air. That was why his hands quivered the way they did. Soon his head throbbed, too, because his brain was bouncing around in the newly desiccated space. By sunset he was hallucinating that his couch was an exam table. On a nearby table lay his cancerous mother, awaiting news of who would live and who would not. He clenched his fists and kicked and turned, his ringing phone pitching him into further visions where Mary hung shackled to that wall he'd dreamt. Her presence there rendered the place horrific, a torture chamber, which he supposed it had always been. Desperate to be helped, he gripped the phone, but everyone fell into three untenable categories—alcoholics, relatives, and ex-boyfriends. He powered it off and watched a spy movie. After that one, another. During a commercial for beds, his shakes gave way to something worse.

"Tchoupitoulas Mattress Madness at Chuck's Tchoupitoulas Mattress at 5300 Tchoupitoulas," shouted the TV.

Hearing that garishly unparallel name repeated, Victor thought he might be suffering a heart attack. His breath tightened. Then, as the man bellowed it all again, the ghastly elegant truth struck Victor. Although he'd lived half his life near Tchoupitoulas Street, he'd always been drunk.

He hadn't outgrown his attacks at all. He'd merely been stifling them.

Since he was already lying down, half in nightmare, he barely noticed his brain shutting off. He passed out cold. The next morning he awoke into a period he would think back on as a new and outsize childhood. Looking around at the squalor of his basement apartment he saw cobwebs in the corners, piles of garments, cluttered trash. He couldn't take it; he shut his eyes again until he was too parched to lie still. He stood up to find water. Landing on his right foot, he stopped, sat down, rose again on the other side.

"Just a test," he said aloud, as if his mother now spectated in heaven. He made a point of arriving on his right foot at the sink.

He would clean the apartment, he promised himself, gulping water, but scanning the room he saw there would be no way to scrub out its sheer lopsidedness. There were low ceilings, half windows up to the street. If he was to remain sober, he would just have to suffer through it until he found a salaried job. How to do that, though, when everywhere he turned there was only ugliness: the phlegmy French names of the avenues and neighborhoods, his unclassically proportioned apartment, the Uptown bars where whole years had dwindled away, the men who lived in them, the names of liquors—*Dewar's*—the name Gary, Gary's white beard, Ernest's gray one, the name Ernest, all of it so suddenly, viscerally nasty that he dreamt of a lobotomy just to soothe himself into a breath?

The prospect of AA meetings, where drunks would speak their names aloud and he would say "I'm Victor," gave Victor such apoplexy that he cut an index card to wallet size and listed

Blackouts
Drunk nose
Prediabetic
Fat
Unemployed
Barebacking
Reflux
Credit cards
Drunk driving
Shat pants

along with three more columns of dire reminders. If he felt like drinking, he took the card out and read it. After a week its edges were worn and he'd spoken only to store clerks. He wondered if he could have befriended anyone, ever, without liquor's aid. Within minutes of his first drink, he'd made a first friend, and all other friends had derived from that one. There'd been a domino effect, he was thinking when a FedEx man arrived with an envelope from a Yazoo City probate court.

Of course, thought Victor as he tore into it: he was his mother's next of kin. He skimmed through reams of papers. He would inherit the house, sell it, live off the income. Everything happens for a reason, he was telling himself when he read the executor's name.

Now he fell into a vision. On the body of a strapping teenage Albert Alfsson Victor saw a rheumy-eyed and hoary head. Floating near it was a disembodied hand, slapping him. He let the papers fall, and sat down. It wasn't a pleasant vision. The quality of his sight was deteriorating, along with the fantasy itself. The old parts aged, the youthful ones regressed. Soon he beheld an aged infant Albert in the air before him. He didn't faint, though. He sat still until his legs went to sleep. Finally he collected himself enough to stand up. He collected the papers, too, threw them into the trash, carried the trash out, came in again, locked the door, lowered the blinds, and lay down.

Law and Order proved most useful: twenty seasons, five hundred hours. It had mostly neutral names, disyllabic, Scots-Irish or English. Aside from his walks to the corner for DVDs and cigarettes, he stayed home ordering delivery. He watched the spin-offs, gaining weight. He watched *The West Wing, Deadwood, 24.* When characters spoke words he didn't like, or called each other by ugly names, his breath caught, but that was better than not watching. During *Lost* he struggled to button his jeans. By *Six Feet Under* he'd stopped wearing them except on cigarette runs. On the day his Visa card quit working, he was cinching his pant waist up with his left hand.

"Got another card?" the clerk asked Victor, but his wallet was in his left pocket. His right hand held the pen, ready to sign a receipt.

"Maybe," he said, leaning against the counter. Using the pressure as a sort of belt to free up his hands, he retrieved the Discover. It felt like a divine gift for that one to go through. He looped the grocery bag around his pants hand and headed home, smoking with his right hand until he saw a ruddy-faced blond man by his apartment stairs. The adrenaline of recognizing Albert Alfsson felt like a hit of pure cocaine.

"You're home," Albert said. He seemed younger than he should be.

Clutching his waist, Victor approached. "Who are you?" he said, falsely. "You seem kind of peaked."

"I've got food poisoning," said Victor, going for the stairs.

Albert followed him in as he hurried to the couch. "It's been hard to find you."

"I've been designing a museum."

"Let's get down to brass tacks. Your mom didn't have many folks caring for her. I was there a lot. I read her rites."

Victor sat on the couch. He put his head in his hands. Albert's words were fading in and out, and it was hard to follow his drift, at least until he held up a paper.

I have a whole new life, it read in Victor's loopy scrawl. *We were immature kids. I don't miss you. I never loved you.*

"This is a copy. My lawyer has the original."

"I thought Sievert was lying," said Victor, his skin clammy.

"Sievert's a Jehovah's Witness."

"If you kept it—"

"Your mom kept it."

"I don't understand."

"I needed Mary to explain why you'd said those things."

"Take the house," said Victor at once, as if that would cancel out a decade of his behavior. "It's yours." His fingers were tingling again. He wished Albert would hit him, slap him silly. Those fucked-up fantasies, the hook-nosed villain: his mind had known it should be punished for what he'd do. It had sought preemptive redemption, Victor thought, as his body hummed with a nearly electric vibration and silvery specks blotted out Albert's handsome face.

He awoke to Albert pressing a compress to his forehead. He'd been laid out on the couch. All these years later, blond fuzz still dotted Albert's sinewy arms.

"Are you awake?"

"Please go away," Victor said.

"Do you want to hear her answer?"

Shaking his head, he could see movement in the far left of his vision. He had left the TV on mute. It was showing a close-up of the stricken face of Ruth Fisher, the brittle mother in *Six Feet Under*. Albert would leave, he thought with a thrill, and he could rewind the DVD and watch what was happening to Ruth.

"She said, 'A pediatric psychiatrist warned us he'd be this way.'"

Now he sat upright. "The house is yours," he said again. Albert could raise boys of his own in it, teach them the Bible, slap them. Anything to shut him up.

"She knew it's not your fault. She pitied you. She used to drive down here and watch you from across the bar."

"Albert, stop talking."

"I want to sell it on your behalf, set up a trust. Do you know what that means? A trust like Sievert's?"

That was when a wild idea grew in Victor.

"You don't even have a twin," he said. "You and Sievert are the same." Sievert had liked Victor because Sievert was Albert. Sievert had posted that letter to himself, locked himself indoors, gained weight and lost it.

"Oh, come on. Don't be stupid, Micah. You watched us play ball. We saw you every day, sticking those pliers up your nose."

"I did no such thing," said Victor, bowled over to recall renaming himself after all those years. It hardly seemed real. I am Micah, he'd said over and over into the mirror, yearning to swap names with a man who had died of AIDS.

A line came into focus: the one he'd drawn to cleave the present from the past. It wasn't a line of aesthetic pleasure; it was a line of shame. Horrified by his words, his deeds, his very nature, he'd drawn a line to sequester himself from the people who loved him. Until today, it had seemed structurally viable, because no one had ever breached it. No one had bothered trying. He imagined a stronger one, the one Albert must have drawn across his own world. That was what people did: they drew lines across their worlds. But Albert's was a line of capability—a circle, it seemed, with Victor and Sievert trapped inside, and Albert peering across at them.

How wrong the old Yazoo City shrink turned out to have been. The swapping of names had been a metaphor all along. It was all metaphor. What was the shrink called? He let Albert's speech blur into a droning din. He exhaled. By the time the name of Dr. Dolf Pappadopolous came bursting forth, he had only to conjure his favorite gin label—*Bombay Sapphire*, words more honeyed to him sober than he'd ever noted drunk—and the spell subsided.

"Please go," he said, taking his list out of his wallet. He scanned over the ugly words, waiting for a concerned query. If Albert read the card, he thought, he might refuse to leave, well up with tears, declare his abiding love.

Here it comes, Victor was thinking when his friend stood up and offered a hand.

"Sorry for your loss," said Albert, arm extended, reaching into the space between them until Victor laid down his list to receive a farewell shake.

GAUSTINE'S PROJECTS

by GEORGI GOSPODINOV

Translated by Angela Rodel

But despite everything, the '90s were the most lively decade, the best decade, a time when it felt like anything could happen. We were young for the last time. And it was around then that Gaustine appeared, a philosophy dropout, with his ingenious projects (and failed projects), which fill an entire notebook of mine.

Why does Gaustine continue to be important to me? I've rarely had friends. Empathy draws you closer to people, but not in my case: the weight of others' sorrows presses down on me like a sickness. No women, no relationships, no friendships. But Gaustine seemed to be made of different time and different matter. I didn't know anyone like him: translucent, yet simultaneously opaque. I could pass through him like he was thin air, or run into him like he was a glass wall. Despite this, or perhaps precisely because of it, he was the only person I could call a friend.

MOVIES FOR THE POOR

One day we were hanging around by the movie theater to see which new films were out. We were poor—it was hard to earn money honestly then— and the tickets were unattainably expensive, so we just gaped at the posters and photos in the display window. Then Gaustine had an ingenious idea: we would retell movies. A detailed retelling over the course of thirty minutes for a minimal fee. His Movies for the Poor project. A complete subversion of the film industry. He got really worked up: What a historical reversal, he said! Moving from the visual back to the narrative. Here's what you'll do: you'll stand in front of the movie theater, mingling with the folks hanging around outside, and you'll strike up a casual conversation, saying how amaz- ing the film was, but how it's so expensive, how these movie-theater types are motherfucking bloodsuckers; however, you'll tell them, you've seen the film already, and you'd be happy to retell it for an absolutely negligible price of seven hundred lev. Tickets cost ten times that amount. All we have to do is gather up a group of fifteen or so and we're good to go, he concluded.

Wait, wait, I interrupted him, when are we going to watch the movie?

We'll watch it afterward, after we get the money, Gaustine replied.

But then what will we tell them?

We'll make it up, he replied innocently. How hard could it be, you're a writer, right? You've got a title, a few lines from the poster, and a couple photos in the display window. What more could you want?

He was something else. He wasn't kidding. He had absolutely no sense of humor, like all obsessive people. Like all those who stray from the beaten track, as my grandma would say. Like revolutionaries and women. Nietzsche said that.

Movies for the Poor. Like those Tamagotchi for the Poor, that old joke. Tamagotchi, if anyone still remembers, were those pager-like (perhaps I need to explain what a pager is, too?) gadgets that allowed you to take care of your electronic pet: feed it at certain times, give it water, play with it when it started whining. And when you got sick of it, you'd ditch it for a few days, until it starved to death. Where have all those Tamagotchi gone? All those old pagers? A person has no idea how much death he is capable of generating.

I know I'm getting sidetracked, but let's have a minute of silence for the souls of:

The pagers of yore
Tamagotchi
Videocassettes and the VCR
Cassette tape players,
which buried eight-tracks,
which buried record players
Audiocassettes
Telegrams (and the rituals that accompanied them)
Typewriters (allow me to add a personal farewell to my Maritsa, filled with cigarette ashes and coffee from the '90s. Writing on a typewriter required physical exertion, a different type of movement, if you recall)

Okay, the minute's over. What were we talking about? Movies for the Poor, yes, but first let me explain the Tamagotchi for the Poor joke. Do you know what it was? A cockroach in a matchbox. That's it. It may not be funny anymore, but I insist on gathering up these odds and ends, all these things that have passed away, that are gone and dead. Which I guess is the opposite of what is written: "to carry them through the flood alive and to go forth and multiply again"... I've gotten completely turned around. I don't know whether the things I've chaotically and hysterically saved from my own flood will be able to live, let alone go forth and multiply. I know that the past is as fruitless as a barren mare. But that makes it all the more dear to me.

That idea about movies for the poor didn't bear any fruit, either. Let me just say that, after I tried to tell the first group the story of a film I hadn't seen, we barely escaped unscathed.

PERSONAL POEM

The Personal Poem project met a similar end.

There's no such thing as shameful work, Gaustine said one morning, repeating that old chestnut. You'll sit there like those street artists who draw people for money. You'll hold a pencil and paper, and you'll say, Would you like me to write a poem for you? Every pretty girl has the right to a poem. (I think that was a quote.) It'll only take ten minutes.

So there I was on a bench in the park, in front of Café Crystal downtown, with a few sheets of paper, a pencil, and a discreet sign in front of me offering PERSONAL POEM SERVICES. Toward the end of the second uneventful hour, a woman of around fifty came up to me. This wasn't the way we'd imagined it. We had imagined, of course, that all of our clients would be twenty-year-old girls.

She was plump and she looked like a bad guy from a Soviet cartoon. She asked for a personal poem. The designated ten minutes passed. Nothing. My head was empty, hollow as a basement. I started feeling worse and worse for both of us. She started sweating, took out a tissue, asked if she could move positions. Yes, of course, I said. I'm not drawing you, after all. Where should I look? she said. It doesn't matter, slightly off to the side, I told her. You don't need to look at me, it's a bit distracting.

She was either romantic or nouveau riche. And with every passing minute echoing in the void, my failure gleamed ever brighter. Finally,

I decided to grab the bull by the horns. I raised my head, looked her straight in the eye, and said: Actually, today you have such a strong aura that it's very difficult for me to concentrate. Would you mind stopping by some other time?

At that time, all the newspapers were writing about auras and aliens. And it worked: instead of slapping me across the face, the woman beamed. She said I was a true poet, and that she had immediately recognized this. Only a natural-born poet could catch auras (as if auras were carp). She announced that she lived nearby and invited me to her place for a glass of wine. I agreed, mostly out of a sense of guilt.

It turned out that she lived alone. When I got there, she took out a wine bottle, sat down quite close to me on the couch, and pressed her body against mine. I beg your pardon, I'm a poet, I said, quickly standing up, as if wanting to remind her that I worked mainly with auras, and that bodies did not enter into my sphere of competence.

Ssssmaaack! The slap came quick and hard, and it knocked the Personal Poem project into Gaustine's growing heap of misunderstood ideas.

CONDOM CATWALK

He took the lead in the Condom Catwalk project himself.

All he needed to do was go to the people with the cash and explain what a deal he was offering.

A fashion revue for rubbers. A revolution, Gaustine said, enthused.

A revue-lution, I chimed in.

That's good, remember it, he noted in passing before going on.

But he came back crestfallen. We sat down and poured ourselves green cows (crème de menthe with milk), and he told me how, as soon as he set foot in that obscenely rich agency, he knew they wouldn't appreciate the idea. I told them that no one has ever done this kind of fashion show, he said. People have put everything imaginable on the catwalk, but never this accessory. Total minimalism. Condom producers will pour crazy cash into it. But they were like, How would the whole thing work? They said the state would slap them with a huge fine for pornography. They said TV stations would never broadcast the show. And if they did, they would have to put little black squares right over the most fundamental aspect of the event. And lastly, they said—and they were just rolling with laughter when they said this—who's gonna guarantee nonstop erections backstage, huh? Who? Do you have any idea what a huge job that'd be? Like changing tires at a Formula 1 pit stop. Ha ha ha. We're talking serious pumping!

So this idea, too, was sent to the repository of failures. Fine, put it down in the notebook, Gaustine said. Clearly we're ahead of our time. Someday they'll be fighting each other tooth and nail for that idea. And so he piled up his treasures for the future. I was his treasurer.

Here, in the Brown Notebook of Failures, also rest Gaustine's other unrealized projects:

Vault for Personal Stories. We could take other people's stories and safely store them for a certain period of time. If the client so desired, after his death, his story could be willed to his heirs.

Projections on the Sky. One of his most monumental projects. An ultra-powerful apparatus would project on the whole "screen" of the sky. In the beginning, he wasn't sure what he would project, but the idea of a celestial open-air cinema filled him with excitement. Such a huge space can't just sit there empty and unused, he said. Just imagine everyone in the hemisphere craning their necks and looking up at the same moment.

A month later the project had taken on more concrete parameters. When there's low, dense cloud cover, he said, let's project clouds onto the clouds themselves. Clouds on clouds. Let's see how nature reacts to the duplication, to the tautology. And it'll be best if we project rain. Just imagine: cinematic rain from real clouds. At first, the audience will scatter, frightened. Like in *The Arrival of a Train at La Ciotat Station*. At the beginning and end of all great cinema there is a natural scare, he concluded.

Garden of Novels. Classic novels will be planted in rich soil, watered, and fertilized with manure, in order to see which of them bear fruit. This is a project for reestablishing balance, Gaustine said. What is made of wood should once again return to the earth.

À la Minute Architecture. Small wire sculptures that would recreate a few seconds of the trajectory of the flight of an ordinary housefly. The wire should accurately reproduce all the twists and turns of the flight.

Skies Over Various Cities, Photographed at Three in the Afternoon. This would be a photo exhibition, clearly.

And Lord knows what else…

But Gaustine's only successful project was his own disappearance. One evening he came to say good-bye, and I asked him where he was going. I was positive that he had some new scheme up his sleeve. To 1937, he answered simply. Drop me a line, I said, playing along with the joke. The '90s were in full swing then—there was never a more interesting time—but that's when he disappeared. I had no idea (and still have no idea) where he went. But when I got the first letter, followed by two or three postcards, all of them written in 1930s-looking handwriting—yes, I think every decade has its own hand—I realized that, this time, unlike all the other times, he had managed to pull it off.

I saw him one winter afternoon, years later, at a café in the London airport. He was holding a magazine in his hand and looking worried, as far as I could tell. My plane was about to take off, but I ran over to say hi. He looked at me coldly, and I noticed his white turtleneck sweater—the type of sweater that had long ago gone out of style. Excuse me, but are we acquainted? he said. I stood there stunned for a few seconds, and then I heard my name called over the loudspeaker and I dashed back to the gate.

He had been reading a *Time* magazine from 1968, I realized as I boarded, an article about the war in Vietnam. It was January 2007.

A text message at 3 a.m., years later: *I found out that cat urine glows in the dark. I thought this might interest you.*

There was no name, but it could only be from one person.

Recently the London *Times* mentioned a new invention designed for rich, harried businessmen with a taste for pinching pennies and leading double lives: a tourist agency for virtual tourism. The agency supplies you with all the material evidence of a journey—stamps in your passport, photos, ticket stubs from the Louvre, for example, or shells from the Cote d'Azure, maybe even sandwiches from the Sandwich Islands—without you ever taking the journey. They tell you how your vacation went, outfit you with a whole set of memories. It's enough to make you believe that you've taken the trip. For a moment it crossed my mind that Gaustine was giving me a sign.

GooDeed

by ETGAR KERET

Translated by Sondra Silverston

A rich woman hugged a poor man. It was totally spontaneous. Absolutely unplanned. He went up to her and asked for some money for coffee. There were no homeless people in her own neighborhood, so he caught her completely unprepared. And he wasn't your typical homeless guy, either. He was white and spoke good English, and even though he had a supermarket cart and clearly lived on the street, he looked clean and shaven. The rich woman couldn't find any coins in her wallet, only hundred-dollar bills. If she'd found a ten-dollar bill, even a twenty, she would have given it to him without a second thought, but a hundred seemed to her like too much to give, and maybe a little awkward to accept, too.

There are clear rules governing the relationship between the homeless and the average person on the street: speak to each other politely; don't look each other in the eye; don't ask for names; and don't give more than twenty dollars. Anything up to twenty is still in the normal range of generosity, but more than that is an attempt to attract attention, to impress, to force the recipient into saying, "Ma'am, you're a wonderful human being," or else seem ungrateful. The rich woman didn't want to go there, but she didn't have any coins or small bills, either, so she said to the man with the supermarket cart, "Wait here a minute, okay? I'll just go into the grocery store and break this."

"He won't break it for you," the guy said. "He doesn't break bills for anyone. And he doesn't let you drink water or use the bathroom either."

"Ah," the woman said. "But should I try anyway?"

"Don't bother," the homeless guy said. "It doesn't matter. You can give me something another time. What did you say your name was?"

The rich woman hadn't mentioned her name, but now she felt she had no choice, and so she told him.

"You're a good woman, Dara," the homeless guy said. "You have a good heart. But I'm probably not the first person to tell you that."

"You are the first person to tell me that," Dara said. "I help my older brother a lot. Mainly financially. And my parents, too. My father, that is. My mother I can't help anymore; she's dead. And none of them ever said I have a good heart, or even thanked me."

"That's shitty," the poor man said. "It's frustrating. Makes you feel invisible. Or like a slave. An invisible slave. Someone who gets noticed only when he doesn't give people what they expect to get."

The rich woman nodded. She wanted to tell the poor man that she used to love her family so much, that she'd like to love them now, too, but that she didn't seem to have the strength anymore. She wanted to tell him that when she first met her husband he'd said "No kids," because it was his second marriage and he already had a fourteen-year-old daughter with issues. So they didn't have kids, and that was actually fine, because their life was good without them. Full. But what kills her is that she never even told him that she actually did want children.

The poor man said, "Let's go and sit somewhere. There's a bench on the corner and a take-out coffee place not far from it. The coffee's on me." But the rich woman didn't want coffee and she didn't want to go anywhere that wasn't her house because she knew it was the only place where she could close the door behind her and cry. She didn't want to hurt the homeless guy, though, didn't want him to think she was being condescending. What finally emerged from all the wanting and not-wanting was a hug. A surprising hug, a hug that was giving, but that also set boundaries. As if she was saying, "I'm with you," and at the same time, "I'm me." It felt good. Then she handed him seven hundred dollars without giving the slightest thought to how it looked or whether it broke the rules. They'd already broken them anyway, when she told him her name. The man said, "This is too much," and she said, "No, it's exactly the right amount." After he took the money, she gave him another hug and left.

She had planned to take a taxi in order to get home as quickly as possible. But now getting home quickly was no longer a priority; she just wanted to enjoy this special day. Besides, she had no money in her wallet. So she walked all the way home, and every step she took in her red Jimmy Choos felt as if she were strolling on a cloud.

Later, she told her friends about it. About that sensation of doing what you want, of allowing yourself to feel good. Of giving seven hundred dollars to someone who then said, "Thank you, Dara. You made my day, maybe even my week." When was the last time someone had said that to them? They all understood immediately. They wanted to feel something similar. They were tired of making donations at those dreary charity balls their husbands always dragged them to, where they ended up getting a gold pin and a generic thank-you from the mayor or an aging movie star dragged out of mothballs for the occasion. They wanted the look, maybe even the hug—if it felt natural—from a man whose life they'd rescued from the sewer. Or, if not rescued, then upgraded significantly. They wanted to see him cry or thank Jesus for sending them to him, as if they were saints and not just very rich women.

Dara took two of her friends to the southern part of the city in her silver Mini Cooper. It wasn't an ideal car for three—Susan had to fold up her long legs to squeeze into the backseat—but they managed. When they found a homeless man, a guy with a dog and without a leg, Susan and Karen argued about which of them would give him the money. It was one of those arguments in which each person insists on letting the other win. In the end, Karen got out and approached the man, who was sitting next to a cardboard box with VETERAN written on it in black marker, and put twelve hundred dollars into his disposable plastic cup. The man, the amputee, saw how much money it was—maybe not the exact amount, but he recognized the hundred-dollar bills, for sure. He didn't say anything, just looked her in the eye for a long moment and nodded a thank-you. That evening, as Karen lay in bed after everyone had already fallen asleep and pictured that nod behind her closed eyes, she felt her entire body quiver. It had been a long time since anyone had looked at her like that.

The next day, they found one for Susan. But it didn't work out so well for her. That is, the man took the money and even said thank you and gave her a toothless smile, but Dara realized immediately that he was an addict who would piss it all away on drugs, and that there had been no real moment between him and Susan. Which isn't to say it was a bad experience, either.

They tried it again a few times, and while they never felt the way they had the first time, they still felt good. And the people who received the money felt good, too, or at least better than before. It didn't take long for Karen to come up with the idea for the app.

It was brilliant. It took off. The software processed all the data about the homeless, or just the beggars, that people uploaded into it, and then it would tell you, at any given moment, where to find the neediest person nearest to you. People just ate it up. *Time* magazine interviewed them about it, and all kinds of people wanted to buy the company from them. They refused to sell, but eventually agreed to give it to Mark Zuckerberg— though only if he promised to donate any profits it made and not keep them for himself.

Zuckerberg looked offended when they said that. "You think I'm getting into this for the money?" he asked. "I already have enough money. I'm getting into this to do good." He said it so beautifully that Dara choked up. This man is special, she thought. It was no accident that he'd gotten where he was. She told him she wanted a minute alone with Karen to discuss it, and before she could get a word out, Karen grabbed her arm and said, "We have to give it to him."

They had called their app One Good Deed a Day, but Zuckerberg immediately changed the name to GooDeed, which was shorter and much catchier. Within a few months, it became an even bigger hit. Not Whats-App, but big.

Six years later, right outside the mall, Dara bumped into the man she'd hugged on the street. She and her husband had signed their divorce agreement only a few weeks earlier, but when the man asked her how she was, she said that everything was fine. Part of her wanted to tell him that she and Walter had split up, and that for the first time in her life, she understood what it meant to be alone, but instead she told him about the app. He couldn't believe it. He knew about it, of course, everyone did, but he hadn't made the connection to himself and their first encounter. Before saying good-bye, she took out her wallet and offered him some money.

"I'm not homeless anymore," he said with a smile. "And you have a lot to do with that. I took hold of myself, stopped drinking, and now I teach classes at the community center. My aunt died a few years ago, and left me a small inheritance. I used it to buy a studio apartment not far from here. Hey," he said, waving his hand in front of her face, showing her the gold band on his finger. "I even got married. And guess what? We've got twin girls now."

Dara was still standing there with the bills in her hand.

"I don't need that anymore," he said, half apologetically. "I did back then, but I'm fine now."

"Take it," she pleaded, tears welling up. "Please, take it. For me."

She had a few hundred dollars in her hand—she didn't know exactly how much, she hadn't even counted it—and it wasn't till she began to sob that he took the money.

ST. E'S

by **PAULA WHYMAN**

The last time I took the train, the boarding was like always, a veneer of orderliness followed by people lunging for seats, clipping ankles with their rolling luggage. Two of the cars were shut, dark, guarded by men who were intimidating in the way guards can be when they're chatting with each other and pretending they have no real concerns about anyone else. We were crammed into the remaining cars, no chance of a place without a seatmate, no chance, in my case, of a real seat at all, except at a table in the crowded café car. A woman ahead of me was slowing things down, trying to drag two wheelie bags through an aisle only wide enough for one. You could see it on people's faces: There's always one like that. Her hair was short, and I watched the tendons in the back of her neck bulge and recede as she looked nervously around for a place. She was calling attention to herself. These days that was the last thing you'd want to do. I felt sorry for her, that no one offered to help. And yet I didn't offer to help. I had my own bags to carry.

I turned and went the other way, which was how I ended up in the café car. Bench seats with shot cushions, sticky tables that smelled like institutional ketchup and burned coffee. And there were loud talkers, some louder than others. The first voice I heard, and the one that would continue to sound in my skull, belonged to an older black gent who'd gathered four strangers to his table. "Here's the party," he was saying. And then he told them about the time he took the train in a snowstorm, and halfway through the trip they had to stop to pick up passengers from a broken-down train. Instead of people getting upset, they drank beer and told jokes, and what a great experience all around.

I didn't understand people like that, who could do the proverbial lemons-into-lemonade shift. I wanted them to go live on an island somewhere away from me, an island of the jocular and easygoing, so I wouldn't have to feel bad about feeling bad. There must be some part of reality they were missing. Or some part I was missing. Laughter from the man's table punched the air, his voice over it, and all I felt was lonely.

Like in a high school cafeteria, the only empty seat in the café car was at the outcast table. I sat facing two hulkish men, strangers to each other as well as to me. They were careful to leave space between them so as not to risk accidentally touching. The one sitting by the window was white, with a buzz cut and muscular arms covered with tattoos I couldn't decipher, except for the one that said GEORGIA on a banner waving between two rose blooms. He had perfect handsome Ken-doll features but on a head that was too small for his body, a thick stump of neck and a chest puffed up and laminated inside a tight T-shirt. I decided he was either a vet a few months back from the Yemen conflict or the Azerbaijan action, or a bodybuilder, or both. Was he from Georgia, or was his girlfriend named Georgia? Or his mother, or his sister or his daughter or his gun? His music, which I could hear but not make out, was leaking softly from his earbuds, a squeal and whine that sounded like Chinese opera. His head drooped forward, his eyes closed. He was short, a full head shorter than the black man who sat next to him. Despite my staring, Ken doll never looked at me, not once. Gay, I decided. And then I remembered that I was too old to be looked at that way, at least not on purpose. It was easy to forget, because inside I still felt like I was in my forties, still borderline lookatable. I had the urge to tell him to turn down his music so he didn't ruin his hearing. At least he didn't hum along, like my sister used to do, even when there was no music playing besides what was in her head. Back then, we were both lookatable, though her looks never did her any good.

Both men had gotten on in New York, same as me, though the train originated in Boston. I played a game where I tried to guess where they were from—were they going home to DC, or were they stopping along the way? The white guy looked like Virginia, and I decided he was going on to Richmond. Maybe Roanoke. There were so few trains these days, ever since the government sold out Amtrak to the Brazilians; now all of them were crowded and went too far. I imagined they just kept going until the tracks ended at water, and anyone who was left climbed onto rafts and paddled to Cuba. That was where everyone used to want to go because you couldn't, and now that you could no one really cared.

The black man across from me stuck his legs out under the table so that his feet were resting on either side of mine. It was a strangely intimate position, being essentially trapped between his legs. When I moved more than an inch, I kicked one of his shoes by mistake. It felt like kicking a tire. I apologized but I don't think he noticed. He was staring at a spot above my head and blinking rapidly. I finally figured out he was playing a video game. Every so often, he'd poke a finger at one of the lenses of his glasses. It must have been an old version; with the new ones you didn't have to do that anymore. He was from DC, I decided. Or Baltimore. His size and his dreadlocks made him look tough, but his face was too round, and his eyes were deep brown and soft. He lived with his mother, and he was around nineteen. He went to UDC, was taking classes to be an accountant. He grew up in Anacostia, where he'd worked hard and tested into a slot at the good charter school, the one that was like an oasis amid weedy vacant lots. On the other hand, maybe he was from Wesley Heights and had gone to St. Albans. He was studying engineering at Hopkins. He had a girlfriend his parents didn't like. She wasn't in school; she wanted to get married. They wanted their son Anthony—named after the saint—to go to graduate school and come to work for his dad's engineering firm, where he could build advanced weaponry simple enough for Georgia, sitting next to him, to figure out in the middle of a firestorm. Maybe Georgia was only home on leave until his next tour. Who knew where it would be this time? The new administration liked to mix it up.

Devin's engineering firm had an opening now. He'd taken early retirement. That was the official line. In fact, they'd fired him. He hadn't told me; I'd heard it by accident from his assistant and pretended I already knew. His last design, the K4, was beset with problems. Not that this was unusual; the more complex the design, the more likely there would be trouble with it.

"I can design a miracle," Devin would say. "But it's only as good as the people who fly it."

He'd gone to Qatar to try and fix it. He'd been there for a month. He came home, and a week later, over Yemen, the K4 missed its target and blew up a school.

The support he'd been paying me had been cut in half, and two months ago, at the age of fifty-eight, I was forced to move in with my father. Being back in my childhood home, besides the unavoidable regression, a certain stasis set in. Capitulation. I could pretend I was there to take care of my dad, but the idea was ludicrous. Every day another "lady friend" would pick him up and take him to play bridge and see a matinee and have a four o'clock dinner. He was having the time of his life.

Of course he must have missed my mother. Maybe.

My father was a good housemate, despite the baggage my mother's litany of minor complaints had assigned him. ("He never lifts his head out of the newspaper!" "He talks with his mouth full!" "He tells dirty jokes to company!") He was neat, didn't play his music too loud, and didn't ask me a lot of personal questions. He even appreciated my cooking.

If my mother were alive, she would have said, "There's still a chance you'll get back together. Nothing's final until it's final. Don't make it final. You'll regret it."

In fact, this was approximately what she said the first time Devin and I separated. It was my mother getting sick that stopped us that time, as if she'd orchestrated her illness with that kind of precision. We presented a united front for the duration of her cancer, and after she died, a respectful number of months later, Devin left. He wasn't coming back.

My father didn't try to discuss any of this with me. My mother had been in charge of the talking. While I did miss her, I didn't miss that. Me and Devin, our last couple of years together had been marked by discussions that never seemed to end. Sometimes I thought we split up just so no one would have the last word. Devin packed up and moved while I was out one day. His note said, "I don't want to discuss it." I understood.

I'd thought of moving closer to Gabriel, my son. That had been a reason to go to New York. He'd invited me to stay as long as I liked, to move in with him until I found a place. I couldn't do that to him. And realistically, if I couldn't afford DC, I certainly couldn't afford New York. But there was a part of me that couldn't stop dreaming.

Awake in the middle of the night, I'd taken to spinning the globe on a bookshelf in my parents' den, closing my eyes and stopping it randomly with my finger. If I were brave and adventurous, I told myself, I'd go wherever it landed. Then I'd see that I'd touched Albania, or a country somewhere in Central Asia that didn't exist anymore, or a spot in the middle of the unbroken blue of the Pacific. If I moved my finger a little to the right, I'd hit Hawaii. But that was cheating. And Hawaii was expensive.

When Devin and I sold the house, I looked around at apartments that were inevitably marketed for young single people, not AARP members whose lives had suddenly shifted into neutral. The one thing I had in common with young singles was a reluctance to commit. My friend Maureen asked me to move in with her. We'd met in a Mommy and Me class when Gabriel was born, forever ago. Now when we got together for lunch, we'd put our phones out on the table and no one would call. She was a widow and living in an adult community. She said, "Just until you find a place." I couldn't do it. I told her it would ruin our friendship, which it might have. "Adult community" seemed to me the last stop before you climbed into Charon's boat.

Before Devin and I separated I found myself walking alone in Rock Creek Park on a beautiful fall day, amid the best weather Washington ever sees, the air that has a bite to it, the weakening but still warm sun, the smell of decaying leaves and smoke from a last-chance cookout. The kind of weather we'll get for about three days before the air dips below freezing overnight and a layer of ice coats the leaves everyone has illegally piled at the curb. It was a weekend, and the roads were closed for biking. I watched people with dogs, people on scooters, rollerblades, skateboards. People pushing strollers. They all knew where they were going, I thought. True or not, it was what I felt. I couldn't remember the last time I'd had to make a conscious decision about the direction of my life. Spinning the globe was just another cop-out.

* * *

I'd put my bags next to me on the bench seat, hoping no one would think to ask if the space was free. When the conductor stopped to scan my ticket, he squinted at my bags.

"You people," he said, shaking his head, not looking at me. "Think you're above it all."

I told myself I wanted to read my book, not socialize, but for a moment I wished I'd been invited to sit with the King of the Café Car. I wasn't eavesdropping; it was impossible to not hear him. He talked about Marion Barry, who used to be mayor of DC. Dead now. I remembered the day of Barry's funeral—the city government closed, his body driven slowly through the streets, throngs of well-wishers on the sidewalk trying to climb over barricades as the hearse passed. Nearly as big a crowd around the Capitol as when they buried George W. Bush. But I remembered Barry's funeral, because while I watched the procession, a realtor planted a for-sale sign on my front lawn. And then I signed the divorce papers.

I wondered if I could think differently than I had all my life, if I concentrated hard enough, if I could let things go.

The café car was the third car from the front of the train. There was the engineer's booth, where the superfluous driver played online poker, then the first-class car, and then, in order to insulate the first-class passengers from the smell of bad food, there was a coach-class car in between. People were lined up in the aisle now. When I looked up, my nose was in someone's elbow. If the other passengers looked down and saw an actual physical book in my hands, they edged away from me. I closed it and put it on the table, so the sticker that said CERTIFIED BEDBUG-FREE was clearly visible.

The cashier behind me was taking orders. Eighteen dollars for a green salad. Nine dollars for a bottle of water. Eighty-six the Pepsi products. Eighty-six the burgers. Nope, sorry, all out of pizza, too. There was nothing except water and Caesar salad and Doritos. Doritos would always be plentiful. I don't know why they bothered to post a menu.

Of course they hadn't announced in advance that the train would be running at diminished capacity. An announcement was unnecessary because the trains were always overcrowded. I was old enough to remember a time when train travel was at least comfortable, if not luxurious. There used to be twenty trains a day on the DC route. Now there were four. Leaving New York City, we'd stop at Newark, Trenton, Philadelphia, Wilmington, Baltimore, Baltimore airport, New Carrollton, Union Station. The stations all looked pretty much the same from where I sat—the same graffiti, the same crowded platforms, the same strangers pressed together trying not to make eye contact. The way up to New York was always good, because at least at the other end I'd see my son. The way back was always a drudgery.

An announcer said, "There will be officers with trained dogs doing a routine security check on this train. Please don't pet the dogs." No one listened to these announcements anymore.

My book dated me. When the TSA men boarded and did their walk-through, their German shepherd sniffed and panted in its direction.

"Whatcha reading?" the officer asked me. Before I answered, he read the title aloud to himself: "*Lost in the City.* Any good?" I nodded. It was thirty years old, out of print. A real find, a book redolent of DC history, of the people and places. You could almost make a map from the information in the stories, and find the neighborhoods where people used to live, where now there were office buildings and upscale retail theme parks and fancy condos for noncommittal young singles.

The TSA guy picked up my book and said, "Mind?"

"Please," I said. Be careful, I was thinking.

He was dressed a lot like a policeman. I wondered how real police felt about being confused with people who had no real crime-fighting skills and were trained only to go through luggage, or mill around in crowds at public events asking to look inside your backpack. Or was this part of the endless anti-terror strategy, to appear token and arbitrary? I guess there were cops who did nothing but write tickets and other cops who stood around all day near shopping centers, so there could be cops who did nothing but look through your stuff. The men with dogs were looking for explosives. The dogs were doing the work. It made me think of Italy, where there were many different kinds of police, and it was important to know the difference, because some of them you could ask to pose for photos, and some you couldn't.

"Has this been heated?" he said. I said yes, even though there was a big sticker on the front saying just that. I didn't know TSA was also the bedbug police. He flipped through the pages and held it out to his dog. The dog snuffled it, licked his chops, and turned away in disinterest.

"Enjoy," said the officer, and put the book back on the table.

"Thanks," I said. There was a damp spot where the dog's nose had touched the page.

The two men at my table had remained assiduously absorbed in their electronic devices during that exchange. As soon as the TSA man passed, they relaxed. The black guy shook his head slowly, watched as the officer and his dog left the car. As he turned to look down the aisle, I got a peek inside his glasses. He was playing *Gitmo Escape XI*. He glanced at my book and at me.

"Going to DC?" he said.

"Yeah," I said. "You?"

He nodded. That was the end of the conversation. Also the end of his hopes for more space for his gigantic feet. Something could open up around Philly, though. All of us might be able to breathe a little by Philly. We were at Newark just then. No one gets off at Newark, only on. There are better ways to get to Newark from New York.

"No more pizza," the café clerk was saying to someone new.

The TSA used to bring on the dogs only in major cities, like DC and New York. Now their appearance was supposed to be unpredictable, which from a certain standpoint seemed more logical. They got on in Newark. They got on in Wilmington, even in New Carrollton once. In fact they might have boarded at every stop; I didn't notice anymore. I did notice their guns. Before the train pulled out, I saw the officer and his dog walking away along the platform.

My left leg had fallen asleep. I hadn't realized how tense I was, frozen in position so as not to jostle my seatmate. The bodybuilder had extricated himself and gone to the bathroom. When the train pulled out of Trenton, I stood. Usually I'd leave something on the seat to show I was coming back. The café seemed less secure than a regular car. I took my purse but left the shoulder bag in which I was keeping my work papers and my lunch. I brought the precious book even though it was the last thing anyone would steal. I said to the black guy, "I'll be right back." He nodded without taking his eyes off his game.

I had no intention of being right back. I needed to walk. I walked from car to car in no kind of hurry. There were people standing in the areas between the cars. Most of them didn't look at me; they were messing with their iWhatevers. One guy was smoking an electronic cigarette. I wondered if he needed to stand there, or if he could smoke it at his seat. I mean, there was no actual smoke.

The announcer said, "Philadelphia, next stop, thirty-five minutes."

I passed the woman with two wheelie bags. She'd found a seat in what I thought was the last car. She was skyping someone, a man with a bad mustache. I walked to the end, thinking I'd be able to look out the back window and see the track stretching out behind us. But I'd forgotten about the closed-off cars. Through the glass in the door, all I saw were the two guards. They were watching the preseason football game on a tablet. My walk seemed anticlimactic now that I couldn't go all the way to the end. In the other direction, I knew, the first-class car would be off-limits, too. I stood and looked out the side windows instead. We were passing through a rare empty space between cities. There was brush, and then grass, and then a field or more like a once-field, where the dirt had been churned up. I thought we must be approaching Philly, that next there would be an industrial area, and then the strip with Taco Bell and 7-Eleven and Public Storage and a Kwik-Lasik franchise, and I should go back and guard my seat. You didn't want to be away from your seat when people were getting on and off.

I started back, but the train lurched and I grabbed onto the railing behind the seat of the woman who was skyping. The man on the screen said, "I promise I'll pay you back."

With another lurch, the train stopped. This happened all the time. I looked out the window, waiting. Now that we were stopped, I could see that the field was part of a farm, and that the churned-up dirt was arranged in neat rows, as if it had been troweled, an old crop turned under to prepare for a new one. But there was a large sign off to one side that said, COMING SOON: THE GATES AT RIDGE FARM — CUSTOM HOMES FROM THE LOW 900S.

The train hadn't jerked again, so I let go of the seatback. People were starting to look at their watches and roll their eyes. Then the air conditioning cut off, and someone groaned. It was freezing when it was on, so I didn't mind. This happened all the time, like I said. What didn't happen all the time was what sounded like a shriek, too distant to know for sure. It might have been brakes, if the train had been moving. But it wasn't. I wondered if someone had jumped onto the tracks. It had happened before, a jumper,

but usually from a station platform. If someone had jumped, the conductor
would stop the train. And they might say engine trouble because it seems
like a bad idea to note a suicide over the PA. "Unavoidably detained" was
the euphemism that came to mind. Like when Devin had called to say he'd
be late coming back from a test flight when my mother was in the hospice,
dying; or the time my daughter, Liana, was trapped in Alaska by the fires
she was covering for AP, and she didn't want to say she was in danger of
being burned alive. There was no euphemism that seemed sufficient when
my sister died. My sister who jumped, so many years ago, from a balcony,
not from a train, but what's the difference when you come down to it?

My sister's body had been fixed up for us to see her one last time in the
hospital. She was under a blanket, it was tucked all around her, up to her
neck. But I could see her chin, her head, which they'd bandaged, her face,
which they'd tried their best to clean up. Her eyes were closed. One hand
was uncovered, resting on the blanket, the blue cast of her skin on white.
I stood at the end of her bed, and while my parents held her hands and gazed
at her still, battered face, I held onto her foot through the blanket. It felt like
clay. For years after, I couldn't look at my children in bed, their feet shifting and wriggling underneath their blankets, and not think of my sister.

"Assume every stranger is crazy," my mother used to say, "until proven
otherwise." After President Reagan closed St. Elizabeth's and kicked the
mentally ill to the curb, my mother began to insist that every person asking
for money on a street corner and any stranger who looked at her crosswise
was a former patient there—the guy shelving boxes at the grocery store, the
gym teacher at the school where she substitute taught, the bank manager
who wouldn't approve her loan. "St. E's," she'd say. "Mark my words." As
if we'd be waiting around until something happened that could confirm
the diagnosis.

My father talked to everyone he encountered in public places, while my mother stared straight ahead, pretending she didn't know him. "St. E's," she'd say to me, pointing at my father.

I made my way slowly back in the direction of my car. All the passengers were grumbling. Why hadn't there been an announcement? Usually the conductor would come on and say something self-evident like, "There's a problem with the train. We're trying to solve it. We'll update you as soon as we know something." And then it might be a half hour before they said anything else, at which time they'd say they were still working on it. An hour-long trip delay was normal. Inadequate explanations were normal. But nothing?

Finally, an announcement: "We've encountered a safety problem. Stay in your seats." Just a safety problem. No need for panic.

There was no open seat for me to stay in, so I kept going. Without the HVAC system, the train was too quiet. I went to the restroom, and when I flushed it was like an explosion going off. When I came back out people were standing up and stretching in the aisles and chatting with each other in that fake-relaxed "here we go again" way.

"Stay put," said the same announcer. What choice did we have, unless someone wanted to get out and push? I was hungry. There was a sandwich in the bag I'd left at my seat. Otherwise, I was in no hurry to sit in a silent, smelly café car.

When I was about halfway back, the engine rumbled to life. It was a shock and a relief. A murmur of voices rose to a clamor, but as I got closer to my car the sounds made by the passengers died down and I couldn't hear much at all over the idling train engine. It was like someone was holding seashells over my ears.

The door to the café car wouldn't open. I must have smacked the button a dozen times. I peered in through the glass, but I couldn't see anything inside the car. Something was blocking my view. A large, dark shape. I tried knocking.

"Hey," I said. "I need to get in there. Could you not lean on the door like that?" No answer. The guy—it had to be a guy, he was so big—he didn't even turn to look. Confirmed: I was at that age now, invisible. And then the darkness fell away. The doors opened, and I stepped into the car and nearly tripped over him.

It was my seatmate, the black guy, lying on the floor. He was moaning softly, and acting like he wanted to get up but couldn't even get an elbow out. A uniformed man, an Amtrak employee, crouched near him and spoke into his ear, his arm over the black man's shoulders. It was the conductor I'd seen walking through the car earlier, the one who'd scanned my ticket.

"Can I help?" I said. He waved me away. He kept his face close to the prone man's ear and seemed to be hugging him. Then there was a sound, a plink, a flat piano key, and the black guy's body jerked.

"Is he having a seizure?" I said. That was when I noticed the woman at the table with the loud talker. He was bent over now, with his head in her lap. Her hand was over her mouth, her face was flushed. The loud talker wasn't talking. No one was talking. There was only what might have been loud breathing, whimpering. I glanced over at my seat, two tables away, and there was Georgia, head down, arms splayed across the table. And a puddle, was it—

I looked again at the black man on the floor, his wild, sinuous hair fanned out in the aisle. There was a hole in his back.

"What," I started and stopped.

The conductor who had been tending to him looked up at me.

"Has anyone called for help?" I said. I held my book in one arm tight against my chest while digging for my phone in my purse.

"Give it to me," said the conductor. His voice was familiar, too.

At first I thought he meant the book. He stuck out his free hand. He was official; I handed him my phone. And then his other hand came out, the one with the gun. He held it against the man's head.

"No, no, he needs help." I think I really said that. But he shot him in the head anyway. That plink sound, and something sprayed onto the bare calves of the woman nearby, and she screamed. He pointed the gun at her, and she stopped screaming.

The conductor stood up in front of me. "Go to your seat," he said. "I told everyone to stay put."

I nodded, but it wasn't the agreeing kind of nodding, it was the kind of nodding that goes with full-body shivering.

"Move it," said the conductor. "See what happens to heroes?"

I think I'm moving, but I'm not. I try to shake myself out of it. The dead man at my feet, he stood in front of the door, why? To keep the conductor from going to the next car? I look at my table, at Georgia who survived Yemen to die in a train that smells like Doritos. And at the table across from mine, where a man lies half in the aisle, his laptop still running, and at the man who was working in the café, slumped against the cash register. And at the women who have been spared but not spared. That boy at my feet whose brains are on a strange woman's legs, where is his mother? Where? Waiting in Shaw or Capital Heights or Glover Park?

I must have said it out loud, because the conductor says, "I've had enough of you," and plink, I'm knocked hard into the door and drop my book and he shoves past me and disappears. I'm sitting on the legs of the man with the giant tennis shoes. Big red drops are spilling onto his white shoes and onto the cover of my book, where my hand is resting. The bookmark has slipped out, but I know where I left off. I want to know what happens.

An excerpt from

ALL MY PUNY SORROWS

by MIRIAM TOEWS

O ur house was taken away on the back of a truck one afternoon late in the summer of 1979. My parents and my older sister and I stood in the middle of the street and watched it disappear, a low-slung bungalow made of wood and brick and plaster slowly making its way down First Street, past the A&W and the Deluxe Bowling Lanes and out onto the number 12 highway, where we eventually lost sight of it. I can still see it, said my sister Elfrieda repeatedly, until finally she couldn't. I can still see it. I can still see it. I can still… Okay, nope, it's gone, she said.

My father had built it himself back when he had a new bride, both of them barely twenty years old, and a dream. My mother told Elfrieda and me that she and my father were so young and so exploding with energy that on hot evenings, just as soon as my father had finished teaching school for the day and my mother had finished the baking and everything else, they'd go running through the sprinkler in their new front yard, whooping and leaping, completely oblivious to the stares and consternation of their older neighbors, who thought it unbecoming of a newly married Mennonite couple to be cavorting, half dressed, in full view of the entire town. Years later, Elfrieda would describe the scene as my parents' *La Dolce Vita* moment, and the sprinkler as their Trevi Fountain.

Where's it going? I asked my father. We stood in the center of the road. The house was gone. My father made a visor with his hand to block the sun's glare. I don't know, he said. He didn't want to know. Elfrieda and my mother and I got into our car and waited for my father to join us. He stood looking at emptiness for what seemed like an eternity to me. Elfrieda complained that the backs of her legs were burning up on the hot plastic seat. Finally my mother reached over and honked the horn, only slightly, not enough to startle my father, but enough to make him turn and look at us.

It was such a hot summer and we had a few days to kill before we could move into our new house, which was similar to our old house but not one that my father had built himself with loving attention to every detail, such as a long covered porch to sit in and watch electrical storms while remaining dry, and so my parents decided we should go camping in the Badlands of South Dakota.

We spent the whole time, it seemed, setting everything up and then tearing it all down. My sister, Elfrieda, said it wasn't really life—it was like being in a mental hospital where everyone walked around with the sole purpose of surviving and conserving energy, it was like being in a refugee camp, it was a halfway house for recovering neurotics, it was this and that, she didn't like camping—and our mother said Well, honey, it's meant to alter our perception of things. Paris would do that too, said Elf, or LSD, and our mother said C'mon, the point is we're all together, let's cook our wieners.

The propane stove had an oil leak and exploded into four-foot flames and charred the picnic table but while that was happening Elfrieda danced around the fire singing "Seasons in the Sun" by Terry Jacks, a song about a black sheep saying goodbye to everyone because he's dying, and our father swore for the first recorded time (What in the Sam Hills!) and stood close to the fire poised to do something but what, what, and our mother stood there shaking, laughing, unable to speak. I yelled at my family to move away from the fire, but nobody moved an inch as if they had been placed in their positions by a movie director and the fire was fake and the scene would be ruined if they moved. Then I grabbed the half-empty Rainbow ice cream pail that was sitting on the picnic table and ran across the field to a communal tap and filled the pail with water and ran back and threw the water onto the flames, which leapt higher then, mingled with the scents of vanilla, chocolate, and strawberry, toward the branches of an overhanging poplar tree. A branch sparked into fire but only briefly because by then the skies had darkened and suddenly rain and hail began their own swift assault, and we were finally safe, at least from fire.

That evening after the storm had passed and the faulty propane stove had been tossed into a giant cougar-proof garbage cage, my father and my sister decided to attend a lecture on what was once thought to be the extinct black-footed ferret. It was being held in the amphitheater of the campground, and they said they might stick around for the second lecture as well, which was being given by an expert in astrophysics about the nature of dark matter. What is that? I asked my sister and she said she didn't know but she thought it constituted a large part of the universe. You can't see it, she said, but you can feel its effects, or something. Is it evil? I asked her. She laughed, and I remember perfectly or should I say I have a perfect memory of how she looked standing there in her hot pants and striped halter top with the shadowy eroded Badlands behind her, her head back, way back, her long thin neck and its white leather choker with the blue bead in the center, her burst of laughter like a volley of warning shots, a challenge to the world to come and get her if it dared. She and my father walked off toward the amphitheater, my mother calling out to them—Make kissing sounds to ward off rattlesnakes!—and while they were gone and learning about invisible forces and extinction, my mother and I stayed beside the tent and played What Time Is It, Mr. Wolf? against the last remaining blotches of the setting sun.

On the way home from the campground we were quiet. We had driven for two and a half days in a strange direction that took us away from East Village until finally my father had said well, fair enough, I suppose we ought to return home now, as though he had been trying to work something out and then had simply given up. We sat in the car looking solemnly through open windows at the dark, jagged outcroppings of the great Canadian Shield. Unforgiving, said my father, almost imperceptibly, and when my mother asked him what he had said he pointed at the rock and she nodded, Ah, but without conviction as though she had hoped he'd meant something else, something they could defy, the two of them. What are you thinking about? I whispered to Elf. The wind whipped our hair into a frenzy, hers black, mine yellow. We were in the backseat stretched out lengthwise, our legs entangled, our backs against the doors. Elf was reading *Difficult Loves* by Italo Calvino. If you weren't reading right now what would you be thinking about? I asked again. A revolution, she said. I asked her what she meant and she said I'd see someday, she couldn't tell me now. A secret revolution? I asked her. Then she said in a loud voice so we could all hear her, Let's not go back. Nobody responded. The wind blew. Nothing changed.

My father wanted to stop to see ancient Aboriginal ocher paintings on the rock escarpments that hugged Lake Superior. They had endured mysteriously against the harsh elements of sun and water and time. My father stopped the car and we walked down a narrow, rocky path toward the lake. There was a sign that said DANGER! and in small letters explained that people had been known to be swept off these rocks by giant rogue waves and that we were responsible for our own safety. We passed several of these signs on our way to the water and with each dire warning the already deep furrow in my father's brow became deeper and deeper until my mother told him Jake, relax, you'll give yourself a stroke.

When we got to the rocky shore we realized that in order to see the "pictographs" one had to inch along slippery, wet granite that plunged several meters into the foamy water and then hang on to a thick rope that was secured with spikes driven into the rock and then lean way back over the lake almost to the point of being horizontal with your hair grazing the water. Well, said my father, we're not about to do that, are we? He read the plaque next to the trail, hoping that its contents would suffice. Ah, he said, the rock researcher who discovered these paintings called them "forgotten dreams." My father looked at my mother then. Did you hear that, Lottie? he asked. Forgotten dreams. He took a small notebook from his pocket and wrote down this detail. But Elf was completely enchanted with the idea of suspending her body on a rope over crashing water and before anybody could stop her she was gone. My parents called to her to come back, to be careful, to use some common sense, to behave herself, to get back now, and I stood silent and wide-eyed, watching in horror what I believed would be the watery end of my intrepid sister. She clung to the rope and gazed at the paintings, we couldn't see them from where we stood, and then she described to us what she was seeing which was mostly images of strange, spiny creatures and other cryptic symbols of a proud, prolific nation.

When we did, finally, all four of us, arrive back alive in our small town that lay just on the far western side of the rocky Shield in the middle of blue-and-yellow fields, we weren't relieved. We were in our new house now. My father could sit in his lawn chair in the front yard and see, through the trees across the highway to First Street, the empty spot where our old house had been. He hadn't wanted his house to be taken away. It wasn't his idea. But the owner of the car dealership next door wanted the property to expand his parking lot and made all sorts of voluble threats and exerted relentless pressure until finally my father couldn't take it anymore and he buckled one day and sold it to the car dealer for a song, as my mother put it. It's just business, Jake, said the car dealer to my father the next Sunday in church. It's nothing personal. East Village had originated as a godly refuge from the vices of the world but somehow these two, religion and commerce, had become inextricably linked and the wealthier the inhabitants of East Village became the more pious they also became as though religious devotion was believed to be rewarded with the growth of business and the accumulation of money, and the accumulation of money was believed to be blessed by God so that when my father objected to selling his home to the car dealer there was in the air a whiff of accusation, that perhaps by holding out my father wasn't being a good Christian. This was the implication. And above all, my father wanted to be a good Christian. My mother encouraged him to fight, to tell the car dealer to take a hike, and Elfrieda, being older than me and more aware of what was going on, tried to get a petition going among the villagers to keep businesses from expanding into people's homes but there was nothing that could be done to assuage my father's persistent guilt and the feeling that he'd be sinning if he were to fight for what was his in the first place. And besides, my father was thought to be an anomaly in East Village, an oddball, a quiet, depressive, studious guy who went for ten-mile walks in the countryside and believed that reading and writing and reason were the tickets to paradise. My mother would fight for him (although only up to a point because she was, after all, a loyal Mennonite wife and didn't want to upset the apple cart of domestic hierarchy) but she was a woman anyway, so very easily overlooked.

Now, in our new house, my mother was restless and dreamy, my father slammed things around in the garage, I spent my days building volcanoes in the backyard or roaming the outskirts of our town, stalking the perimeter like a caged chimp, and Elf began work on "increasing her visibility." She had been inspired by the ocher paintings on the rock, by their impermeability and their mixed message of hope, reverence, defiance, and eternal aloneness. She decided she too would make her mark. She came up with a design that incorporated her initials E.V.R. (Elfrieda Von Riesen) and below those the initials A.M.P. Then, like a coiled snake, the letter *S*, which covered, underlined, *and* dissected the other letters. She showed me what it looked like, on a yellow legal notepad. Hmm, I said, I don't get it. Well, she told me, the initials of my name are obviously the initials of my name and the A.M.P. stands for All My Puny... then the big *S* stands for Sorrows which encloses all the other letters. She made a fist with her right hand and punched the open palm of her left hand. She had a habit then of punctuating all her stellar ideas with a punch from herself to herself.

Hmm, well that's... How'd you come up with it? I asked her. She told me that she'd gotten it from a poem by Samuel Coleridge who would definitely have been her boyfriend if she'd been born when she should have been born. Or if he had, I said.

She told me she was going to paint her symbol on various natural landmarks around our town.

What natural landmarks? I asked her.

Like the water tower, she said, and fences.

May I make a suggestion? I asked. She looked at me askance. We both knew there was nothing I could offer her in the way of making one's mark in the world—that would be like some acolyte of Jesus saying Hey, you managed to feed only five thousand people with one fish and two loaves of bread? Well, check *this* out!—but she was feeling magnanimous just then, the excitement of her achievement, and she nodded enthusiastically.

Don't use your own initials, I said. Because everyone in town will know whose they are and then the fires of hell will raineth down on us, et cetera.

Our little Mennonite town was against overt symbols of hope and individual signature pieces. Our church pastor once accused Elf of luxuriating in the afflictions of her own wanton emotions to which she responded, bowing low with an extravagant sweep of her arm, *Mea culpa,* m'lord. Back then Elf was always starting campaigns. She conducted a door-to-door survey to see how many people in town would be interested in changing the name of it from East Village to Shangri-La and managed to get more than a hundred signatures by telling people the name was from the Bible and meant a place of no pride.

Hmm, maybe, she said. I might just write *AMPS,* with a very large *S.* It'll be more mysterious, she said. More *je ne sais quoi.*

Um... precisely.

But don't you love it?

I do, I said. And your boyfriend Samuel Coleridge would be happy about it too.

She made a sudden karate-chop slice through the air and then stared into the distance as though she'd just heard the far-off rattle of enemy fire.

Yeah, she said, like objective sadness, which is something else.

Something else than what? I asked her.

Yoli, she said. Than subjective sadness, obviously.

Oh, yeah, I said. I mean, obviously.

There are still red spray-painted *AMPS*s in East Village today although they are fading. They are fading faster than the hearty Aboriginal ocher pictographs that inspired them.

Elfrieda has a fresh cut just above her left eyebrow. There are seven stitches holding her forehead together. The stitches are black and stiff and the ends poke out of her head like little antennae. I asked her how she got that cut and she told me that she fell in the washroom. Who knows if that's true or false. We are women in our forties now. Much has happened and not happened. Elf said that in order for her to open her packages of pills—the ones given to her by the nurses—she would need a pair of scissors. Fat lie. I told her that I knew she wasn't interested in taking the pills anyway, unless they were of such a volume that their combined effect would make her heart seize, so why would she need a pair of scissors to open the package? Also, she could use her hands to tear it open. But she won't risk injuring her hands.

Elfrieda's a concert pianist. When we were kids she would occasionally let me be her page turner for the fast pieces that she hadn't memorized. Page turning is a particular art. I had to be just ahead of her in the music and move like a snake when I turned the page so there was no crinkling and no sticking and no thwapping. Her words. She made me practice over and over, her ear two inches from the page, listening. Heard it! she'd say. And I'd have to do it again until she was satisfied that I hadn't made the slightest sound. I liked the idea of being ahead of her in something. I took real pride in creating a seamless passage for her from one page to the next. There's a perfect moment for turning the page and if I was too early or too late Elfrieda would stop playing and howl. The last measure! she'd say. Only at the last measure! Then her arms and head would crash onto the keys and she'd hold her foot on the sustaining pedal so that her suffering would resonate eerily throughout the house.

Shortly after that camping incident and after Elf had gone around town with her red paint, making her mark, the bishop (the alpha Mennonite) came to our house for what he liked to call a visit. Sometimes he referred to himself as a cowboy and these encounters as "mending fences." But in reality it was more of a raid. He showed up on a Saturday in a convoy with his usual posse of elders, each in his own black hard-topped car (they never carpool because it's not as effective in creating terror when thirteen or fourteen similarly dressed men tumble out of one car) and my father and I watched from the window as they parked in front of our house and got out of their cars and walked slowly toward us, one behind the other, like a tired conga line. My mother was in the kitchen washing dishes. She knew they were coming but was intentionally ignoring them, passing off their "visit" as a minor inconvenience that wouldn't interfere too much with her day. (It was the same bishop who had reprimanded my mother for wearing a wedding dress that was too full and billowy at the bottom. How am I to interpret this excess? he'd asked her.) My sister was somewhere in the house, probably working on her Black Panther look or re-piercing her ears with a potato and rubbing alcohol or staring down demons.

My father went to the door and ushered the men into our home. They all sat down in the living room and looked at the floor or occasionally at each other. My father stood alone with panicky eyes in the middle of the room, surrounded, like the sole remaining survivor of a strange game of dodgeball. My mother *should* have come out of the kitchen immediately, all bustle and warmth, and offered the men coffee or tea and some type of elaborate homemade pastry culled from *The Mennonite Treasury* cookbook, but instead she remained where she was, clanking dishes, whistling with a forced nonchalance, leaving my father to fight alone. They had argued about this before. Jake, she'd said, when they come here tell them it's not a con-venient time. They have no right to march into our home willy-nilly. He said he couldn't do it, he just couldn't do it. So my mother had offered to do it and he had begged her not to until she agreed but said she wouldn't bounce around waiting on them hand and foot while they laid out plans for her family's crucifixion. This particular visit was about Elf planning to go to university to study music. She was only fifteen but the authorities had heard from a local snitch that Elf had "expressed an indiscreet longing to leave the community" and they were apoplectically suspicious of higher learning—especially for girls. Public enemy number one for these men was a girl with a book.

She'll get ideas, said one of them to my father in our living room, to which he had no response but to nod in agreement and look longingly toward the kitchen where my mother was staked out snapping her dish towel at houseflies and pounding baby veal into schnitzel. I sat silently beside my father on the itchy davenport absorbing their "perfume of contempt" as my mother described it. I heard my mother call my name. I went into the kitchen and found her sitting on the counter, swinging her legs and chugging apple juice straight from the plastic jug. Where's Elf? she asked me. I shrugged. How should I know? I hopped up on the counter next to her and she passed me the jug of apple juice. We heard murmuring from the living room, a combination of English and Plautdietsch, the vaguely Dutch-sounding and unwritten medieval language spoken by all the old people in East Village. (I'm called "Jacob Von Riesen's Yolandi" in Plautdietsch and when my mother introduces herself in Plautdietsch she says "I am of Jacob Von Riesen.") Then after a minute or two had passed we heard the opening chords of Rachmaninoff's Prelude in G Minor, Opus 23. Elf was in the spare bedroom next to the front door where the piano was, where her life mostly took place in those days. The men stopped talking. The music got louder. It was Elf's favorite piece, the soundtrack to her secret revolution perhaps. She'd been working on it for two years nonstop with a teacher from the conservatory in Winnipeg who drove to our house twice a week to give her lessons and my parents and I were familiar with every one of its nuances, its agony, its ecstasy, its total respect for the importance of the chaotic ramblings of an interior monologue. Elf had described it to us. Pianos weren't even allowed in our town technically, too reminiscent of saloons and speakeasies and unbridled joy, but my parents snuck it into the house anyway because a doctor in the city had suggested that Elf be given a "creative outlet" for her energies to prevent her from becoming "wild" and that word had sinister implications. Wild was the worst thing you could become in a community rigged for compliance. After a few years of having a secret piano, hastily covered with sheets and gunnysacks when the elders came to visit, my parents grew to love Elf's playing and even made occasional requests along the way, like "Moon River" and "When Irish Eyes are Smiling." Eventually the elders did find out that we were harboring a piano in our house and there was a long discussion about it, of course, and some talk of a three-month or six-month excommunication for my father who offered to take it like a man but when he appeared to go down so willingly they decided to let it go (meting out punishment isn't fun when the victim asks for it) as long as my parents oversaw that Elf was using the piano only as an instrument for the Lord.

My mother began to hum along, her body began to sway. The men in the living room remained silent, as though they were being reprimanded. Elf played louder, then quieter, then louder again. The birds stopped singing and the flies in the kitchen stopped slamming up against the windows. The air was still. She was at the center of the spinning world. This was the moment Elf took control of her life. It was her debut as an adult woman and, although we didn't know it at the time, her debut also as a world-class pianist. I like to think that in that moment it became clear to the men in the living room that she wouldn't be able to stay, not after the expression of so much passion and tumult, and furthermore that to hold her there she would have to be burned at the stake or buried alive. It was the moment Elf left us. And it was the moment my father lost everything all at once: approval from the elders, his authority as head of the household, and his daughter, who was now free and therefore dangerous.

The opus came to an end and we heard the piano top slam shut over the keys and the piano bench scrape the linoleum floor in the spare bedroom. Elf came into the kitchen and I passed her the jug of apple juice and she drank it all, finished it off and chucked the container into the garbage can.

She punched a fist into her palm and said finally nailed it. We three stood in the kitchen while the men in suits filed out of our house in the order they had filed in and we heard the front door close softly and the men's car engines start and the cars pull away from the curb and disappear. We waited for my father to join us in the kitchen but he had gone to his study. I'm still not sure whether or not Elf knew that the men were in the living room or even that the bishop and the elders had paid us a visit at all, or if it was just a coincidence that she chose that exact time to play the Rachmaninoff piece to fierce perfection.

But shortly after the visit from the bishop and his men Elf made a painting and put it in an old frame she'd found in the basement. She hung it in the middle of our living room wall right above the scratchy couch. It was a quote. It read:

> I know of a certainty, that a proud, haughty, avaricious, selfish, unchaste, lecherous, wrangling, envious, disobedient, idolatrous, false, lying, unfaithful, thievish, defaming, backbiting, blood-thirsty, unmerciful and revengeful man, whosoever he may be, is no Christian, even if he was baptized one hundred times and attended the Lord's Supper daily.
> —Menno Simons.

Okay, but Elfie? said my mom.

No, said Elfie. It's staying right there. It's the words of Menno Simons! Aren't we supposed to be following them?

Elfie's new artwork hung in our living room for about a week until my father asked her: Well, kiddo, have you made your point? I'd really love to put Mom's embroidered steamship back in that spot. And by then her righteous indignation had blown over like so many of her wild personal storms.

All My Puny Sorrows *is available now from McSweeney's Books.*

THE DENTIST ON THE RIDGE

nonfiction by **DAVE EGGERS**

The dentist, Marko, a swaggering, wide-smiling man in his late thirties, runs a modest family practice in a small Croatian city called Metković, about ninety minutes north of Dubrovnik. The operation consists of himself and an older couple, Ema and Luka, who serve as his assistants, helping him with teeth cleanings and the making of molds. Ema and Luka live in a clean modern ranch house in Metković, and they rent out a crumbling villa in Kremena, a tiny village in the nearby hills. This crumbling villa is what they've rented to my wife and me for the month of July.

Marko has invited us out to eat at what he says is the best restaurant in town. Here they cook the meat outside, in a stone dome with a steel cover, while the guests watch. The process, called *pod pekom*, usually takes three hours, but in this case, Marko called ahead, got the roasting started, and so we are sitting on the patio with him and Ema and Luka and their young daughter, all of us with drinks in hand, in the early evening, and the food, lamb, will be ready momentarily.

"How do you like the rental?" Marko asks. His English is better than that of our landlords, Ema and Luka, with whom we've been communicating haltingly, with gestures and smiles, for the last week.

The rental is easily a hundred and fifty years old, made of stone, and is tiny in all ways, made for smaller people from an earlier time. The rooms are cramped, the hallways are narrow, the stairway seems made for elves. It is also possibly haunted. We have not slept well since arriving, because we are sure that a child died in the old stone home, and this child does not want us to rest.

We have not asked Ema and Luka about the child. We don't know how to ask about the child, but we assume a child passed away there, because on the second floor of the crumbling house there is a shrine. We assume it is a shrine: a bare tree, three feet tall, decorated with baby shoes and baby clothing and pictures of angels and infants, and a miniature suitcase. We assume this is a tribute to a child who died too soon.

The tree makes standing or walking or sleeping upstairs very upsetting. After the first night, which was humid and made the second floor stifling, we have decided to sleep, or attempt to sleep, on a pull-out bed on the first floor. It is cooler there and there is no shrine.

"The home is beautiful," we tell Marko.

Marko conveys this to Ema and Luka, and they are relieved. As landlords, they have been very hospitable. A few days after we arrived, they took us to a restaurant where we were given a tour, by motorboat, of the nearby marshes. We followed a winding route, through eight-foot reeds, as the sun dropped and soaked the landscape in yellow linen light. Their daughter, eight years old, a tomboy, a soccer player, an imp-faced adventurer, sat at the bow, as if on the lookout for sandbars or icebergs. At the end of the ride, the restaurateur pulled up two traps from the bottom of the marsh. The traps were round, squat and ribbed; they looked like landmines. Inside each was an eel, black and shiny, curled neat and tight. Ema and Luka and their daughter ate them for dinner; we demurred, and instead worked our way through the bread and deli meats.

We have seen the family only a few times since that day. Otherwise we've been driving around the Dalmatia region, a gorgeous area of hills and rocky outcroppings and a nearly empty Mediterranean coast. We have seen white homes with salmon-colored roofs, and have swum in lagoons where Roman ruins lay unheralded in shallow waters. We have seen few people in the countryside, but when we do see people, they are invariably beautifully well made, tall and strong and thin, and always wearing snug clothing from a decade earlier. This is some kind of genetic jackpot, we tell Marko, and he seems pleased.

"Why didn't you stay in Dubrovnik?" Marko asks.

Metković is not a tourist city. In fact, it surprises everyone we meet that we are here. We did go to Dubrovnik when we first arrived in Croatia. Dubrovnik is stunning; it's the Europe everyone wants: cob-blestoned, castle-fortressed, ocher-colored, unspoiled by commerce or crowds. There, we watched a fireworks show in the center of the medieval city, the stones underfoot polished so smooth that they reflected the bursting white lights of the celebration above. In a gift shop we bought a DVD called *War in Dubrovnik!*, which told the story of Dubrovnik being shelled by nearby Montenegro. Walking around the city, which appeared untouched, pristine even, it seemed impossible that it had ever seen conflict of any kind. And the idea of Montenegro sending missiles toward Dubrovnik seemed as likely as Santa Monica shelling Malibu.

This is 2004, and Croatia is a peaceful place, and Dubrovnik is thriving, so much so that staying in the city, or near it, is prohibitively expensive. So when we typed the words *villa Croatia cheap near water* into a search engine we found rentals only in places like Metković and Kremena. Kremena overlooked an inlet of the Mediterranean, and Metković is an inexpensive, unassuming place, so we sent our money through the internet and arrived to meet the aunt and uncle at the old villa. The whole process seemed ill-advised, even insane: such a thing should not, in theory, work. *Come across the sea, internet stranger, and into my home. You will sleep here, and over here is a tree that celebrates the life of a child who died in infancy. Oh, and here is the path down to the bay where you can swim.* That this worked, and we are here in Croatia, with a home and new friends cooking us a lamb, proves that for every boundary, physical or cultural, between people, for every instance of misunderstanding or suspicion, there are a thousand instances of senseless trust.

On the restaurant patio, Marko is drinking beer in a bottle and seems very happy. He is a cheerful man, a confident man not bothered by much. He has a successful dentistry practice, and he's single and wealthy in an area where money is tight. He looks out on the small soccer field slightly below the restaurant patio. It's a small field, walled in like a hockey rink. On one of the walls, the words GO HOME AMERICAIN have been spraypainted in three-foot letters. It's not clear what Americans the artist hoped to expel, but we choose to assume it's not us.

"So what else have you seen?" Marko asks.

We tell him some of the things we've seen. We saw, while driving down the coast the other day, a beach town called Neum, located on a fifteen-mile stretch of coastline owned by Bosnia-Herzegovina. This arrangement, going back a thousand years, cuts Croatia into two non-contiguous parts, and makes for an interesting experience when entering the parking lot driving a car with Croatian license plates. It was not that we were unwelcome, but we had been warned that it was not ideal, to enter Neum with Croatian plates, given that Croatia has its own thirty-six hundred miles of coast, so why would a Croat find it necessary to come to the only beach available to Bosnians? But we parked with our Croatian plates and we were unbothered. The beach was festive and bursting with children, and men in bikinis, and teenagers watching each other furtively, and elderly women swimming in the dark blue sea on a hot day ten years after the region sought to destroy itself.

We also saw Mostar. We were on our way to Sarajevo and stumbled upon the reopening of one of the most historically significant structures in the region. We saw balloons and flags and thousands of people congregating on and around what seemed to be an old stone bridge spanning a narrow stretch of the Neretva. Only when we asked around did we realize this was the Stari Most—the Old Bridge of Mostar, which after much international effort had been rebuilt exactly as it had been before the war; the unveiling had happened the previous day.

The bridge had been built by the Ottomans in 1566 and at that time was an architectural astonishment. An Ottoman architect, Mimar Hajrudin, spent nine years designing and constructing it of white marble, but when he was finished, he wasn't confident it would stand, so he fled before the scaffolding was removed, fearing for his life if the bridge didn't hold. But it stood, and flabbergasted all travelers. A seventeenth-century explorer, Evliya Çelebi, wrote in his journal: "The bridge is like a rainbow arch soaring up to the skies, extending from one cliff to the other... I, a poor and miserable slave of Allah, have passed through sixteen countries, but I have never seen such a high bridge. It is thrown from rock to rock as high as the sky."

For four hundred and twenty-seven years it stood as emblematic of the span between the Christians living on its west side and the Muslims living to the east. But in 1993 a Croatian commander, Slobodan Praljak— before the war he was a theater director—decided to destroy it, and after some artillery strikes it fell into the river below. Mostar had long been a multicultural place, a mixture of many faiths, so when the militants destroyed such a decorative bridge—it could not be used for any strategic purpose—the statement made was clear.

So we arrived unwittingly the day after the bridge had been reopened, reuniting, to some degree, Muslims and Christians, Croats and Serbs, amid great fanfare and international celebration. The festivities included divers leaping from the bridge to the water below, and fireworks, and Prince Charles, and other dignitaries from around the world. We walked across with thousands of others on a bright sunny day, the water below cerulean and moving quickly over ancient stones. A group of young boys was jumping in from the rocky riverbank.

From Mostar we drove north along the Neretva to Sarajevo, the road winding through low hills and clogged with UN convoys, passing the other way, hundreds of cars waiting behind them, wanting to move faster. The hills above were dotted with minarets and crosses, defiantly sharing the landscape, but when we arrived in Sarajevo the city still bore, on virtually every building, the markings of the four-year siege and the hatred that fueled it. The crude grey sunbursts of mortar wounds were on municipal structures, hotels, apartment buildings, boutiques. From the surrounding hills the Serb forces fired mortars, artillery, antiaircraft guns, rocket launchers, and sniper rifles at the largely civilian population, killing about twelve thousand people, including more than fifteen hundred children.

We drove into these hills, which had been largely untouched since the war. Cement platforms, where the Serbs had set up their artillery, were now vacant and covered with graffiti. The hills were heavily wooded, and the woods were still heavily mined. Everywhere, signs bearing skulls and crossbones warned of stepping into the trees, death possible everywhere. We looked for the bobsled run, built for the 1984 Olympics, which had been used by the Serbs as a sniper nest, but we didn't find it. That night we dropped back into the city and saw the facade of Zetra Hall, a skating rink that had served as a morgue during the war; coffins had been fashioned from its wooden seats. But outside, on the street, there was optimism in the city that night; there had just been a film festival, and the markets were glittering, a wildly diverse group of travelers bustling through, buying expensive clothes and food, believing in rebirth.

Marko orders another round of drinks. He does not seem particularly haunted by the war. He was a young man at the time, he says, and the fighting was not heavy in the Neretva valley, where we are. There was a war hospital in Metković, but otherwise the Croatians' limited reserve of weapons and other resources were not directed here. Still, appearances needed to be kept up, and the Croatian defenses had to create the illusion of impenetrability.

"They had no gun for me," Marko says. "So they gave me a piece of wood carved in the shape of a rifle. Have you seen those hills outside of town?" We say we have. "I was stationed up there. I had to make sure the wooden gun was visible." He gets up and stands at attention, holding an invisible rifle against his shoulder. It was crucial that his silhouette look formidable, he says. "Every hill had a guy like me on it, everyone with wooden guns. That was my war."

He sits down, laughing at himself. Ema and Luka smile tentatively. Maybe they don't know what Marko is talking about. Maybe they're uncomfortable with his irreverence for the war, the speed of his forgetting.

But peace is made possible by the forgetters.

"Ah," Marko says, pointing to the arrival of our food. The lamb is carved up and we take our plates. A young girl comes to our table, offering fresh peaches, and we each take one.

ALIENATION AND ABSURDITY, AT HOME AND ABROAD

STORIES FROM CROATIA

With photos by Boris Cvjetanović

THE NEW WAVE OF CROATIAN WRITING

an introduction by **JOSIP NOVAKOVICH**

Size doesn't matter, in some things. As I write this, Croatia is about to play the first match of the World Cup against Brazil, in São Paulo—a David fighting Goliath on his home turf. Here, meanwhile, *McSweeney's* has chosen six Croatian writers to compete for your attention amid the literature of the United States. And yet, even after the inevitable losses of translation (all the regional idioms, the words from Turkish, German, and Italian that have been transformed, in Croatia, into local flavor), these stories offer a vivid picture of one part of the world, and probably not the picture you expect. Despite having only four and a half million Croatians to choose from, we've found a set of deeply entertaining texts.

From the somber narratives of Miroslav Krleža and Ivo Andrić, to the government-sanctified writers who presided after World War II and until Tito's death—before which a predictable crew of a dozen authors were the only ones allowed to publish—to the postwar feminist writing of Slavenka Drakulić and Dasa Drndić, to the realistic and ironic work of Miljenko Jergović and Robert Perišić, Croatian writing in the last seventy-five years has taken quite a journey. And no wonder, as the country writhed through Serbian monarchy, totalitarian socialism, liberation and nationalism, free-market democracy (that is, the mafia), and EU and NATO coddling. Our writers have had a lot to keep up with.

After the war for independence in the 1990s, nearly a hundred new publishers emerged. Desktop publishing made things relatively swift and inexpensive, and hundreds of writers came out of the woodwork—many of them, of course, writing about the war, and about postwar trauma. It was a celebratory time, for some, as well as a kind of death for the old writers, with a fair amount of ageism to accompany it. Being young was a plus—it meant you had something new to say. Enough of the old stuff from the old stuffies, was the attitude. And now, nearly a generation later, we have a new batch of writers for whom even the postwar writing, with all its obsessions, is already a bit alien. The young have become the old young, and we have the new young to attend to now. I suppose it's a worldwide phenomenon, reflected in one small country.

Still: the remarkable thing in this issue's batch of writing by relatively young Croatian writers is that almost none of them address the recent wars. There's been a backlash against war writing as a kind of straitjacketing, or profiteering. The perception in Croatia, from what I have observed, is that such writing is the expected thing—especially for editors abroad, in Germany and Austria. And while Germany, at least, has taken a strong interest in writing from Croatia and other former Yugoslav countries,

English-speaking countries have been much slower to pay attention to the region. For that reason, many young Croatian writers take it as a challenge—to be somehow noticed and translated in England and the States. After all, if you grow up listening to Zappa and the Stones, to publish in English is a big trip.

So, the war. There's almost no mention of it in the writing here. The new Croatian writers avoid what they perceive to be the obvious shot. You want war from us? Guess what—you won't get it, and not only that, you won't get much love, either. Sex sells, but there's not much of it in these stories. Instead, in this batch, you'll find a lot of funky wit—strange encounters and absurdities, all related in highly personal styles. Five of the stories here are told in the first person, and even the one that isn't has a highly subjective, individualistic, interior slant. And while they can't be neatly reduced thematically, there are three stories here that deal primarily with childhood, and the loss of a mother; three others have to do with travel to far-flung places. (Norway and Brazil, in one; Canadian suburbia, in another; and little-explored Moldova, for a literary tour, in a third.) The emphasis on travel may reflect the fact that, because of relative poverty during the war and after it, international trips are still something of a novelty for the new generation.

No matter what, all six of these stories dig deeply into the fabric of current Croatian life, at home and abroad, and find alienation, chaos, ruthlessness, and absurdity beneath the surface. But there's a great emotional range here: Zoran Ferić depicts a boy who has to deal with delivering bribes to the doctors attending to his dying mother, mixing comic elements and huge sadness in a touchingly charming sequence of scenes. Gordan Nuhanović's metafictional story of that literary tour in Moldova starts out as an absurdist and cynical tale about publishing and translation, and ends up as a tribute to Pushkin. And Olja Savičević's narrative of anorexia becomes a beautifully written meditation on food and body image.

Formally, too, we have different approaches—from the essayistic trav-elogue style of our Moldova story, to Tea Tulić's brilliantly strung-together vignettes, to the dramatic evocations of Zoran Ferić. Overall, though, one suspects that autobiographical concerns strongly inform many of these pieces. In that you might see a kind of central European influence or mentality, as in writers like László Krasznahorkai and Thomas Bernhard. Rumination and introspection is part of the Croatian aesthetic, some-times to wonderful effect, and in cool contrast to the American school of minimalism, in which introspection was vilified and to be avoided at all costs—although, of course, there has been a backlash against minimalism in the States as well. I know I am contradicting myself—I have general-ized too much already.

Anyway, read, or don't, and form your own conclusions, or don't. There are, besides the writers featured here, dozens of other memorable voices in Croatia, and it's a shame not to have enough space to include them all—or, for that matter, to have enough space even in this introduction to mention every one of them. Besides the bohemian, essayistic work of Edo Popović and Miljenko Jergović and Robert Perišić (whose *Our Man in Iraq*, an antiwar parody, has recently been published in the States to much acclaim), there is Ivana Simić Bodrožić (who does write about the war, having been displaced from Vukovar as a child), and Marinko Koščec, and Roman Simić, and—well, and many others.

But for now, for a change, you can travel not to the Croatian islands (as the cool and hip travel sites lately advise you to do), but to six Croatian minds—which, after all, are not so insular as you might think.

AUTHENTIC MOLDOVA

by GORDAN NUHANOVIĆ

Translated by Celia Hawkesworth

Awriter from a small country naturally looks to the big nations: to France, England, Germany. He fantasizes about print runs in the millions, about pocket editions sold at airports. Meanwhile, the experienced agent shakes his head skeptically.

"We don't have a hope in France. With the best will in the world they can't remember who we are. If you say, I've got an interesting writer from Croatia, it sounds risky. It's like a guy coming to us from Africa and presenting himself as a writer from Mali. You'd start looking for the number of the police station straightaway."

"How do you mean?"

"Literature comes into being in familiar locations. Ours, stuck between so many borders, strikes them as too narrow even for children's fiction. And no one reads short stories anymore, as you know."

"Okay, so what are the chances in England?"

"Something could be done there, perhaps. I've got some contacts, but for the moment they respond to our proposals with polite rejections. At book fairs, their agents ask me whether we were ever anyone's colony, and how that's reflected in the second- and third-generation writers. They want to read about the consequences suffered by oppressed nations—you've heard of neocolonial literature?"

"And the Germans?"

"Listen, some things can't be changed overnight, but don't go immediately sinking into despair…"

"They're only interested in Kusturica as well, aren't they?"

"I'm telling you, it takes time to change these things."

"Well, fuck it. I can't and won't ever do a Kusturica."

"Hang on. That's not the end of it. There are Czech Republics, Polands, Slovakias… Let's have a think about Hungary. The average print run there is several thousand."

"Those new Russians have done pretty well in our country."

"As far as the Russians go, for the time being it's all one-way. We haven't managed to get their attention yet."

"They're investing quite a lot on the coast…"

"Don't mix up the hotel business with literature."

"Ukraine? That's a big market."

"Big, but disorganized. A lot of the addresses I have there don't work anymore."

"Where else is there? Spain, Portugal—why wouldn't we go in that direction, and through them into Latin America?"

"In principle—yes. But we're still an unknown quantity there—that's why everything is going so timidly. I've sent them a preliminary list. You're on it, obviously."

"What's the situation in Italy? They must be interested in what their neighbors are writing."

"I've had some inquiries, but life's not a bed of roses there either. Several big houses have declared bankruptcy, and now they're only going for sure bets."

"Maybe we should turn to the small, independent states?"

"Look, what I can offer you at the moment is Bulgaria. Don't make a face—we're the West to them. The Serbs traditionally do well there, for instance. They want us as well, on the condition that they're not mentioned in a bad light. I hope you don't have any clueless Bulgarians in your novel?"

"No."

"We're talking about around a dozen million potential readers."

"I don't know... What about the narrower region?"

"The Serbs? Forget the others for the time being."

"Even the Slovenes?"

"Only if we're supported by foundations and endowments. No one relies on the market there anymore."

"Wait—I haven't even asked you about America."

"I'm *glad* you asked me about America. I'll tell you what I always tell your colleagues when they ask me about America: so..."

In the Republic of Moldova I'm presented as a respected writer from Croatia. This first happened at an impromptu afternoon tea party in the elite district of Kishinev. Although my host Branko and I had originally set out to visit the medieval monastery of Old Orhei, a telephone invitation from the lawyer Kornel Iluminescu changed our plans. We were now on a hill above the city, where mansions were crammed together side by side. We didn't see any guards, maybe because the streets were so narrow that they could be defended by one well-armed plutocrat.

Branko, who had, at that point, sold the largest number of diapers ever retailed in the history of the young Moldovan republic, spoke about Kornel as a big shot whose name opened many ministerial doors. When Branko had arrived several years previously, he had been offered Kornel's services immediately. He's costly, but exceptionally effective, Branko said.

Kornel couldn't have been more than thirty-five: short, swarthy, volatile. He greeted us in his luxurious living room. A very young girl was sitting with a poodle in her arms in front of a vast plasma screen. She was watching a National Geographic documentary about a black tribe in the rainforest. Kornel introduced her as Natalija. Then he led us on a tour of the house, which was crammed with works of art and hunting rifles. Kornel was a fox hunter.

"It's good for business," he said, which I didn't doubt for a moment.

Poor Kishinev. From the upper terrace it looked like a rag, half buried in clay. Kornel, however, seemed moved by the sight of the city of his birth. He decided that we must quickly have something to drink. And so I clinked glasses with the big shot. When he admitted that he was still drinking beer to sober up from the previous night's binge, Branko shot me his first anxious glance of the day.

Kornel asked what I was doing in his wonderful country. I told him the truth: I was shooting a ten-minute documentary about the cultural and social life of Kishinev.

"He's a writer," Branko announced somewhat solemnly.

"Of history?"

"Not quite…"

"What exactly are you writing about?"

It was easy to spin that, even in bad English.

"Love and midlife crises. Lots of emotional relationships, scattered around the city."

"Interesting," replied Kornel. "Why not publish something here in our country? Have you considered that? My friend has a large shop in the middle of town. I think he even sells books."

"You could be the first writer from Croatia published in Moldova," Branko pointed out quietly.

"In Romanian?"

"Romanian, indeed!" Kornel snarled at me. "No, in our language: Moldovan! Or perhaps that's beneath you?"

"Oh no, good heavens, not at all. That would be excellent." I hurried to express my enthusiasm before he changed his mind.

Kornel then dedicated himself to conversations on his cell phone. It seemed as though he had decided to fix all the details of the publication that very afternoon. Who would have thought that things could happen like this? I tried to conceal my excitement. Moldova was, admittedly, the poorest country in Europe, but it would be a way of getting into Romania—and then the publishing route stretched in an arc toward France, along the well-trodden path of love and understanding between our two Romance peoples.

The lawyer paced around the room, talking for a long, long time in his native language. The short winter afternoon was nearing its end when Kornel finally wound up his conversations.

"Okay, it's all sorted. We'll pick up the guys from the conservatory by the Academy," he announced. Branko coughed modestly.

"What guys?" he asked in Russian.

"Weren't you headed for Old Orhei?"

"Yes," we replied in unison.

"Well, when you're done there, you'll be the guests of my old friend in the forester's lodge. I want you to experience the real, authentic Moldova."

* * *

Kornel and the girl with the poodle set off immediately in his striking off-road vehicle. Branko and I followed them. At an intersection, four students from the state conservatory really were waiting for us with their instruments. Kornel sent one of them, a clean-shaven violinist, to our car, as our guide.

"Have you been to Orhei before?" I asked him.

"As a kid," he replied.

"And you know how to get there?"

"Yes."

"Can you make a living from music in Kishinev?"

"No."

"It must be very beautiful here in the spring and summer, when the parks turn green."

"Yes."

At first I attributed his curt answers to his poor knowledge of English, but nothing could be got out of the boy in Russian, either, so I concluded the following: he was born when the Russification of the country was waning, and grew up in the atmosphere of the war for Pridnestrovie or Transnistria, so that in his nationally conscious school he learned only Romanian—or, pardon, Moldovan.

The darkness was already deepening when we started on the bad road toward Old Orhei, Moldova's medieval capital. We couldn't reach the monastery by car, so we set off on foot up a small hill, beneath which lay several villages with no lights. The whole region gave the impression of being pledged to the distant past. Not a trace of investment, just earth and the lowing of livestock on the move. We went through a wooden door into the rock, walking through what appeared to be catacombs. Real torches along the walls lit our way.

Our passage through the hill soon brought us out into a small underground church. The ambiance reminded one of places of worship from the time of the persecution of the first Christians; the priest, with his long gray beard, looked like a contemporary of Methuselah's. Nevertheless, he was energetically waving a censer over a basket of food that some of the villagers had brought. The torches, the aroma of incense, the priest in his robes, these mysterious trenches under the earth—I was reeling from so many impressions when Branko signaled that it was time to move on. Outside, beneath the Central Moldovan mountains, it was now completely dark. Instead of the livestock from the valley, all that could be heard was a high-pitched barking, as though a dog had swallowed a piece of chalk.

The violinist's instructions took us to the main road. The heavy Bessarabian rains that had fallen recently had more or less ruined it, and the car had serious trouble rounding the bends. I presumed that the otherwise sharp Branko, at the wheel, must have been temporarily befuddled by the poetry of Old Orhei. The Moldovan villages with no electric light fit perfectly into the whole atmosphere. People emerged out of the dark, in front of our headlights. Festively dressed young men and women stood at the dark village intersections.

It was a chilly Saturday night in the week before Christmas. We crossed the empty road toward Tiraspol and Odessa and entered a wooded area. The reserved violinist pointed out a small light on the opposite bank— but between us and the forester's lodge there was a river. The violinist couldn't remember if there was a bridge. Perhaps it had been swept away by the torrent, he said. He proposed turning round and going back to Kishinev, but Branko didn't want to do that without letting Kornel know. Who knew when he would be in need of his contacts in the government again? His diaper business was not going to last forever.

At that moment we caught sight of Kornel's jeep on the far bank, setting off toward the river. He went down to the shore in the vehicle and then disappeared into the darkness of the water. For some minutes nothing could be seen but the shapes of moving water, and then two beams of light emerged from the river directly in front of us. In a state of shock, the three of us climbed into the jeep, now glistening in the moonlight.

Kornel was in the grips of an adrenaline rush. His short legs barely reached the pedals. He looked like a little boy with an enormous toy in his hands. He turned around, shouted "Let's go, Moldova!" and steered us into the river.

I watched the level of the water rising up the windscreen as we sank deeper and deeper. When we were half submerged, we had yet to reach what seemed to be the deepest point in the riverbed. We all listened tensely to the wheels struggling against the mud. The windows were under the water now, and the jeep was all but floating.

What a writer from Croatia had to endure in order to be published abroad, I thought bitterly, while the opaque mass of water swirled around us.

I was interested to know what was going on in Branko's mind at that moment. Perhaps he was cursing all those diapers he had intended to sell before the country opened its doors to Müller and Happy Baby? Or else, like me, he was trying to remember how people in films open doors under water, and wondering whether he should perhaps break the window with his elbow. Was that even possible in an armored vehicle? At last the jeep's wheels connected with something firm beneath them. Gravel. It seemed that Kornel had, after all, found an underwater corridor. He stepped on the gas and we all felt the magnificent power of the jeep gaining traction. It just needed a little solid material under it to bound toward the opposite shore. Soon we were poking out of the river, our headlights lighting up the tops of the trees.

Two tracks in the mud led to the forester's modest lodge. A little ways ahead, before the lodge, a Lada Niva was stuck in the mud. There was virtually no empty space around the house; it was pressed in on all sides by forest, bushes, and the all-pervasive mud. A thin old fellow in a greenish uniform was waiting for us on the porch. He and Kornel immediately launched into a conversation about the drive. It seemed that the forester was explaining where he had gone wrong and where he hadn't. Branko and I sneaked into a small room inside.

The musicians were there, each with his instrument in his arms. They had stretched out over a big, antique bed frame beside a bread oven. Pale Natalija, the young woman from Kornel's mansion, was stroking her little poodle and saying nothing. When Kornel entered, the boys leapt to their feet and started with neutral pieces, to warm up. Violin, cello, bass, and harmonica. Meanwhile the forester brought out what was, presumably, everything he had in his fridge: preserved cucumbers, preserved carrots, preserved watermelon. Kornel explained that these were authentic Moldovan specialties, which, unfortunately, it was no longer possible to find in town. We were also given some cold chicken—the remains of an authentic forester's lunch. And then the wine arrived as well.

Kornel pointed out that this was an above-average wine, made from forest berries, and that we should be careful with it. As he spoke, he drained his whole glass. The obliging forester replenished his sponsor's glass conscientiously, like a page. Perhaps all the foresters' lodges in the country survived on sponsorship, I thought, waiting to be affected by the wine so that I could abandon myself to Kornel's bragging.

It didn't work. Each mouthful filled me with a bitter unease. I had the impression that we had too easily deprived ourselves of a way back to Kishinev. We would have to face returning by the same underwater route. What would that look like, with a drunken Kornel? The question gave me serious concern. In the meantime, I had to sit in this pseudo-lodge, eating preserved watermelon, and admire an aspiring dandy whose behavior was growing worse and worse.

And it had all begun with Steven Seagal. Kornel had been personally responsible for Seagal's stay in Moldova, apparently, which had inflamed a great deal of false hope in the people. Seagal had promised to raise funds for a Moldovan Hollywood, Branko explained, while Kornel lambasted the famous actor.

"I've got his number, but he never picks up."

"He probably changed it long ago."

"He made me look an idiot."

"It's got nothing to do with you," Branko soothed him.

"Of course it does. I had the president receive him as a friend of our country, at his summer place! I laid my reputation on the line!"

"And what came of it?" I asked Branko quietly.

"He ate and drank here for a week, made all sorts of promises in the media, and then was never heard from again. That's why Kornel thinks that he's damaged his standing."

Kornel was shouting at the musicians, who were trying desperately to find a song that suited him. They were young men, and they played with their eyes wide open, under stress.

It soon emerged, however, that the problem was not with the music, not even so much with Steven Seagal: the problem was me. I realized this when Kornel, on his fourth glass of wine, asked me who I worked for. I talked lengthily about my interest in the culture and history of this poor, but proud—I stressed—country, and in the phenomena common to all countries in the wider region. It seemed to me important to be diplomatic. It would be catastrophic to touch on the poverty that was everywhere in Kishinev, although my skirting round it was also risky, because a fox like Kornel knew perfectly well that I wanted to mention it, but was deliberately avoiding doing so because I was surrounded by woods and a river, some fifty kilometers from town, at the mercy of him and his foresters.

"You know nothing about my country," he interrupted me.

The others in the room seemed stunned by this change in Kornel's tone. They bowed their heads a little lower.

"He doesn't know much, it's true, but he arrived only two days ago—give him time to learn," Branko leapt in. But Kornel shook his head. His eyes had sunk back into his dark face. They glinted from there like two little icebergs.

"You haven't answered my question," he said.

"I told you—he's a journalist."

"He even reminds me of someone—does this guy look like someone?" he asked the forester, who was measuring me up and down disagreeably.

"Sure, he looks like someone," the man confirmed.

"Only who? Hmm."

I tried not to look directly at Kornel and his private forester, but it was all so cramped that it was difficult for our eyes not to meet.

"Branko, I'm very sorry to have to tell you this, but there's no place for your friend at this table," Kornel concluded.

"Kornel, please, he's..."

"He's an immoral man who has come to spread lies about my country."

"Kornel..."

The musicians, genuine virtuosos, responded to all these slanders with more lively traditional music. Now and then I became momentarily aware of the ease with which they played, despite the fact that Kornel was talking about how many Moldovan parliamentarians had met their end in the forests around us. Eventually even Branko realized that things had taken a turn for the worse.

At a certain moment the two of us found ourselves on the porch, where some silent types with coarse features were now milling around. I was certain that they had come as reinforcements. Maybe they really did plan to do us in and leave us to rot in the forest. We went out onto the muddy road to consult.

"I didn't realize he was mad," Branko apologized.

I suggested that we should try to reach some kind of bridge. We'd walk along the river until we found one. At that moment my cell phone rang.

"Yes?"

"Look, there's a chance of a spot at San Vigilio in Italy. Eight runs, two black, three red, four-star apartment with sauna—it's not far from Madonna di Campiglio either, if anyone wants…"

The voice of a friend from Croatia sounded bizarre.

"Look, Pape, I can't talk now," I said.

"I'm not hearing you, where are you?"

"Abroad."

"Sorry?"

"In Moldova."

"Don't fuck with me. Come to the Apple tomorrow for a drink—we've got to sort out this skiing thing this week."

"I'll get back to you."

I used the phone as a light and stepped decisively into the darkness. It seemed to me that there must be something nearby connecting the two banks, despite the poverty of the place. Branko shared my thinking. From the lodge we were accompanied by a wistful violin solo, but after just a few steps we sank up to our ankles in mud. Water filled our shoes. Branko's car on the other bank was bathed in moonlight, glimmering like an inaccessible beauty. With every step my idea sank ever deeper into the clay.

The worst thing was that there would be no one who could tell our loved ones back home what had happened to us, I thought as we climbed pitifully back onto the porch. A crowd had formed there while we'd been away. All the musicians were standing around, smoking. The forester was there too, smiling a little foolishly.

In the dining room an unexpected scene awaited us. The girl with the poodle was now addressing Kornel very energetically over the remains of dinner on the table. It was clear why the whole company had gone outside. We didn't understand what she was saying, but it was obvious that she was the only one allowed to speak such sharp and reproachful words to him. Kornel looked like a little boy who knew that he was getting his just deserts. He was staring dully at the preserved watermelon, deprived even of a drink in his glass.

When she finished, Natalija stretched out her hand toward the little poodle, which jumped obediently into her lap. Kornel spent the rest of the evening in offended silence. The only time he seemed reanimated was when he, with us in tow, got behind the wheel of his jeep and charged at full speed out of the mud, straight at the barbed-wire fence behind the house. The wheels dragged part of the fence away as he tried to extract himself, pulling several concrete posts out of the ground. We all had to get out of the car while the forester snipped the wire caught beneath the car bit by bit with wire cutters. It was a lengthy, difficult job.

It was growing light when we finally plunged into the river. There, under the water, Branko apologized again for everything that, fortunately, had not happened. But I was thinking only of the skeletons of the Moldo-van parliamentarians rotting somewhere in that barely accessible forest, above that house of terror.

On the following morning, still in the sunniest Soviet republic, as they used to call it, I waited in vain for the sun. It didn't appear. I roamed around the main square, where I was supposed to be picked up by a local film crew. The traffic on the main thoroughfare was dense; from time to time the monument to King Stefan the Great would appear behind the trucks and streetcars. The longer I looked at it, the more I began to feel that something was missing. Then I realized what it was: a horse, you idiot. The king was standing on his pedestal without a horse. Throughout the entire world, kings (and governors) wave their sabers belligerently from horses of supreme breeding—but this historical luminary was on foot. Perhaps, I reflected, this should be the starting point for my story of Europe's poorest country—its pedestrian-king hidden behind a truck stopped at a traffic light. In that case, one would also have to say something about the structure some hundred meters farther on, probably the most modest triumphal arch in the world. It would be hard for any horseman in a dignified posture to ride through that baby-arch. But there was too much symbolism there for one who had driven underwater through a river the previous night, and then endured several hours of fear. Although what I chiefly remembered was the preserved watermelon. My body shook at the thought of it.

I knew that I needed to forget the lawyer from hell as quickly as possible and focus on my job as a journalist. There were a multitude of meetings in store for me that cloudy morning. Admittedly it was Branko who had reminded me of most of them. He had even succeeded in reaching the minister of culture, for whom I did not have a single question. Branko had set it all up while I was sleeping. The people, the time and place of the meetings—and then, like a proper manager, he had confirmed it all once again. Over the telephone he had sounded so hale and cheerful that I didn't have the heart to tell him that none of it would be included in my piece.

That was the worst thing about this job, besides the near-drownings: you went around, you asked questions, you nodded, you raised your eyebrows, you endeavored to be enthusiastic about what you were being told, and all along you knew that you would be using just one or two minutes of the whole hullabaloo you'd created. Tasting the famous Moldovan wine, visiting the national museum, conversing with the director of a theater— that was all nice, but more or less pointless. Soon we would shoot pictures of the bookshops, the streets, the pavement flea markets, the stray urban dogs, things that I knew in advance I wouldn't need. Then we would visit the pride of the city of Kishinev: the railway station, "the last stop in the Balkans," as the Moldovans called it. After that came Eastern Europe and the Caucasus, which many people here shrank from, much as Croats shrank from the Balkans. The Moldovans wanted to be treated like the outer wall of the region. In keeping with this, all the entrances of the station were guarded. The building looked like a marble monument on a poor grave. Only travelers with tickets were allowed onto the platforms, and then only just before embarking. When a foreigner comes to Kishinev by train and emerges from the circle of the station, he may experience a considerable shock. After we had passed through all the security and emerged onto the platforms, I stood in front of the camera and said: "If this is what the last stop in the Balkans looks like, then the Balkans have a bright future before them!"

After my meetings, I took the cameraman and driver for an American cappuccino to think about what to do next. Toward the end of the day I finally realized that what I needed was a writer. I turned for help once again to Branko, the one officially registered Croatian in Moldova. I will never be able to repay him for everything that he did during those days. He contacted me within the hour. He didn't have particularly good news. He told me that both his secretaries were trying to find me a Moldovan writer, that they had dialed several dozen numbers, but despite their best efforts, they had gotten nowhere. Even Branko sounded despondent as he explained where things stood. One writer was currently on a scholarship in Luxembourg, another had been killed the year before in a traffic accident. A shame.

Nevertheless, we already had seven hours of recorded material. Branko joined us as night was beginning to fall. Although I was heartily sick of it all, he insisted that we visit the Pushkin Museum, where the director had been waiting eagerly for us since the early afternoon.

* * *

In 1820, the Tsar sent Russia's best-loved poet, Alexander Pushkin, to
the south of the country, to the then barely accessible Bessarabian prov-
ince. It was the court's response to Pushkin's sympathies for the rebellious
Decembrists. Pushkin was accompanied by quite a substantial library,
something of which has remained at the memorial house in Kishinev.
Unlike Ovid, Pushkin had not sent whining requests to his monarch, but
instead accepted his exile as a spell of leave in the country. In the course of
his four years in Kishinev he wrote several works, including *The Prisoner
of the Caucasus*, and also got the idea and inspiration for *Eugene Onegin*. His
study still looks today as though the poet has just stepped out: the pen
steeping in the inkwell, a small samovar, a cup, his yellowing books, and
his notes. When the museum director, a Russian woman, began to talk
in her native language about Pushkin, it seemed to me that I would not
be able to bear the onrush of passion. It was quite a torrent, and here and
there took on lyric qualities. Branko managed to translate every fifth or
sixth word. At one point I stopped paying attention to his mumblings;
I didn't need a translation, just the music of that Russian speech. I realized
how risky it would be to ask any questions. We would not have left the
museum until morning.

After two good hours, with Branko and I both spent, the director sat
down at the piano beside the poet's bust and treated us to a dessert of
several compositions. Just as she had talked with full lungs about Pushkin and Russian culture, so she launched passionately into renderings of
"Moscow Evenings," "Rabinushka," "Ochi Chorniye," and, as a gesture
to the cameraman, a Moldovan, "Smuglyanka Moldavanka." It was the
depths of night outside, and the museum's working hours were long over.

As I listened to her, I thought of all those Russians I had come across
in the Baltic countries, in Asia Minor and in the Caucasus. They were,
for the most part, people of advanced years who had been sent to the
highest peaks that could be occupied: Alma Ata, Tbilisi, Baku, Bishkek,

Kishinev. An Englishman in India doesn't look as uprooted as, say, a Russian in Kazakhstan. If you ask him for directions, he will very likely give you the street names from Soviet days. That's also their whole commentary on the situation in which they've found themselves.

The lady director of the Pushkin Museum was one of that colonial breed in which a spark of the old order still smolders. After talking for two hours, her face was almost serene. She thanked us lengthily for the time we had devoted to Pushkin. As we left, the cameraman made an ironic comment about her; it seemed to me that he was expressing doubt in her reason. I, meanwhile, thought how fitting it would be if, in another life, she could come back as Pushkin's inkwell.

HAIR

by **TEA TULIĆ**

Translated by Ellen Elias-Bursać

MOM

On the day Grandma didn't die, Mom had a strange headache. Her eye began wandering to the left. My brother took her to the emergency room. He came back without her. Mom is a strong person with fine bones. She had been in the hospital twice before. Once she peed out a stone, the other time, a stray child.

On the day Grandma didn't die, I was shopping. Books, balms, bubble bath. In my hair I wore week-old damp. I passed through the square where a handsome boy died just the other day. They say he was an athlete. A good student. Not combative. He had been beaten to death.

I wondered what foreigners make of our word for death. *Smrt*.

GRANDMA

Grandma says I should pull out the green cash box where she stored some banknotes. We need to see whether they are still legal tender. We are particularly anxious about the high denominations.

Meanwhile, Grandma needs to be changed into dry clothes. My sister peels off her three pairs of tights while I hold her. The banknotes are current. Grandma is dry now.

We finger the little box. It has three gold chains with pendants in it, as well. One is for Mom, the second for my sister, the third for me. Grandma intended for me to have the one made with links. It is yellow, like her urine in the plastic bucket.

Our brother won't get anything. He is a man.

GROUP PORTRAITS

There is a picture. In it are Grandpa, Grandma, Mom, and her sisters. Mom is in a gray-black, thick cotton dress, and she has blue highlights in her hair. Grandpa is sitting in the middle, with his hands on his thighs.

There is a second picture. Mom and her sisters again. This time with their husbands. My aunts are rosy-faced and wearing blouses with pads sewn into the shoulders. The husbands wear colorful sweaters.

A third picture. With us. The grandchildren. Our faces are serious, our hair almost combed.

We sent all three pictures to our uncle who lives in Canada, in a house with a pool. While we were getting ready to have the pictures taken, someone said to Mom:

—Don't use so much makeup, Uncle will think we're well off, and he won't send us any money!

I believed that if we looked beautiful enough, our uncle would frame us, put us on the mantel, and think of us often.

GHOSTS

At night, ghosts keep Grandma awake. They trip over her bed, pad across the parquet floor, and knock over things that aren't there. I go to her room and take away the framed photos of those who have died. She has a bunch of plastic flowers in a vase. I ask her where she got them.

—I bought it at the open market, I swear! she shouts from the armchair.

—Fine, I say. —Just remember that you're the one who's not letting them rest in peace. Not the other way around.

I go off and leave her praying to her rosary. The plastic one. I haven't seen the pearl one for a long time.

THE NURSES (DON'T KNOW)

No one knows why Mom is in the hospital. That is why we run up and down the stairs. The nurses are all upstairs. They have ergonomic clogs and mascara on their eyes. They have no information. They also have no plastic cups.

—A doctor went down just now, they say.

No one runs up and down the stairs except us. The coffee machine is below. The smell of soup is also below. Below there are no doctors. There haven't been doctors here for days.

Grandma threw up last night. It would have been better if she hadn't. But she did, so I had to throw up too.

A SHORT CONVERSATION ABOUT OUR GOD

Once, I came home and told Mom and Dad that I was impure. That I could not die unbaptized and that this needed to be changed right away. Grandma said she would have baptized me long ago if she'd been asked. Then we all got dressed up and went to church.

Mom dressed me in a white blouse. Dad was silent through the "Our Father," and everything was over in fifteen minutes. After that, immortal and safe, I played the organ, delivered sermons to the pews, cleaned the altar, read the many-colored book, and chimed the bell at noon. In thin sneakers, betrothed to God, I asked the priest:

—How can God send my father to hell when he loves me?

He said nothing. After a while they moved him to another church, me to another school, and God to a phone line.

DREAMS

They say that when you dream of a snake, it's not a good sign. It means you have a friend who is not your friend. That his true face is hideous.

When you wake up, take a good look around. Look out for he who eats from your hands. The demon you caress. Whether you find him or not, beware. He is someone you know.

There are other things Grandma and Mom really don't like dreaming about, aside from snakes. When one of them dreams that her teeth are falling out, the other always says:

—Someone will die in the next few days.

Then, usually, an acquaintance of ours—or somebody else's—dies.

NUDITY

Once, we could fit in the same tub, Mom and I. We'd bathe together. I would put foam on my nose and she'd laugh. We'd sit facing each other. I remember our bony knees. How they resembled cliffs. Then Mom began to put my brother into the tub with me. His finger got stuck in the drain. He screamed until he was blue. Eventually Mom decided the time had come for us to bathe separately.

At the beach, Mom swam half naked. I said to her:

—Why can't you be like the other moms, and swim with your boobies covered?

—Well, why do you have to be like the other little girls and wear patent leather shoes? she said.

In first grade she had my hair cut like a hedgehog and said:

—You are my little punk girl.

Dad says we will collect all the hair that falls from Mom's head and make her a wig out of it. And maybe we'll shave our cat for the wig as well. Cats don't care about nudity.

AUSTRIAN PHARMACY

I call a doctor in Austria. He is from here, but he works abroad. He writes on the internet that he heals everything. He has compounds that are made from plants that grow at unheard-of altitudes. In the pure air. People are satisfied with his products. They write to him to tell him how well they are walking, pissing, sleeping, eating, drinking, ever since they started ingesting his pure plants.

It is a family pharmacy, very old, he says. He speaks a little bit of Italian. I tell him that Mom is in a lot of pain. That the doctors don't believe she'll survive. That we are in a hurry. I ask how much his plants cost. He says three thousand. I ask whether they really work. He gets angry. Very, very angry. He says that I am rude and he is going to hang up.

—Please don't! What did I do?

—You insulted me, young lady.

I plead with him to let me order the medicine.

—You'll get it in two days.

I hang up and am ashamed of my tears.

HAIR IN THE DRAIN

When Mom unscrewed the bathtub drain and pulled out a ball of hair, she said to me:

—See, this is all your hair! I'm going to cut your hair short.

In her wet hand she held my long, brown strands. Once they had been loved, but now they were loathed.

—It's as if we have a dog in the house!

Once we did have a dog in the house. I found it in front of the school and brought it home while Mom and Dad were at work. It ate all the minestrone and all the bread. It was big and hungry, like Dad was later that evening. So it had to go.

WASHING HAIR

I want her to let me help her wash her hair. She has given me everything. The last ten kunas from her wallet. A massage, during *those* days. A little bra. A sweet potato with drumsticks. Cigarettes. A note for school saying I had a fever of ninety-nine degrees. Apricot juice with whipped cream. A black eyeliner pencil. The Netherlands. Chamomile tea. A hairdresser. A dress with Mickey Mouse on it. Instead I ask her:

—Why are you so edgy?

She called me to help her wash her hair, but she doesn't even let me shampoo it. I stand over her and watch her posthumous back. She still does everything herself. What she wants is a witness.

Let me help you wash your hair. Rinse your teacup. Don't smoke. You are my child now.

SISTER

A doughnut. She was so small when Mom squeezed her out. That is why they laid her out in a container for little doughnuts. To rise like bread in the warmth until she was ready for our tasting. For our kisses and cuddles. So little then, and now so ready to say:

—Guys are yuck!

I was fifteen and had five coins for my midmorning snack in my pocket when they let me look at her from far away, through the hospital window. I am too old to take a bath with her, I thought. And she stuck her finger in her ear, softly, not crying.

A HOME FOR HANGING

When I was born, Dad broke the ceiling lamp. By swinging on it. After-ward Grandma used to say:

—Men, when they are overjoyed, are not normal.

She'd say: —Men!

Once we heard a story of a lady living in a five-story building who had hanged herself on a coat rack. That's how tiny she was. That's how sick of everything she was. Like an old hooded jacket, hanging in her cookie-cutter apartment. Grandma said:

—Women never hang themselves for no reason.

In Mom's hospital room there are no hooks on the wall, so we often sit on her bed in our jackets and coats.

THE GREAT HEALER

The Great Healer arrives in the capital from the Middle East. He is quite large. His face is covered with little black spots. He has a wide-angle grin. He has bodyguards. Politicians, athletes, artists visit him. They say he heals everything, even souls. He has healed hundreds of thousands of people, apparently. Though the newspapers exaggerate.

Everyone from the smaller cities goes to him. Everyone except beggars on crutches. And us.

ROOMS FOR CRABS

Summers on the island were fragrant, sonorous, and salty. I would wake up in the morning, put on slippers, and race down the long street. I'd toss my towel down by the water's edge and jump butt-first into the shallow sea. That was when I was there alone with my aunt. When Mom came, I spent my time with her at the beach. She would sunbathe her little breasts, and in the shallows, I would build a home of sand and pebbles for the dozens of crabs in snail shells. Unlike the cancer crabs at the hospital, each crab on the beach had its own room. But neither kind of crab would ever leave their little houses, once they were in them.

HAIR EVERYWHERE

Hair everywhere. On the pillow. On the floor. In her hand and my hand. We talk about colorful Indian head scarves. About thick soup. Bad weather. Discipline. We talk about dry skin. We talk about everything, but we grieve for the hair that has fallen out. It's a symbol of the predatory creature in her head. The skin spills off her, too. When she changes her undershirt, tiny flakes waft through the air.

BIRDS FROM HELL

We find Grandma in the corner of the kitchen. Her plastic rosary around her neck. She says:

—Hell has opened! There are things in the room falling all over the floor, rolling! These flowers are not from the cemetery, I swear!

My sister and I go into the room. Two doves, short on breath, sit on the top of the wardrobe. We chase them away, but they slam into the walls. We call the tall neighbor who gives us dried cod at Christmas for help. He comes in and turns off all the lights. He turns off the television set. He grabs first one bird, then the other, and releases them out the window. Later, Grandma sleeps with the rosary around her neck. She places a three-dimensional picture of Jesus on her breast.

NICE THINGS

The book says nicely, THINK OF NICE THINGS. So I think of nice things. I buy a nice dress, love myself in it, take it off, lie down in bed, and chide myself for buying something in these screwed-up times. Then I think of nothing, and when I leave the house, nothing becomes everything. And everything bends me double. The book says that when we say No, we actually get Yes. Like when a boy rapes a girl. That is what the Universe ordained, it says.

BAREFOOT

They say that when people jump from windows and balconies, they first take off their socks, shoes, sneakers, slippers. They jump barefoot. With their ingrown toenails, corns, calluses. They go to their barefoot ancestors. Some leave behind platform clogs, some patent leather shoes.

Bare feet are free. They draw letters in the sand. They go for a scoop of vanilla in a cone. They walk along sea-urchin paths. They crush the crabs in their houses. But from these rooms one leaves in socks.

There is no fall. No thump.

IT'S ME

by **DAMIR KARAKAŠ**

Translated by Stephen M. Dickey

I

Philip was standing by the window in white long johns. From time to time he sighed through his nose, blew on the glass to melt a misty layer off the window, and then looked through that little hole, as if through someone else's eyes, at the row of tall willow trees covered with so much snow that their limbs sagged under the weight. What Philip liked, almost obsessively, was the moment—he once called it the moment of true feeling—when the willows, with almost stylized movements, cast off that weight, shaking off the snow, and the branches slowly sprang back up, releasing themselves, as if growing again.

As he watched that scene of liberation, everything seemed to Philip to separate from what it had just been connected to.

* * *

"Please, honey, fix that cotton on the Christmas tree," Philip's wife said in a tender voice. "You might pay a little more attention."

Philip turned around slowly; she was mixing dough, rolling it out, sprinkling flour onto it. Her arms were covered in flour up to her elbows.

Philip went slowly up to the Christmas tree in the corner of the room, where the afternoon shadows were thickening: he looked at it. Then he spread out the fluffed cotton on its edges, which was supposed to imitate snow.

Philip's wife stopped kneading the dough for a moment, looked straight at the tree, tilted her head, and then moved back, trying to find the right angle.

"Good, now it's much better," she said.

Shortly afterward she stopped what she was doing again.

"Did I hear something?" she asked.

Then she said: "Please, go take a look."

Philip got up and went to the little room whose door was painted blue, with little golden stars scattered over it: inside, two children were sleeping next to one another. They had pacifiers in their mouths and their little noses twitched like rabbits' snouts. Philip covered them a little better with the blanket, went up to the window of the room, and continued looking into the white, at the cars that passed at regular intervals.

A truck came down the street with its turn signal on, as if it were winking. Philip thought that someone was mocking him. He returned to the living room, went up to the window again, and stared, motionless, at the willows.

The two of them had come here to Canada, to this city that some still call "the Chicago of the north," when the war had started in their country. His wife's older sister had already been living here. They'd been here for a long time, now, snow- and icebound.

His wife had been trained as an elementary school teacher. Now she worked as a cleaning lady in the neighboring houses. He had an electrical engineering degree but worked in a bus factory, screwing in screws. He focused on the last twist of each screw. His boss, a wire-haired Dane, constantly repeated the same thing: "Concentrate on the last twist! Concentrate on the last twist!"

Philip, not wanting to think about anything, would just nod.

The house that they'd rented with the help of his sister-in-law was a simple, one-story house. His wife dreamed of having her own house or apartment, someday. Philip just nodded. Even before she would finish what she was saying, he nodded.

All he'd cared about was avoiding conscription, but now he regretted it. Leaving. He would have rather been in a war than here.

A child was crying in the little room. His wife said: "Please, Philip, go take a look."

He went back to the room. The pacifier had fallen out of one child's mouth, and then its crying had woken up the other child, whose pacifier had been lost as well. He restored the pacifiers to their places and waited a little for the children to fall back asleep.

"You know what occurred to me?" his wife asked when he sauntered back out. He sat down on the couch to leaf through some newspaper advertisements and nodded to signal that he was listening.

"Did you know that the Indians here can get free credit?" she asked, kneading the cakes, putting all of herself into those movements. "And you have that Indian friend." She stopped, looked at him, and blew a lock of hair from her brow. "He could say you're an Indian, and we could get free credit, too. I asked around—actually my sister asked around. It's a great idea, isn't it?"

He looked at her, and then looked away, at some point beyond the wall. His wife spread out the dough as far as the ends of the table, then sprinkled flour on it in wide motions, as if she were sowing a field.

"I know it's immoral," she said, "but think of our children a little. We can't let a chance like that slip by."

He still didn't say anything. He was thinking about that Indian, George Welcome; what a strange surname, he'd said to himself when he'd met him. He'd thought that the man was joking about it, at first, but George was always dead serious. He always had his arms folded over his chest. Once Philip had even seen him walking like that.

"Philip...?"

He lifted his gaze to her and sat up on the couch.

"My sister is coming in half an hour. She'll explain everything to you. And I forgot to tell you, she and her husband are inviting us to a New Year's Eve party. That's nice, right?" she said, removing her apron and throwing it carelessly over the nearest chair.

"It's at some fancy hotel," she added.

They heard a car outside. Its muffled sound was drawing nearer. He stood up and slid his feet more firmly into his slippers.

"Please, just go change out of that underwear," his wife said from the door.

He went to the closet, pulled a pair of jeans over his long johns, sat down in an armchair, and played with the slippers on his feet.

"Philip...?" his wife said. She sat down on the couch and stretched out her legs. "You know what I think? You should start thinking about taking some vacation and going to your brother's place when the weather gets a little better there, so you can get that house of yours sorted out. Enough time has passed, and we need every dinar we can get. It's time to divide up the property. And then we'll figure out about that free credit. I'll take a look at plane tickets tomorrow."

2

When the plane landed, he took a taxi to the bus station.

He bought a ticket for the bus to Brinje. He was lucky; he would catch the only one leaving that day.

The bus was old, with paint peeling off its sides. It was almost empty, but it moved so slowly that it seemed weighted down, or as if it were dragging the road along with it. Philip sat up front near the driver, who wore a cap and drove with one hand while he switched radio stations with the other.

After two hours of driving they arrived at Brinje. There was no one on the main street except a man hauling sacks of cement on a wooden wheelbarrow, weaving back and forth. In the middle of the town, up on a hillock, stood the ruins of a medieval castle. Wooden scaffolding had been erected all around it. It occurred to Philip that he'd never actually seen that castle without the scaffolding.

Philip turned off the main road, onto a side road that went up toward gray, jagged mountains, their peaks piercing the sky. He walked with his rucksack on his back, looking at the straggling villages. He breathed in the air and recognized the smells of his childhood. Around him people were dressed in a mixture of civilian and camouflage clothing. The houses cast elongated shadows across the road.

In the yard of an old farmhouse he saw a Gypsy who'd knocked a sorrel horse down onto its side. The Gypsy was sitting on the horse's head and smoking nonchalantly. A different, older Gypsy was picking at the hoof of the horse with the tip of a knife blade. Philip could hear female voices inside the farmhouse, and the crying of a small baby. Both men greeted him with a nod. He nodded back. He knew most of the Gypsies here; he'd gone to school with many of them. But he didn't know these men. They'd probably settled here after the war.

Farther on, the houses near the road disappeared. Philip continued walking, passing reddish-yellow pools, the choruses of frogs resounding in the air. He marched through denser and denser woods, the birds in the trees droning like a well-tuned orchestra.

He used to walk to the cinema through these same woods, in spite of the sinister howling of wolves. Strangely, his father hadn't forbid him to go to the cinema. It was only drawing that he'd hated. Whenever he'd seen something Philip had drawn, he'd gone wild, tearing it up and thrashing Philip good with a switch.

His father hated sketching and anything that reminded him of it from the depths of his soul. He would say: "You should eradicate bad things from a man while he's still young."

Andrija, Philip's older brother by four years, took this advice to heart. Whenever he caught Philip drawing, he'd tear up his sketch and beat him up. Then he would report it all to their satisfied father. He was his father's little soldier. Once Philip saw him literally saluting their drunken father as he reported having torn up two of Philip's sketches. Andrija had slapped him, that time.

Their father approved of all this; their mother didn't get involved. Andrija had even gone as far, once, as to undress Philip and toss him naked into a bed of nettles. Another time he'd walked on top of him, furious; Philip had begged him to stop, but his brother had just stepped on him harder, and added in a few kicks and punches.

Philip had tried to run into his mother's arms, once. But when Andrija came over to beat him, his mother said only, "Don't hit him on the head, just don't hit him on the head." Her breath stank of slivovitz. "Whoever deserves a beating should get it," she would say. She thought he wasn't sufficiently obedient to his father, who, to her mind, only wanted what was best for him.

With time, Philip stopped drawing. In art class, at school, his hand would tremble so that he couldn't make a straight line.

After he'd finished eighth grade, Philip's father called him in for a talk. He told him that he would go to school to be a precision engineer, to be someone who repairs televisions. That was the future. His father said that Andrija would repair cars and Philip would repair televisions. Philip simply shrugged his shoulders.

He ended up studying electrical engineering in Zagreb. He remembered how, on his first day in the big city, he saw a graffito on a wall: THEY WON'T GIVE ALEX A PIANO, it said. He averted his gaze quickly. He felt pressure in his chest for two days afterward.

Later he met his wife, and had children. Sketching and the desire to sketch had long since left him.

He arrived in the village after nightfall. Ten or so old houses, nestled in a valley between two mountains. Someone's dog started barking, followed by all the others, as Philip approached. He stopped in the middle of the village, beside a wild apple tree with forking branches. Lights were on in a few of the houses, but it was dark in his family's home. After a while the dogs stopped barking, as if they had finally realized he belonged there. He adjusted his rucksack and followed the winding trail down to the house.

There were junked cars scattered around the property. A white car was parked by the front door. Philip took off his rucksack, stood for a while motionless in front of the door, and then finally knocked.

No one answered. He knocked again.

"Who's there?"

"It's me."

"Who's me?"

"Your brother."

* * *

They sat in the kitchen, in a thin mesh of light. On a glowing burner on the stove hissed a battered tin pot, something inside of it simmering. There wasn't anything on the walls except a Catholic calendar, smeared with traces of dead houseflies. Andrija was telling Philip that his wife had left a month before. She had taken their two children and gone to her parents.

"Bitch," he said.

He repeated his sentences when he spoke, as if stressing their importance. The older he got, the more he reminded Philip of their father. Philip mainly listened, glancing around and nodding. Andrija crushed out a cigarette in the ashtray, then got up and went to stoke the stove. He dragged a low table with squat legs along with him, the same table their mother had sat on when she milked the cows. Now Andrija sat down on it, opened the metal door beneath the burners, and pushed in one more piece of wood. Some red-hot coals fell out, but he knocked them back in with his hand.

"Tomorrow there'll be vegetables and meat on the stove, so help yourself," he said. "I'll be gone all day. I have to go repair a truck."

"Bitch!" he hissed once more over the pot. Then he came back to the table, sat down, and passed his palm over the plastic tablecloth. He looked at Philip.

"The old man really loved you," he said, turning his eyes back to the stove and gazing at it for a long time. "He admitted that to me before he died. He said that he was afraid more than anything of you becoming an artist, and then turning into a faggot, like our uncle. He was really afraid of that. You can imagine how he felt when it came out that our uncle had been living with some other faggot in Belgium," he said, turning toward the wall. "What a shame that was for our family!"

Philip said nothing. He could barely remember Uncle Mile. All that came to mind were black-and-white photographs in which their father and uncle were mowing hay and smiling at one another tenderly. He knew that his uncle had studied to be a stonecutter: he'd made portraits, and various ornaments on gravestones. Later he'd gone abroad and never come back. Only rarely did they mention him at home, even when word came that he'd died of a stroke. He was buried somewhere in Belgium.

"And then, when you went to Canada," Andrija was saying, "Papa always boasted: 'I made a man of him! I made a man of him!' And he did, when you think about it." He got up and leaned with his palms on the table. "If there had only been someone to beat me like that, who knows what I could have been," he said, and looked away, lost in thought.

Then, little by little, Andrija began to talk about the war, in which he'd taken part from beginning to end. He said that he expected the police to burst in and take him away at any moment, because someone in the village had accused him of having thrown two old women into a well during the fighting in one of the neighboring Serbian villages.

"That tells you what kind of people live in this wretched village of ours," he said. "They live just to make your life hell..."

He fell silent, and started toward the stove. He grabbed the pot by its handles and moved it to the edge of the burner.

"And how long are you thinking of staying?" he asked, moving the pot a little more. "Did you have some reason, or did you come just because?"

Philip started to say something but stopped. He didn't want to start talking about selling the house—at least not yet.

"I'll be here for a while," he said.

Andrija looked at him curiously, then glanced at the clock and gave an audible yawn.

"Let's go to bed," he said. "I've got a lot of work to do tomorrow. I've got a lot of work to do tomorrow, and you must be very tired."

Philip got up, and Andrija patted him softly on the shoulder. "You know what?" he said. "I'm very proud of you." He began slowly twisting the various buttons on Philip's shirt. "You live in the West, you've had success. Papa would be very proud of you if he were alive. Papa would be very proud. Now be good and go to sleep. You've had a long trip, you must be very tired." Andrija paused. "If you happen to hear someone walking around up in the attic, don't be afraid, that's our old man stopping by. You know how he always liked rummaging around in the attic. I went to the priest, and he said it's normal, that it will stop with time, and there's no reason to be afraid. And besides, Papa always leaves peacefully." He ran his hand across Philip's back. "Good night," he said. "Tomorrow or someday soon we'll go to the cemetery."

Philip nodded and walked up the stairs.

He dropped his things in the little room that their deceased grandma had used. After she died, Philip had begun to sleep there. Before that he'd slept with Andrija on the couch in the kitchen, where Andrija still slept now.

Philip turned on the light. He put his rucksack into the dry, brittle closet, pressing down on it with his knee so that he could close the door. Then he opened the cobweb-covered window to ventilate the room a little. He sat down on the edge of the bed and lifted his head. His gaze passed slowly around the room. Everything was as it had been before. Sagging walls of indeterminate color, a woodstove, a tattered blanket on the bed, across which Philip ran his fingers nostalgically. He turned out the light, listened for a bit, and then slipped under the warm blanket, feeling the familiar indentation in the mattress, which had a bad spring.

In his dream Andrija told him to go to the cemetery. Philip got his shotgun and put in two shells for bears: one red and the other blue. He slung the gun over one shoulder and hoisted a pickax over the other. When he reached the cemetery he walked up to a fresh mound of earth, set the shotgun down, and started digging a grave with the pickax. After a while he struck something hard. A coffin. He deftly opened up the lid with the tip of the pickax.

His father was lying inside, wearing a white shirt with a starched collar that didn't suit him at all. He was smoking a cigarette and smiling.

How are you? his father asked.

Good, said Philip. *And you?*

A coffin is the best bed. Never makes you sore, Philip's father answered cheerfully.

Why did you beat me? Philip asked him quietly.

Because you turned out better than me, his father said, and laughed.

Philip's eyes rolled back in their sockets. Eyeless, he took the shotgun and pulled the triggers, firing both barrels at his father at the same time.

A light flashed.

Philip awoke, bathed in glistening sweat. He got up and sat on the chair for a while, with his head in his hands. Afterward he fell back asleep, and didn't wake until noon.

Later he slowly went down to the kitchen. Andrija wasn't there. Philip strolled around the house for a bit, and then went back into the kitchen.

He sat at the table and looked out the low window. He had no desire to take a walk through the village and talk with the neighbors. He had no desire to talk to Andrija. He had no appetite, and no desire to go to the cemetery. He didn't feel like doing anything.

He sat the whole afternoon by the table, leaning on the plastic tablecloth with his elbow. Now and then his elbow slipped, and once he almost banged his head on the table. At one point he thought it might be best to kill himself; nothing made any sense anymore.

A phrase repeated itself in his head: *Merciful bullet.*

He left the table and pulled open a drawer mechanically. Inside was a screwdriver, cellophane tape, stress tablets. His gaze stopped on a stone-cutter's pencil.

He looked for a long time at that pencil and its dull point. Then he took it in his hand, went to the dresser, and pulled out some brown, oily packing paper. He tore off a rectangular piece and went back to the table. He began turning the pencil in his hand, lost in thought.

He stood up, grabbed the paper, and went up to his room. Darkness fell. He turned on the light. He sat on the edge of the bed and looked through the window. Then he went into the hall, carefully lifting his feet from the floor as if he were walking on the rungs of a ladder, and grabbed a board from the attic. He brought it back to his bedroom and put it on his knees. His pulse quickened, and he felt the paper trembling.

He began to draw.

The moon hung outside the window like a giant white animal. The tip of the stonecutter's pencil stubbornly followed its long shadow. Philip's eyes gleamed as he drew, as though they were emitting moonlight themselves. He drew the Gypsy who'd been sitting on the horse's head, and the other Gypsy who picked at the horse's hoof. After he added the last few lines, he decided that he was never going back to Canada, not alive nor dead.

He went down to the kitchen and found some tape. Then he went back upstairs and taped the sketch onto the wall above his head.

In the morning Philip heard the noise of a car outside. Someone was revving the engine. He looked through the window.

Andrija was standing next to a yellow car and pulling on his work overalls. A man Philip didn't know was sitting in the driver's seat.

"Do you need anything from town?" Andrija called up when he spotted Philip at the window.

Philip waved and then said, "No, nothing."

"I won't be back till late. I'm going to repair something," Andrija said.

Philip nodded, watched the car drive away, then lifted his head and looked at his sketch.

Later, Philip walked around the village, glowing. He visited their neighbors. There were only ten or so of them, now. When he'd been a kid, there had been more than a hundred and fifty men and women in the village. They asked him when he'd gotten there, though they all knew exactly when he'd arrived. They asked about his wife and children, and about life in Canada. Philip smiled and nodded. He hadn't ever said much, so the neighbors weren't surprised.

He visited the old woman who lived on the very edge of the village last. Her eyes were watery and she was lying in bed, grinding coffee with a coffee mill on her chest. Her neck was lined with deep wrinkles, as if she'd had her throat cut a hundred times. He took the coffee mill and ground the coffee for her.

"Nobody comes here anymore," she said, getting up with difficulty. "Not even my sons. Such are the times. The only one who stops by is your brother. Sometimes he brings me something from the store, and asks about my health. God will repay him."

She went shuffling to the wall and kissed a wooden crucifix on it.

When he left the woman's house he went off into a fragrant field and lay down in the grass. Everything seemed wild, pure, and untouched, as if it were the first day of creation. His eyes followed a flock of birds until they disappeared into a part of the grainy sky. Then he went to the woods and strolled among the trees, touching their branches.

At a tree stump he thought of his wife and children. Every time they came into his mind he felt for a moment as if he were trapped in a hemp sack, with no air, and staggered. He couldn't think about them anymore. Instead he thought of his sketch, and felt great happiness.

He would work some job, start studying at the art academy, and begin a new life. They'll be better off without me, he thought.

When he returned to the house, he saw Andrija lying under a gray car. Only his legs were visible. There was another guy there as well, the same man he'd seen that morning. He had a flat face and he greeted Philip with a nod. Darkness was already gathering in the corners of the house.

Philip went into the house cheerfully, hurrying up the stairs to his room. He wanted to see his sketch as soon as possible, to enjoy it. As he skipped up the stairs, he thought about how this evening he would tell Andrija that they didn't need to divide the house or the property, that he would leave him everything. When he got into the room, though, he saw that the sketch wasn't there.

At first he thought it had fallen under the bed. He knelt down in a panic, but he couldn't find it there, either. He looked outside—perhaps the wind had carried it away—but he didn't see it on the ground by the window. He ran his hand along the wall where the sketch had been. There was nothing.

Outside Andrija was repairing the car by the light of a flashlight. Philip stood in the yard and watched the darkness settle over the house like an even layer of molasses. His brother opened the car's hood, stuck his head inside, and tinkered with something, increasing and decreasing the gas. Then he shut the hood and the man with the flat face paid him, got in the car, honked, and drove off.

Andrija snorted audibly as he left, counted the money, and put it in his pocket.

"Andrija?" said Philip.

Andrija looked at him.

"My sketch is gone."

"What sketch?" he asked.

* * *

The next day the two of them went out behind the house. Andrija cast glances around the field and led Philip to a hole in the ground.

"Here," he said. "It was a morning just like this one, and those dishes, the dishes that had been in the kitchen, were right here. Clean, clean as can be." He repeated this in a whisper as he paced back and forth. It was the same thing he'd said to Philip the night before.

"But I know, I know that I had, after my supper the previous evening, I had left them dirty. So the first thing I thought was, Maybe it was our dear departed father. Maybe he washed the dishes.

"And then, about ten days later, I was standing right over there," he said, pointing to the corner of the stable with his chin. "And I see that weasel stealing an egg from the stable and carrying it in its paws. It was walking on its hind legs, like a human. So now I think—maybe it went into the kitchen that evening, and licked those dishes and brought them back out here. But who knows? And who knows what else it took out of the house?" His last words were barely audible; he was staring down into the hole.

"See what I'm talking about?!" he exclaimed. He called Philip closer to the pit, crouched down, and reached inside.

He held up a piece of brown paper between his thumb and index finger, showing it to Philip in triumph.

"It's your sketch," he said, and then he knelt down, positioning himself a little better. Philip slowly knelt down as well. Andrija removed two rocks from the pile, laying one next to him and the other one next to Philip.

"We'll wait for it. We'll wait for it. Damn that thing. We'll wait ten years if we have to," Andrija said.

Philip was squatting down and staring into the hole. He put his fingers on the rock, feeling its little indentations and cracks under his fingers. The quiet was absolute, so quiet that Philip could hear that rock breathing beside him.

When Andrija bent over and peered into the hole for the umpteenth time, Philip grabbed his rock, raised it high over his head, and hit Andrija hard with it on the back of his skull. Andrija dropped down gently, his head covered in blood. It was as if he were still peering down into the hole, but now from a much more uncomfortable angle.

Philip hit him again for good measure. In the quiet of the morning all one could hear were the motions of his arm and the dull thuds of the rock when he connected.

At one moment, between two powerful swings of his arm, Philip thought he saw the weasel jump out of the hole in his brother's head. Before he could react, it grabbed his sketch from the ground and vanished back into the pit.

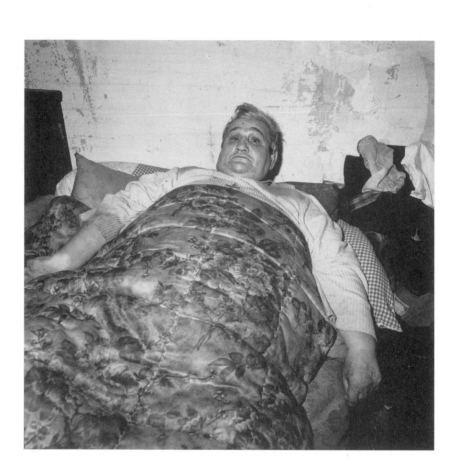

PRETTY HUNGER

by OLJA SAVIČEVIĆ

Translated by Stephen M. Dickey

As your bony fingers close around me...

Everything began on Monday. Usually Sunday is my water day, and I don't eat. But this week, here's what I ate on Sunday: half an apple, half a plate of noodles with no sauce, green salad with a whole lot of vinegar, and some yogurt. I ate all of this stuff because that bitch Carmen made me.

I can't wait till she leaves. She annoys the hell out of me—her and her purple nails, her pitiful looks, those swollen little feet in their high heels. And her obsession with food: always cooking, tinkering with her roux, splattering grease everywhere, chewing mouthful after mouthful of stuffed cabbage, of bacon, of goulash, of tripe. Every day she brings home those bags full of bloody meat—veal brains, pigs' ears, chickens' lungs.

She leaves fish eyes in the sink and a thick yellow skin on some cold milk in a saucepan. Father and her are like two hamsters, dozing all day long and then suddenly coming to life around the table. So much cheerful harmony and family spirit generated by the smashing of rabbits' backbones!

Such are the horrors of our meals together. Their quick, tiny mouths obliterating everything in front of them like little mechanical animals—first the soup, then the meatballs, the mashed potatoes, and the cabbage salad. Smacking, slurping, swallowing, belching, *scherzo, allegro*.

I wonder to myself what they were like as children, my father and his fatty sister, long ago when they still refused mashed carrots. When they were those willowy teenagers from our family photographs, who would sleep through breakfast and often skip dinner. I've seen those pictures, but I still can't imagine Carmen ever having been a child. I bet that even then she suppressed her nervousness with rose-hip jam, just as now she suppresses the idea of her wasted existence on the planet Earth with cooking and eating.

That mass of sebaceous glands and depressive gonads has always gotten on my nerves, but it has been much worse since she resorted to this strategy of phony understanding. Now I can't even tolerate her. There's no way anyone like her could understand the beauty of hunger: how it empowers me, how it makes me clean and fresh on the inside, how it allows me to be the creator of my own body. Its subtle controller. *Just make a wish!* my body says. I want to be as pretty as a moonbeam, I say. And I'm making this wish come true.

Eating serves no higher purpose. The conscious acceptance of hunger, on the other hand, does something wonderful: it promotes the gradual attainment of perfection. After a while you get used to the pain, and begin to see it as part of the beautiful, terrible sacrifice you are making. You begin to worship the hunger.

Hunger makes my body bearable. I'm 5'7" tall, and I'm proud to say that I've kept myself at 101 pounds for the past month. It's not like I want to get sick and die; right now I'm content with my 101 pounds. It's not really unhealthy to be "Ana," no matter what that fat cunt Carmen says. Some girls lose control, but there aren't very many of them.

Dad, of course, is on her side. I'm well aware that he asked her to come on my account. He thinks I need a mother. As if that doughnut could replace my mother—it's not like her gluttony is any healthier! She's getting more and more ugly, while I'm getting prettier all the time. I just hope I haven't gotten any of her genes. I can't believe she gave birth to a girl like Zvjezdana. My darling little blonde cousin Zvjezdana. She arrived yesterday, with her red suitcase full of white shirts and pleated skirts. If it weren't for her, I'd have found a way to get rid of her tiresome mother long ago.

So, to get back to the story: on Monday, I lost it. As I said, Sunday has been my water day for months. I'd love to be like water. Clear, cold, powerful, transparent.

My aunt knows I feel most tempted to eat on Mondays. So what did she do, that old crow? She left a plate of hot meat pie, half uncovered, steaming on the table! When I saw it my stomach turned, and then tears came to my eyes. I grabbed the plate and started for the trash can. I've become skilled at throwing food away. I have so much self-control that I can make smoothies for my father and Carmen, tossing in strawberries, oranges, and bananas—which I have a weakness for, even though they're full of sugar—and still not eat any of them myself. But that fucking meat pie smelled so damn delicious that I took it back out of the trash can, sat down on the tiles, and shoved it into my mouth.

Afterward I licked the greasy paper. I thought I would throw up, but I had sworn to myself that I would never become one of those pathetic "Mias" who eat too much and then vomit.

There were two of those girls in my high school. They make an effort, but they're still the lowest of the low. Vomiting is such a primitive way to gain control. I still respect them, though. After all, not everyone can be "Ana." A moonbeam. A stream of water. A silver thread.

My revenge for the meat pie was fearsome. I dumped salt into the soup. I turned up the dials on the oven until the roast burned. I put Tabasco sauce in the cake icing, toothpaste in the homemade mayonnaise.

I think Carmen got the message. She stopped looking at me like a loggerhead turtle looks at its poisoned young, and something new flashed in her eyes: rage. Dad shrugged his shoulders. I almost felt sorry for him. I must have made him feel like a loser, but what the hell, that's how you cure prejudice.

In any case, Aunt Carmen gave up trying to make me into a pert, ruddy little girl after that. I could feel that I was close to getting rid of her. But I didn't want her to leave before Zvjezdana came. She wouldn't visit us unless Carmen was still here. Zvjezdana lived in some rural backwater with the rest of their family, and Carmen had promised her a weekend in the city, or something like that. Then they would go back home together. I hadn't seen my cousin for almost two years.

Usually I don't like those country girls in their pleated skirts and white shirts or puff-sleeve tops. I just don't get it. Even dolls' clothes are more modern than that. But Zvjezdana was always dressed like she was about to be in some school performance. She was without a doubt the prettiest girl in her school. And now she was fourteen and as tall as me. She looked like she'd stepped out of a picture book or an old film. She looked like a sunbeam.

* * *

They put her up on a cot in my room. I'm proud of my room. I have posters of Calista Flockhart and Kate Moss, a lampshade that I made myself, and a window that looks out on the city marina. Sometimes the moon hangs right above a ship's mast, like some black-and-white lollipop.

Zvjezdana was tired from the trip. We talked about some guys that we'd hung out with the summer before; I hadn't seen them since then. I'm graduating next year, and I've already been out to clubs a few times— those guys didn't go to the clubs. They still kicked soccer balls around and ate big bologna sandwiches. I haven't spoken to them at all since one of them called me Skeletor.

Girls like me don't have problems with the guys in the clubs, but they're usually too high or drunk or ugly to go off with. There's a DJ I kind of like, though. He's got taste, he's cool. The club where he works is like a spaceship; it's fantastic there.

Zvjezdana said she's never been to a club. I told her we could go together tonight.

She fell asleep in the middle of our conversation, still dressed, on the cover of her cot. She looked so precious, not like other girls her age. I covered her with a blanket. Later, when I was in bed, I remembered that I'd forgotten to ask her how much she weighs.

Saturday. The day I go dancing. I'm taking Zvjezdana with me, but, God, I'll have to loan her some jeans—she can't go there in a pleated skirt, even if she is a sunbeam.

All morning I was really nice to her loggerhead turtle of a mother. She kept eyeing me suspiciously. She didn't know what I was up to.

The weather was clear, and I could taste salt in the air, feel the empty spaces in my body. Strong southern sunlight was coming into the kitchen, motes of dust swirling in circles. When the days are clear and cold, my pain is more pronounced, the empty spaces wider.

Zvjezdana was sitting next to me, drowsy and disheveled. She had slept all morning and smelled of apple shampoo. Carmen, whose motherly instincts I had completely fucked up in the last few days, vented her frustration and fed her only child: crepes, milk and cereal, homemade butter and bread—the only thing missing was a slice of ham, but that was probably on the way. The hot pastry disappeared, along with the fragrant hot cocoa, but Zvjezdana only picked at the rest of the food, probably just so she wouldn't insult her mother. I ate a nonfat yogurt and a piece of toast.

Zvjezdana wants to meet up with the guys we talked about yesterday. I'm not crazy about the idea, but I go with her. She's brought rollerblades, and I keep up on foot. She's in a good mood and babbles the whole way to the soccer field, skating around palm trees and along the very edge of the road. She's going to fall into the sea, I think. She's reciting lines from "Dream On," by Depeche Mode; I tell her I didn't know she was a fan of theirs. I didn't think people were into them anymore. She smiles and says she isn't, that she just likes that song and had no idea who sang it. I say the song is cool no matter what, and then we're already at the soccer field.

The guys have rollerblades, too, and she skates alongside them. She's adept at it. The best-looking guy, the one who called me Skeletor, takes her by the hands. I used to like how his bangs fell on his face when he smiled, but now I hate him. My emptiness is spreading. The sun is harsh, the air thin and dry. I leave to drink a glass of water and afterward I don't feel like going back.

* * *

That evening I'm angry. I don't want Zvjezdana to meet the DJ I like. I know she'd like him, too, because girls go crazy for him. I'm afraid she'll catch his eye and I won't.

I make something up about a headache so we don't have to go to the club. We sit for a while in front of the television, while Carmen mixes icing for a chocolate cake and makes more crepes. My cousin eats four with apricot jam. Dad eats two, because he's on a diet or something. I eat one and a half, and now I feel guilty. Today was complete shit. Meat pie and crepes in the same week? And a package of peanuts when I came back from the soccer field, because of my nerves?

So that my cousin won't see me cry I complain about my headache again and go to my room. I'll never be like Kate or Calista, I think. I'll never be a moonbeam.

Around three in the morning I'm woken up by pain in my empty spaces. That damned crepe is to blame, I think. It aroused my appetite. I feel terribly hungry. They say it helps to chew celery, but where could I get celery at this hour? So I do the next best thing and drink a glass of water. That usually helps, if you fall asleep fast enough afterward.

But I can't fall asleep. I can smell Zvjezdana's apple shampoo. Everyone likes her, I think. She looks like a ray of sunlight. I go back to the kitchen and am about to get some lemonade out of the fridge when I catch sight of that beautiful chocolate cake. It's smothered with a dark, finger-thick glaze of chocolate icing. I cut it into rectangular pieces, arrange them on a plate, and take them to my room. Zvjezdana is sleeping like an angel. Her bangs are covering her eyes, so I tuck them behind her ears. With my fingers I open her lips, slowly. I still haven't asked her how much she weighs.

I take the first piece of cake and start shoving it into her mouth. I do the same thing with a second piece. I do it quickly. After the second piece she wakes up and starts choking on the cake, suffocating. I grab her by the arms, firmly, as hard as I can, and with my free arm I grab pieces of cake from the plate and smear them all over her face. She kicks me away and I tumble down from the bed onto the floor.

"Mamaaa! Mamaaa!" she shouts. The loggerhead turtle flies into the room in her white nightgown, like a breathless ghost. She picks up her child as though she were a baby and flies back out of the room, cursing me.

From the hallway, I hear her shouting at my father.

"Your daughter, your daughter!" she yells.

"Look, Papa," I say to him as soon as he enters the room, "I'm eating cake." I'm shoving piece after piece into my mouth, tears and snot running down my face. I feel like I might choke.

The next day he will tear down all the posters of my idols for the third time that year. I will eat breakfast again, but he will take me to the doctor anyway. Carmen will shake her head and its three double chins, and Zvjezdana will only look at me sadly. My father will look tired and worried. But that night I still think I can convince him that everything is all right.

"Why did you do that?" he says.

"Papa, I ate all that cake, all of it…"

I don't want him to hug me. Nothing like that. He doesn't do it, either, not this time. He closes the door softly so that I know that this shame is mine and mine alone.

SALIVA

by ZORAN FERIĆ

Translated by Coral Petkovich

I

When she could no longer walk, they took my mother to the Vinograd Hospital, and I was given a serious duty: I had to deliver an ashtray and a large bouquet of flowers to an address on Mosa Pijade Street.

My father said: "When you get there, pay your respects and hand it all over from the doorway, you hear me? If you're offered anything, say you're in a hurry. You understand? Just make the delivery."

Flower deliveries were very expensive back then. I figured that this was why my father entrusted this job to me.

The night before I was supposed to make the delivery, I couldn't sleep. I had to do it in the morning, around ten, before I went to school, but that evening my father had said: "Don't take your schoolbag, understand? Make the delivery first. Then come home and get your bag and get ready for school. Do you understand? You'll have to leave early, but not too early, understand? It isn't polite to visit people too early, so plan on getting there around ten. You'll need ten minutes to get to Kvatrić, and then the tram to Drašković will take about five minutes, if it isn't crowded. From there you'll get the number fourteen and get out at Đuro Đaković's house. Then you'll have about a five-minute walk to Mosa Pijade. So you should leave at nine thirty at the latest. You understand?"

"Yes!" I said.

I did understand, but I couldn't sleep. I thought it would be obvious that I was my father's son, not the deliveryman, and it was unclear to me what would happen when they realized this. Best not to say anything, I thought. Greet them, hand over the flowers, and leave. But my father hadn't mentioned what I should do if they asked me anything. And how would I find the house? Did they have a dog? What if, let's say, they did have a dog, and the bell in front of the yard didn't work? Or, let's say, the bouquet gets smashed while I'm on the bus? The night was long, but there were enough questions to fill it up completely.

2

In the morning I boarded the number 11 at Kvatrić on time, and I caught the number 14 on time as well. It all went fine, except that in the crowded tram I was constantly tickling someone with the upper part of the bouquet, where anthuriums and prickly green asparagus peeped out of the white paper. I knew the flower because my mother had shown it to me before she'd gone to the hospital.

"You see this flower?" she'd said. "It's called *anthurium*, but it's also called *Adam*."

Then she looked at me knowingly. "Are you not going to ask me why?"
"Why, Mama?"
"Because of the little dick in the middle. Can you see it? That's where
the pistil and stamen are located."
I was embarrassed. Since becoming ill, my mother had changed; she
had become much more unrestrained, telling rude jokes and trying to
show me that which, until a few months ago, she had avoided by saying:
"You'll find that out when you grow up."
And now, all at once, I had grown up.
When I got out of the tram at the place where Đure Đaković used to
live and set off on the footpath next to the tumbledown villas, panic took
hold of me again. The people to whom I was delivering the flowers and
the ashtray, which was now wrapped up like a present, would realize that
something was wrong. They would think that my father, even though he
received high wages, could not pay for the delivery—that we were short
on money now that my mother was in the hospital.
And so what? I thought. Let them find out. What do I care? I had
never seen these people in my life before, and goodness knows I would
never see them again. Why should I be embarrassed? I looked carefully at
the addresses of the villas as I passed them. Their gardens were neglected,
their facades gray, their metal fences rusted. My father had written the
correct address on a piece of paper that morning and left it underneath my
breakfast plate. I kept walking.
My friends and I used to do all sorts of things to people we didn't know:
ring doorbells and then run away, write rude things on the windows of
cars. Lately we'd been spitting on the heads of passersby from the heights
of Davor Zebić's fifth-floor apartment in Maksimir. A neighbor shouted at
us, once, over the balcony—"Shame on you!" she said—but she never told
our parents. Maybe she liked the way we spat on people. Maybe the person
to whom I was bringing the flowers had been walking on Maksimir Street a

week ago, and maybe that very day, while we were skipping school, we had
spat on his head. I could see by the house numbers that I was getting close.

That's it, I thought. What do I care about strangers? And to punctu-
ate this thought, I spat on the asphalt. The phlegm burst on the ground,
an uneven star of foaming liquid. I stopped and turned around. There was
no one on the street. No one had seen me. I gazed at that fluid, which was
congealing in the dust, like a loathsome flower, and immediately I felt disgusted. I felt nauseous even though just a few seconds ago the spit had been
in my mouth. While it was inside me, I thought, it was called *saliva*; but
when it came out, it turned into *spit*. Why should something that had been
inside me, a part of my body, be so revolting when it came out?

I kept walking. I imagined spitting in my soup spoon at some restaurant,
filling it up with saliva. I'd watch the bubbles diminish, like small lives
extinguishing themselves, and then I'd sip it from the spoon like it was white
veal stew. The thought made my stomach turn. Was it possible, I thought,
for a person to become completely disgusted with his own physical self?

3

The house had a relatively new facade; it was the only one that did in that
row of nationalized villas, all built before the war. I stood in front of the
green fence, trying to collect myself. All the gardens were growing luxu-
riantly, and the leaves of the trees were turning red and brown. The house
itself was plain yellow and two stories tall. There was a flight of stone
steps leading up to a small enclosed porch. My mother would have called
it "Maria Teresa yellow."

I rang the bell, but nothing could be heard. For a few seconds my heart
was in my mouth, like my stomach had been just moments before. Surely
I wouldn't have to go alone into a strange yard. And then an old woman
with gray hair appeared on the porch.

She was dressed in a gray cloth skirt and a black polo-neck shirt, on which could be seen a string of false pearls. "What can I do for you?" she said sternly, as though I had interrupted something important.

"I have to deliver some flowers," I said.

"Well, open the door!"

It did not escape my notice that she had addressed me with the familiar "*ti.*"

The door buzzed open and I walked through the yard. When I got close to the woman, I saw that the pearls were almost the same color as her hair.

"Come in!" she said.

"I'm only delivering," I said, speaking the sentence that I had been turning around in my mouth all night.

"Never mind that. Come in!"

The porch was full of indoor plants: philodendrons, rubber plants, palms in wooden flowerpots. The woman walked into the house, and I followed her with the flowers and the ashtray wrapped in cellophane.

"Put on the slippers!" she said when I'd come inside, and placed a pair of unmatched slippers on the floor in front of me. I wanted to repeat that I could not stay, that I was only making a delivery, but she had already taken the bouquet and disappeared. For a moment I hesitated, but then I took off my shoes, put on the slippers, and went into a huge sitting room. Looking at the outside of the house, you would never have been able to imagine that such a big room could fit inside it. The furniture was old but well polished: a chest of drawers with a marble top—very similar to a piece of furniture in my grandmother's house on Medulic Street—a dark brown upright piano, a set of leather upholstered chairs, and a small round table on which sat a lovely porcelain bulldog.

"This is Biedermeier," my mother would have said, referring to the chest of drawers. "And the table is Secession, walnut."

The walls were full of pictures. I recognized a Stančić that one of my mother's friends also possessed, and that as a child I used to copy when we visited. I placed the ashtray on the table and sat down in the armchair. I could hear trams passing by outside, even though the windows were shut.

The old lady came back with the flowers in a vase. She put them on the table and then said:

"Would you like some juice?"

"All right."

She went out again and I heard her in the kitchen, running water. When she returned she was carrying a glass of raspberry juice on a small tray. She put it down in front of me, the glass making a clinking sound when it touched the porcelain.

"Be careful you don't spill it!"

My father would certainly be angry about all this. I should have just turned around and left, I thought.

The old woman was unwrapping the ashtray now. She untied the ribbon and put it aside; the cellophane she took off and crumpled into a ball. It was a cheap copper thing, with a picture of a boy urinating on the bottom, the towers of a cathedral behind him. I had known for a long time what *kitsch* meant, and was sure that this was a prime example.

There was a small white envelope taped to the ashtray. The woman took the envelope and left the room. She came back quickly, in twenty seconds. She didn't count it, I thought.

"Is the raspberry juice good?" she asked.

"Yes," I said, even though I hadn't tasted it. And then, so that everything would be finished more quickly, I gulped it all down. I almost choked. It was tasteless. Then we both looked at the ashtray for a while longer. The situation was becoming more and more uncomfortable. I am here for my mother, I thought.

At last the old woman said:

"It's best you take that home."

She handed me the ashtray. My face must have become very red, because the woman looked up and examined me closely for a moment.

"Give my regards to your father!" she said as I left, ashtray in hand. Somewhere near the bus station I threw it in a trash can.

4

That same day, in the evening, we were supposed to go to the hospital, but my father phoned: "I can't go today, I have a meeting. You go if you want to."

I caught the number 11 and set off for the hospital. I got off at the station in front of the barracks and walked down Vinograd Street. In my head I repeated what my father always said:

"See, my son, there, where there used to be vineyards, today they cure people from alcoholism." And then with a smile he would mention Doctor Hudolin. That was his way of making things easier.

"They're not curing Mama of alcoholism," I always wanted to say to him.

She was waiting for me lying down, with the usual question.

"Did you have lunch?"

"Leek and minced meat," I lied. When I'd returned home from the delivery there hadn't been time to eat anything before school. I noticed that there was now a triangle made of metal tubes hanging over my mother's bed. It hadn't been there the last time. I didn't know what it was for, but I didn't want to upset her with unnecessary questions.

"How was school?"

"We didn't write anything."

"Did you correct your history paper?"

"Yes, I did," I lied, but it was not an outrageous lie, because I had agreed with the professor that I would correct it the next day. Today or tomorrow, it's all the same.

My mother tried to get herself into a sitting position. She took hold of the triangle and slowly sat up.

"Fix my pillow for me."

Her voice was hoarse, and her hands shook from the effort. I placed the pillow so that she could sit properly, and then helped her lean back slowly.

"That's it, now I can see you better. Why didn't Tata come?"

"He has a meeting."

She was quiet for a little while.

"Look after him," she said. "It's not easy for him."

I asked myself why the three of us constantly lied to one another. My father pretended that nothing serious was happening; my mother pretended to forgive him for not coming to the hospital; and I tried hard to pretend that things were getting better. But one day I would tell my father that he was a coward, that he was not brave enough to face the truth—he who'd boasted of charging Batina Skela and breaching the Srijemski Front with the Russians, when only one out of every five men survived.

"That's exactly why he isn't brave," my mother would explain, if I'd told her what was troubling me. Instead she looked at me lovingly and asked again if I had a girlfriend.

"No, what would I want with a girlfriend?"

"You've turned fifteen. It's the time when certain needs appear."

I blushed, like I always did when my mother talked about stuff like this.

"That prostitute on our street, the one they call Pig Head…" she went on.

"What are you talking about, Mama?" I said through clenched teeth. My voice sounded more like squeaking than human speech.

"Soon she'll be trying to tempt all you young boys!"

"Mama, she's a repulsive old woman."

"Never mind that. All I want to say is that human desire is the most elastic thing that exists, you understand? Bodily pleasure can be wonderful, but it can also become something terribly revolting. And I won't be there to advise you."

"Stop, Mama!" I squealed. I couldn't admit to my mother that, for months already, I had been masturbating to the sight of that old prostitute and her fat bottom—the way she climbed up our street from the square, wearing a short skirt, carrying a shopping bag full of vegetables her clients had bought for her.

"But I want you to know," she said, her voice becoming stronger and more determined, "you're the one who decides whether what will happen is wonderful or revolting. Just don't do something you regret for the rest of your life."

"Mama!"

"All right, there you are. That's all I wanted to say." Her voice became weak again, as though she had finished a decisive battle. Her own personal Batina Skela. "I asked the doctor today and he promised to let me go home," she said. "I miss home so much—did you know that?"

"I know," I said.

"They said that the nurse will come to our house every day to give me painkillers and dress me. And Aunt Rada will help too—you and your father won't have to do anything." She paused. "Now go home so you have time to study for tomorrow."

5

But they didn't let my mother go home the next week. And on Thursday I once again set off for the house on Mosa Pijade Street.

This time there were neither flowers nor an ashtray to deliver, only an envelope. An ordinary white envelope, with a surname typed on the front. HUDOLIN. I got on the tram at Kvatrić on time, and caught the number 14 on time again, and arrived at the house even earlier than before. I won't go inside today, I thought. I'll just hand the envelope to the old lady from the doorway and leave. I won't put the slippers on. I won't drink any juice. I didn't want anything to do with them.

I rang the bell three times. Two brief rings and one long one. It seemed like the old woman came out onto the porch faster this time. She was wearing the same black blouse, with a white kitchen apron over it.

"Push the door," she said, but in a friendlier tone.

I climbed the steps. I greeted the old woman and offered her the envelope. She seemed embarrassed.

"We can't do this in the doorway," she said. "Come inside. I've baked cakes."

There was something commanding in her tone, and I gave in. The slippers were already waiting for me in the entryway, and the old woman was there beside me while I took off my shoes. On the round table in the sitting room was a crystal bowl full of vanilla crescents: biscuits dusted with powdered sugar. The woman disappeared again and came back carrying the tray with its glass of raspberry juice. The porcelain and glass clinked together, just like the last time. She put it down in front of me and sat in the armchair, looking at me with a smile.

"Please, help yourself. I made it for you."

I took a biscuit and put my hand under my mouth to stop crumbs from falling on the carpet.

"Jesus, I'm so forgetful," she said, and went again into the kitchen. She returned with an empty plate, which she set in front of me. She watched me while I ate.

"How's school?"

"Good," I said, my mouth full.

"Do you go to high school?"

"Up on the Salati," I said. Now my mouth was emptier, and I could answer her.

"What mark do you have for mathematics?"

I paused before answering. I had lied to my mother about this, but that didn't mean I had to lie to everyone. But why was this woman being so polite? What did she get out of it?

"One," I said, with a note of triumph in my voice.

"That's no good. Mathematics is the most important. Without mathematics you can't do anything."

"It's not the most important. I go to the language school. For us, languages are the most important."

I tried the raspberry juice. It seemed to me that there was more syrup mixed in with the water this time.

"Have another biscuit."

I took one. Why was she worried about my mark in mathematics? It had nothing to do with her.

"If you have any problems, you can come to me. I worked as a mathematics professor."

I raised my head and looked at her in astonishment.

"I'm retired now, but I still give instruction."

"I can manage by myself."

"That's what everyone says, and then all of a sudden you have too many ones, and it's too late. It would be better to start—"

"I can manage," I said, cutting her short.

She smiled. It was as though she hadn't noticed the impertinence in my answer.

"You wouldn't have to pay," she said finally, in a softer voice.

She's embarrassed, I thought, so she wants to redeem herself. She wants to redeem her horrible son, the doctor.

I calmly took one more biscuit and dispensed of it politely, holding the small plate under my chin. I washed it down with the rest of the juice. Then I said:

"Tata has sent this to you." I put the envelope on the table in front of me. I remembered how last time she had taken it into the other room without counting it. So, in front of her, I tore open the envelope.

"You don't have to do that," she said, with noticeable discomfort in her voice.

Out of the torn envelope I extracted a bundle of bank notes and began to count them, putting them on the table next to the tray. One, two, three... There were ten red hundred-dinar notes and five blue fifties. The old woman watched me counting, her face changing color, turning light purple.

"Tata told me to count it."

My father had not told me to do this, but I wasn't worried about my father, that coward. The face of the old lady looked as though it would burst. The whole time she was silent, watching me. Then, finally, she gasped.

"The money isn't for Rudy, if that's what you think." Her voice shook. "It's for the nurses who are looking after your mother in the hospital."

"So why am I bringing the money to you?" I wanted to ask. But I didn't.

6

On Friday evening, when I returned from school, my father and I sat down at the table to eat. He had warmed some goulash that Aunt Rada had made, and I had made a green salad. My father said that the goulash was good, and that it was very kind of Aunt Rada to make it for us, because otherwise we would be hungry. Only when we'd finished eating did I say:

"Are we going to the hospital today?"

My father cleaned the dishes and said nothing. He scraped the leftovers into the rubbish bin, and then he rinsed the plates in the sink.

"You go," he said, still occupied with the plates. "I brought some blue-prints home."

My father had not been to the hospital since my mother had gotten worse, about a month ago. He could not be persuaded to go.

"It's all right," I said. "They're going to let her come home soon anyway."

He stopped what he was doing and turned around, as though he hadn't heard me properly.

"Who told you that?"

"What do you mean who? Mama told me. She asked the doctors to let her go home and they told her she could, and that a field nurse would come twice a day to give her an injection against the pain and to help her change her clothes."

"This is the first I've heard of it."

"Well, it's the truth. She also said she wouldn't inconvenience us at all, that the nurse would do everything."

My old man buried the plates he had already washed under hot water, mumbling, and then tipped half a container of Vim over them.

That evening he ended up coming along after all. When we turned onto Vinograd Street, my father, strangely, did not mention the vineyards or Doctor Hudolin. It was after seven when we passed through the main entrance and turned left, toward the building where my mother lay. The sky was still light but darkness had fallen on the ground, and the weak hospital lights were lit. Even though it was not the time for visits, the ward let us in. The nurses were collecting plates from dinner, their trolley squeaking along the hallway. From some of the rooms we could hear music coming from the patients' radios. In the sitting room, the women who could walk had gathered to watch the news.

My mother was surprised when she saw my father.

"You came?" she said in a weak voice. My father sat beside the bed and seemed unsettled. He didn't know what to do with his hands.

"You need something to read," he said finally.

She just smiled; she hadn't been able to read for a long time.

My father turned to me. "Son, go and buy the newspaper down at the kiosk!" he said.

He took out his wallet and handed me five dinars. I took the money and left the room. I walked slowly; I was not in a hurry, now that my father was finally there with my mother. I went down to the kiosk, drank a can of Dvojni C, and stayed there for a time with the drunks who had escaped from the alcoholism ward. They were all annihilating little bottles of cognac. I knew my father wanted the newspaper so he could kill time while he sat beside my mother's bed; it was not my mother, who was unable to read, who needed it. So I took my time.

When I had bought the *Evening News* and was again in front of my mother's room, I could hear raised voices from within. They were arguing again. Through the door I could hear my mother's words, the ends of her sentences spoken in a deep tone, the same way she had sounded when she spoke to me about Pig Head.

"...because I want to kick the bucket at home!"

My old man was silent.

When we left the hospital I asked my father:

"Did they tell you when they would let her go?"

He frowned as he unlocked the door of the Škoda.

"They won't let her go."

"But she wants to come home!"

"And I want to fly to the moon," he said, and then added, "What would we do with her at home? We can't look after ourselves, much less her."

7

A few days after that conversation in front of the hospital, my father told me I would be going once again to Mosa Pijade Street.

"You don't have to eat cakes this time, or talk to the old woman, do you hear? Just give her the envelope and come home. They are not related to us in any way, and even if they were, fuck people like that who live on the backs of other people. You understand? Just give her the envelope and leave."

He had found out everything, I thought. Maybe it would be better to just leave the envelopes in the mailbox from now on, like any other letters. I thought seriously about this, but then it occurred to me that there was a lot of money at stake. Someone could follow me and steal it.

And so, that night, as I had done every night, I brooded over the whole thing. I hadn't known how to behave, last time, when the old lady was bursting with anger. How could I deliver the money without seeing her? And why, in the end, did I have to be polite to such people? Why put the money into an envelope and not count it out into their hands?

And then I suddenly realized what was going on. I remembered the conversation he'd had with my mother, the argument in the hospital. He was paying to keep her there until the end. The doctors would have let her go—it was her last wish, after all, and they always grant last wishes, even for murderers. My old man was paying them to keep her there. Hatred overwhelmed me. My hands curled into fists.

I squeezed them so hard that I broke the skin on my palms. That revolting old vomit-covered coward. It would be a pity to waste my saliva on him. I thought of his closely shaved double chin, the little soft cushions of his fingers. He disgusted me.

"I fell in love with his hands," my mother used to say.

Now those hands were lumps of fat, from which came pudgy sausages with nails.

8

In the morning, as usual, I found a small plate with a fresh roll on the table. Underneath the round porcelain with the worn gold rim was a white envelope. The name and surname had been typed on it with our electric Olympic typewriter. Again hatred took away my breath. I picked up the envelope and put it inside my jacket pocket.

"When you take money onto the tram," my father had said the night before, "you must put it away safely in an inside pocket. You understand? Trams are full of pickpockets. You can't tell who they are, and you won't feel anything when they put their hand into your pocket, nothing. They practice with dolls that have bells on them."

I did not touch the roll. My father's attempt to be considerate revolted me. He was always like that: he pretended to be good because it made things easier for him. Stinking, revolting coward. When I'd first delivered the money, I had thought that I was doing it so that those in the hospital would take better care of my mother and lessen her pain as much as they could. When I was there she pretended she felt fine, but I had seen how she clenched her teeth, how her whole body cramped. One time, to the nurse who was getting her injection ready, she'd mumbled something like, "Kill me, I beg you in the name of God." I'd heard her say it. At the age of fifteen I was brave enough to hear her say that. If I had not been brave enough, the words would have been unintelligible—my ears would have heard them but they would have been stopped before they reached my brain.

I arrived at the Kvatrić station. I didn't see the point in it anymore, but the tram arrived on time, so I got on. It would have been stupid not to do it. My mother's words followed me the whole way down Drašković Street, and continued with me toward the Đaković house: "Kill me, I beg you in the name of God!" The people who saw me in the last cab of the number 14 would have seen a thin fifteen-year-old with straight, fair hair murmuring nonsensical things to himself. They were not brave enough to hear what I was saying.

"Kill me, in the name of God!"

"Kill me, in the name of God!"

"Kill me, in the name of God!"

And then, when I got to the hospital, when I appeared at her bedside, she would ask:

"Did you do your homework?"

I could see it all, I could hear it all, not one detail escaped me, and meanwhile my old man ran away to his meetings, wandering around town aimlessly. Once I saw him at the West Station, and then again staggering down Vodnik Street, completely lost. He couldn't sit down beside his wife, take her hand, and say:

"It hurts me too, it hurts me..."

I got off the tram near the building where I had been accepted as a Young Pioneer and continued on toward the old woman's house. With each step, my hatred for my father grew. Instead of paying for care and help, my father was paying to keep my mother locked up until she died. When I got close to the house, I spat on the same place I had spat on the first time, gazing with disgust as the spittle bubbled on the tarmac.

"Dear Tata," I murmured, "I wouldn't even waste saliva on you."

A moment later I raised my hand to ring the bell, and then paused. To a bystander it may have looked like a greeting. But it was a decision. If my swine of a father was paying the doctor to keep my mother in the hospital, what would happen if the money never reached that other swine?

I had never in my whole life stolen anything from anyone. Especially my parents. When they sent me to the shop, I brought back the change to the last little coin. Even when my parents began to steal from shops themselves, I never joined them. I would have rather committed murder.

But now I turned from the door and ran across the street. I didn't care where I went—I just wanted to get far away from the old woman, from her slippers and raspberry juice. The money that was keeping my mother in the hospital was still in my inside pocket.

9

And so the money traveled farther away from the yellow house. It went across Nova Ves, began moving uphill, and then, unexpectedly, came back downhill, passing Medvedgrad, passing the shoe factory, and then hurried down Tkalčić Street. For a long time it went by ruined shacks smelling of cheap stewed vegetables and damp, and then, unexpectedly, it climbed up to Dolac by way of Skalinska Street, straight in front of Petrica Kerempuh and the bronze people dangling there.

I found myself at the marketplace. The decision, which had come to life in my legs, had now made its way to my head. If the money did not get to the doctor, there was a chance my mother's last wish would be fulfilled. Around the statue of the old peasant lady, vendors were selling autumn flowers, roses and gerberas. And chrysanthemums, too. I went down those few wooden steps and, all at once, it felt as if the crowded market was embracing me. There, on the ten or so wooden stairs leading down to the lower level of the marketplace, I decided not to go to school that day. A child whose mother is dying has the right to play truant. Before the enormity of death, school was a tiny marble—something that could be lost in the sand. And, in that way, I lost myself in the crowd.

Near the fish shop I saw Pig Head. Actually, first I saw her backside in a short red woolen skirt, her huge bottom bulging out of the stretchy knitted fabric. I looked at her fat, heavy calves, her black high heels covered in mud. She walked along, pointing at items in the stands. An old man with a hat, a peasant, walked behind her and bought whatever she ordered. I went after them, cautiously. We were like a strange little procession. Her outrageously fat bottom gave me an erection, but I was not embarrassed at all. A strange feeling of freedom had overcome me. Previously, when I'd met the gaze of Pig Head in the street, I would lower my eyes, blush, hide in a stranger's garden until she went past. Now I followed her bottom like a dog looking for a mate.

When they stopped at certain stands, Pig Head would put her hand on the fly of the old man and he would stop dead, as though he were trying to prolong the moment for as long as possible. Then she would quickly move her hand away and they would continue walking.

While my mother was still healthy, whenever Pig Head would pass her, she would comment quietly:

"Jesus, how repulsive she is!"

When I masturbated in the bathroom I would whisper: "She's repulsive! She's repulsive! She's repulsive!" and then I would become hard, just because of that word, *repulsive*. I'd promised myself that I would never go near her, even after my mother died.

But I could go down to the Vartek's alleyway, where the prostitutes stood, and watch them for a while.

10

All kinds of things are permitted a boy whose mother is dying. But I just wanted to look. I went down Bakačev Street in order to get to the alley next to Vartek's department store, so that no one who knew me could see me from Republic Square. When a man of a certain age went into that alley, everyone knew what he was looking for. Old, badly dressed prostitutes stood back there, tempting the soldiers that wandered by. Some of them wore very short skirts that showed fatty thighs full of veins. The alley smelled of urine.

Two women stood at the end of the alley, ten meters or so from me, while I pretended to look at men's suits in a shop window. I could feel my heart in my mouth, as though my Adam's apple had begun to beat. I stared at the shop window and did not dare to lift my gaze. But I also wanted to be able to see them better, so I could keep them in my memory as long as possible. I was looking at a male mannequin in a gray suit. The mannequin had a shirt and tie like a very proper person in a terribly improper place.

Soon I heard high heels tip-tapping toward me. I'll just look at her once, I thought. I'll look at her from top to bottom and then I'll leave. I'll fly away from this terrible place—even though my swine of a father deserved for me to spend all of his money there, so that not even one little yellow coin, small as the button on my pajamas, remained.

I turned around and looked. Fat legs in white high heels; a denim miniskirt that was too tight and betrayed the folds of fat on her legs; a light blue cotton blouse hiding huge breasts; a wide face. She looked like Pig Head. Her bright red lips moved:

"What do you want, boy?"

"Nothing," I answered. I was surprised I answered at all. And now I will turn around and leave, I thought. I had seen enough.

But then a second woman arrived. A thin Gypsy woman in jeans, with dark curly hair and a cigarette held in the corner of her mouth. She was squinting because of the smoke.

"He doesn't have any money, he's just looking," said the fat one to the Gypsy.

"They look and then they go home and jerk it," said the Gypsy, smiling.

I blushed, like I had when the old woman gave me back the ashtray.

"I do too have money," I said defiantly.

I'll show them, I thought, and then I'll turn around and leave. I took out the envelope and opened the edge of it with my finger, as I had in front of the old lady. I gave them some time to look at it, and then I put the envelope away and started to leave.

"Wait, where are you going?" shouted the fat one, and hurried after me. "I was just joking, you know. We should talk."

She stood in front of me and took my fly in her hand. My erection grew, and I was frozen. The fat one squeezed my balls and my stiff member.

"For two hundred you can get the lot. I do different positions, front and back."

I stood there quietly, concentrating, like the old peasant with the hat. I wanted nothing more in the world than for her touch to continue. I stared into her eyes: she was a little shorter than me and at least twenty years older. She smiled back at me.

"There, you see, that's better. There's nothing to be afraid of."

"And how long does it last?" I croaked. She was still holding me down there. She was afraid I would bail.

"Until you finish," she said gently.

I took out the envelope and gave her two red notes.

"Give me a little more for luck!"

I gave her a blue one too.

"You want it here or in the room?"

I turned around. People were passing quite close to us. Some had stopped and were looking down the alley.

"In the room," I said.

"That's a different price."

"Okay."

She was still caressing me down there with her left hand while, with her right hand, she put away the notes.

"Come with me. It's over there, on Vlaška."

She walked first, and I followed, ten meters behind her, looking around to make sure no one could see me. I thought about turning and running. That would be the best thing to do, I thought, but then I remembered my father saying:

"Always finish what you start. Do you hear me? Never leave a job unfinished. That's a sign of a weak character."

My father had the gall to talk about weak character.

In the next moment, finally, I decided to leave. And then, in the very next second, gazing at the buttocks in the worn denim skirt rolling on top of her short legs, I changed my mind again. I'll look at her a little longer and then I'll leave, I thought. It was as though she had tied an invisible cord to my member and was now leading me like a poodle.

We walked into the entryway of a run-down house on Old Vlaška Street. She climbed up a wooden staircase in the dark, and slowly I followed her.

"Be careful you don't fall," she said. "Someone stole the lightbulbs."

She led me out onto a wooden veranda on the first floor. On the right I could see a row of doors.

"Give me the money for the room."

I gave her one more blue note.

"Wait for me here," she said, and went through the last doorway. She was inside for some time, long enough for me to think she had tricked me, that she had disappeared and was now running along Palmotića Street. In a way it was a relief. I'll wait another few moments and if she doesn't appear, I'll go back downstairs, I thought. But then a boy, pimply-faced and a bit younger than me, came out of the room and stood near the wooden railing, staring into the yard. Behind the boy the fat woman appeared and motioned for me to come inside. I didn't know whether to acknowledge the boy or not. He had new jeans and torn slippers on his feet. In the end I slipped past him and went through the door.

The room was overcrowded: there was a cooking stove, a double bed, and a desk with books. The fat woman covered the window with a dark curtain.

"Do you need to wash?"

"I don't know."

She undid my belt, took down my underpants and trousers in one movement, bent over, and smelled between my legs.

"You're okay," she said.

Then she took off her skirt and panties, but left the blouse on. She spread her legs and widened her private parts with her fingers, as though airing it out. I could detect a smell. First I got rid of my jacket, then my underpants and trousers. I took off my shoes too, and when I made a movement to take off my sweater, she said:

"You don't have to take off anything up there."

So I still had on my sweater and my socks. My mother had bought me the sweater two years ago in a department store, and we had bought the socks together in Nami. She had looked for the socks with the least amount of synthetic material.

"Son, when you buy socks, make sure they're not synthetic, otherwise your skin isn't able to breathe. Do you understand?"

She was already sick when she told me that. We bought lots of socks that day.

The fat woman was lying with her legs spread out. She took out a condom, bit off the plastic cover, and put it on me. Then she pulled me on top of her and, with her hand, helped me enter her. The thing I had never imagined would happen that day was happening. I went up and down on her and thought of myself like a blacksmith's bellows, filling with air and then emptying. I supported myself with my palms and the tips of my toes, as though I were doing push-ups. I lasted a long time, and she became impatient. She gazed at my face, looking for a trace of something that showed no signs of happening. Finally she said:

"Hey, maybe you finished already?"

She made me pull out and then she looked suspiciously at the tip of the condom. She found nothing there, so she took the condom off, wiped my member with a towel, and then lay down again.

323

"Come on, I'll give you head."

I got on my knees and approached her. She flicked the tip of me with her tongue, and held my balls with her hands. When she pushed her finger into my anus, I began to come. She pulled me out of her mouth and spat everything out. The surge caught her on the cheek.

I left her the envelope with the rest of the money. I didn't know what to do with it. If I took it home again, my revenge would not be complete. I no longer felt revulsion toward my father, which had been choking me until half an hour ago. I let her wipe me with a damp handkerchief, got dressed in a hurry, and went out onto the veranda. I found the boy with the pimply face in the same pose in which I'd left him, staring blankly into the yard. The kid had retreated completely into his own mind and was living in there. I hurried out of the damp entryway, into the brilliant October sunlight, and tried to escape from that repulsive place, from those things that happen by instinct. That morning I found out how easily a person can disgust himself, just as though he were saliva against the wall of a house. I'm still running away from that, even though fourteen years have passed.

A HAPPIER ENDING

by BEKIM SEJRANOVIĆ

Translated by Ellen Elias-Bursać

I

I am sitting in an old hut on my grandfather's "ranch." Night bursts into the valley and splashes across the forest and the shrouded hills. I have been here for some time now, and there is no more turmoil in me. I feel like someone who once meant to write a story but wasn't able to, because the story took control. It was no longer clear what was real: the story or life. Nor whether life was writing the story, or the other way around.

The lightbulb on the ceiling flickers on and off. Above it, a mouse scampers around the attic without permission. One night I woke and saw its tail pop out from under the worn sofa on which I was sleeping. It disappeared into the hole in the wall above the curtain rod. The walls are full of holes, where the plaster has crumbled away.

The "ranch" is a small tract of land, just under two acres in size. My grandfather bought it when he retired, and planted a plum orchard here. Now he and Grandmama and my mother are all gone, and the orchard is overgrown, full of brambles and neglect. The land belongs to Aunt Zika, who has allowed me to stay here as long as I like.

The plums are rotting on the ground because no one harvested them. Summer is nearing its end. During the day the hornets buzz in battle formation and gorge on the juice of the overripe fruit. Birds of different sizes squawk while hopping around the gullies, pecking at the little plums, and at each other, too. Fat grasshoppers are joining the fray now, along with those unbearable tiny flies that buzz straight into your eyes.

2

For some time now I have been hearing voices. There are several. I recognize some of them, and know they belong to me—the others, I'm not so sure. They surface as if from the depths, speak once or twice, and then disappear forever.

One of the familiar-seeming voices goads me, saying it was not entirely convinced by my so-called attempt at drowning. The voice contends that I merely slipped awkwardly and splashed into the mucky shallows. It rails against me, saying I haven't got the balls to do something like that for real. And, reluctantly, I have to admit that the voice is right.

Two years ago I threw myself into the Sava. I can see myself as I stood, distracted, on the bank, a cigarette in hand. I was watching the river, the cawing crows all around me, my heart stabbing in my chest. I knew that one of my attacks was imminent. Panicking, I dropped the cigarette into the mud and went to stub it out with the sole of my tennis shoe. I watched my foot wiggle back and forth and saw the ground under it shifting.

The feel of the cold water brought me back to my senses. I swam in a frenzy toward the bank, about two feet away, before I realized that the water was only waist-deep.

3

When I clambered to my feet that October two years ago my nipples were poking at the damp cloth of my shirt. As I gasped I thought about my former wife and her breasts. They were only a little larger than mine, but their form was poetic and entirely different. Nipples sharp and hard like the tips of Prussian helmets from the First World War. If you bit into them your teeth would crack, your cheap amalgam fillings would fall out.

At the time I was trying not to think about her, to push her away like a bad memory. I told myself that I didn't love her anymore.

—The question is, did you ever love her? piped a voice from some dark corner of my mind.

—No, the question is, can he ever love anyone? rasped the hoarse voice of a psychiatrist from another corner.

—Love yourself, love only yourself, only yourself! croaked a new, unfamiliar voice.

—Love yourself least, interjected the psychiatrist.

The voices began pursuing me when she left. I held on for a few more months in Oslo, working at the university, and then, at the end of the winter semester, I packed up my backpack, took all my money out of my bank account, and fled to Brazil. I wandered for a time without much purpose, then settled down a few months later on the little island of Tinharé, in the north of the country. There I fell in love with a girl who was like a twin to my former wife.

She had the same arched brow, the same impudent eyes, the same full lips, the same lithe body and skinny, nearly nonexistent fanny. The only difference was that she was black. We were in love for more than two months, and the voices inside me stilled. I began to imagine that I would stay on the island forever. I could see a throng of my dark-skinned children chasing each other around on the sandy beaches. And then one day she told me she had to move on. She admitted that her husband was in jail, and that her three children were waiting for her in a little town in Mato Grosso, with her mother. Then she asked me for money. I gave her all I had and went back to Oslo.

The university had fired me because I had taken off for more than half a year without notifying anyone. Perhaps that could have been smoothed over—Professor Pettersen, my mentor, liked me. But there was no point: I knew I would be off again at the first chance I got, as soon as I'd saved enough money.

I managed to stay on in Oslo until the fall, working every day. When there were translations to do, I translated, and when there weren't, I worked in construction. In the fall I was overcome again by the itch to travel, and so I left once more, first for Croatia and then for Bosnia. I thought about what it would be like to throw myself into the Sava and be gone, but it wasn't that easy.

4

I wake with a jolt before dawn, completely soaked in sweat. At first I cannot think where I am; my heart pounds in my chest. The vestiges of a dream are still dancing around the hut. I jump quickly to my feet and pull apart the curtains to draw reality into the room. Light, pale as death, sifts through the window, too wan to chase away the terror.

The dream: I am an evil spirit. Three good spirits are pursuing me. We hurtle, cometlike, around a vast building that reminds me of my elementary school, the National Hero Zaim Mušanović school. They hunt me the way unflagging hunters pursue their prey. While we fly furiously down long corridors, up and down sets of stairs, through familiar classrooms, they tell me what awaits me when they catch me, and I hurl every curse I can think of back at them. One of them chases me lightning-fast toward a closed window; I spin around abruptly, stepping out of its way; it crashes into the window. I push the window open, shove the good spirit out, and slam it closed. Then I zing like a bullet through the school auditorium, where we used to maintain an honor guard by Tito's portrait. The two other good spirits writhe after me in pain and rage. I realize with horror that the waking world is nothing but a dark chimney in which I find momentary respite from pursuit.

I usually have these dreams when I stop smoking hashish. I've smoked for some ten years, every day, with the occasional break. I've stopped sometimes because I couldn't get any, or sometimes to clear my thinking. Then the dreams come back.

5

After the fall into the Sava, two years ago, something akin to hope, a feeble and phantomlike flame, began to burn within me. Two weeks later I flew back to Oslo. On the plane I tried not to look at the faces of the people around me, or listen to their voices. I wasn't interested in their dismal stories of how they'd spent their vacations, how much they'd paid for rooms, how many grilled squid they had eaten in a wine cellar on Hvar. I ordered a beer, opened it, and clumsily spilled half of the contents on the pants of the young Norwegian man sitting next to me, who was speaking somewhat ecstatically to his girlfriend. She was skinny in an unhealthy way, with fake breasts and small red pimples on her face. The young man looked at me first in shock, then in anger. He started to brush the foam from his pants, swearing loudly in his north-Norwegian dialect. I said nothing, and watched him the way a person watches a nit that will ingest a

half liter of his blood as it grows to be a louse. I sipped a little beer, popped
a Valium, and turned to look in the other direction.

Before I sank into the bliss of unconsciousness, I thought about how
it would be best if the plane were to crash while I was asleep. Somewhere
in the Alps, if possible.

6

Whenever I was in Norway, everything got on my nerves: Norwegian
music and musicians, literature and writers, newspaper headlines, television news, the language and all its dialects, the mountains and the fjords,
the endless, dark Nordic winters, the endless summer days, the king, the
queen, the people on the street, the obnoxious, precocious little boys and
stuck-up little girls, the frustrated women with pumped-up buttocks and
pushed-up tits, the self-conscious, natty young men, the soccer and the
politics and the history and the laws.

Meanwhile, everything having to do with the Balkans seemed so right:
the people were genuine, warm, defiant; they didn't have that sheeplike
Norwegian obedience; they were not constrained by a spider's web of reg-
ulations. Negligence, carelessness, and chaos ruled the day—that fertile
clutter that, with all its bad sides, is closer to human nature than a cold,
metallic, perfectly organized social structure. Chaos is life, I'd muse in
one of my rented rooms in the eastern part of Oslo, listening to Balkan,
Oriental, or African music and reading books written in my language. I'd
light joint after joint and conclude: to rein in chaos means to step toward
the void.

There was truth in all this bullshit of mine, but no one was forcing
me to stay in Norway. I could have gone back to the Balkans. And it isn't
as if I didn't try. But when I returned to Croatia, or to Bosnia, Serbia,
Montenegro, or Macedonia, after the first weeks, filled with wild parties

and encounters with friends, everything would assume a different form. I would wake up one morning in Rijeka, or in Split, or Zagreb, or Sarajevo, or Mostar, or Tuzla, or Belgrade, or Novi Sad, usually hungover and exhausted, my consciousness narrowed by one drug or another, and all of a sudden everything would flip. I'd be swamped by a mixture of disgust and panic, a feeling of utter failure. After two weeks of that I'd retreat into isolation, listening to Norwegian music and reading books in Norwegian, and if I did drink, I'd start blathering on about the beauty of the Norwegian countryside, about their refined culture, their sophisticated democracy, and other such nonsense.

7

I woke before the plane landed at Gardermoen airport, some fifty kilometers from Oslo. A wave of fear washed over me. That is how it has always been: the fear has been with me forever.

I remember getting off the plane, numbed by the Valium, and walking toward passport control with a yawn. The policeman greeted me kindly, examined my red Norwegian passport, and asked where I was coming from. I answered him in slow motion, through my nose. He stamped a blank page and said: —Welcome home! I glanced at him in wonder.

At customs there was a police officer standing on either side of the passageway, one of them accompanied by a dog of indeterminate breed. As I approached, the animal grew visibly agitated, wagging its tail and jumping toward me. The policewoman, on the right, asked if I might come with her into a room down the hall. I went without a word.

Inside, she asked whether I knew why they had stopped me. I said that I did.

—Do you know what kind of dog that was?

—I do.

—Do you know why it selected you?

—Maybe because I recently had weed in this backpack, I answered, yawning.

She seemed overjoyed. She repeated my sentence, word for word, and then started poking around in the little backpack that I had carried as hand luggage. She asked if I had anything like that on me now.

I looked at her and said nothing. She asked again, and I asked her if I really looked that stupid.

—You smoke hashish, too? she asked, and briefly stopped digging through the toiletries.

—I smoke, I answered, feeling a fleeting but gratifying glee at being so cool. I knew this was from the Valium I took on the plane, but I didn't care. The policewoman asked when I last smoked.

—At the airport in Split.

Another police officer took me to the next room. He kindly requested that I take off my clothes. I undressed without a shred of embarrassment and, for a moment, thought about breaking into dance.

While he searched my jacket, pants, socks, and shoes, he inquired politely about where I had been traveling, what I was doing, and my profession. I stripped off my underwear and handed it to him. I told him I didn't feel like talking; he should just do his job and I'd do mine.

—Okay? I added.

—Okay, he answered.

He examined my mouth, my armpits. In the end, all that was left for him to do was stick a finger up my rectum. But I could tell that, at the last moment, he decided against it.

Better that way, I thought maliciously. Even I wouldn't look there.

8

The door opened with a harsh electronic beep. I stepped across the green line on the floor and entered Norway. A crowd of people was waiting for someone they knew to come out. A young woman walked by me and a young man with a bouquet of flowers strode toward her; she ran into his arms, but instead of kissing they just stood there embracing for a long time, while he whispered into her ear. I stood with one of my backpacks on my back and the other in my left hand and peered around, pretending to look for the person waiting for me. A short man with a mustache held up a slip of paper with the name HELENA written on it. In the other hand he held a little Norwegian flag.

I walked slowly, expecting something, a surge of emotion, memory, someone calling my name, grabbing me by the shoulder... Nothing. Even the voices in my head had stilled. My feet felt soft, as if the black marble floor was transforming into the Sava mud. I started turning, by then completely lost, like a catfish in a trap. From somewhere in my spinal cord, I heard a voice speaking with scorn about the years I'd already wasted in Norway. An elderly couple passed by, peering into my pupils. And then my knees finally buckled.

Someone splashed cold water onto my face. I came around slowly. Above me, several heads nodded knowingly, happy to have witnessed something out of the ordinary, to finally have experienced something beyond everyday life. I reached for the hand that was splashing me: it belonged to a middle-aged saleswoman from the kiosk in front of which I'd collapsed. There was a small sign pinned on her left breast that said CATHRINE. Cathrine was a blonde. She had a haircut like Ljupka Dimitrovska and was chattering on, anxiously, in south-Norwegian dialect. At first I thought she was talking to me, but then she leaned over, thrust her breasts down in front of my nose, and slapped my cheeks, and I realized she was talking to herself. I moved her hand away, but the only thing I managed to say was:

—Sugar, give me sugar...

She brought me a soda. I sipped a little of the sweet, bubbly drink, and then I got up. The people around me began to disperse. The show was over.

9

I boarded a train for the city, got off at Oslo Cental Station, left the station building, and stopped. It was evening, neon lights were going on and off, trams were trundling and chiming, traffic lights were changing from red to yellow to green, people were stopping and going on command. To the left of the station building was the Plata, a spacious green park where the druggies hung out. They rambled in clusters, organized their merchandise, exchanged profanities and the information that mattered to them, mooched money aggressively from passersby, and squabbled with the police who would chase them away from time to time.

I descended into the gloom of the metro and caught a train to the eastern part of Oslo, to the Tøyen stop.

From there I went up the slope at the Hagegate. Three young Somali women passed by. One was wearing a headscarf and a veil over her face; the other two were in skintight jeans, jabbing at the sidewalk with their high heels. They were giggling and gesturing broadly in the air. At Tøyen square, two unnaturally thin young men sat on a bench. One man's head had dropped to his chest; the other was staring at something he was holding in his half-open fist. The first lifted his head for a moment, cursed, then dropped his head again.

Up a side street, on the doorbell of number 52, I found my friend Egil's last name. JOHANSEN. I buzzed, and a voice answered. I gave my name, and the door opened. Egil stood in the open doorway on the third floor and greeted me warmly. There was none of the hugging or kissing that we have in the Balkans.

Egil didn't talk much—he didn't show emotion in a noisy way. When he wore a hat, he looked like Clint Eastwood. He was ten years younger than me; I had taught him South Slavic literature at the University in Oslo a few years back. That was how we'd become friends. We'd light up a joint together or have a beer after class sometimes. I introduced him to Gypsy music. Now he was studying Arabic and working as a DJ.

One of the rooms in the four-bedroom apartment would be available within a week, he told me; if I wanted, I could move in. Until then I could sleep in the living room, on the sofa. Aside from Egil, there were two other men living there, counting the one who was moving out.

I agreed to take the room, and then we had nothing left to talk about. After a few minutes of silence Egil said he was going to go into his room to study, and I went off to take a shower.

10

I made my bed on the sofa in front of the television set. Egil and the two other roommates went in and out of the bathroom, and then withdrew to their rooms. Tomorrow was another workday—they had to get a full night's rest. I lay on the sofa, covered myself with a sleeping bag, and thought about what I was going to do in Norway. Find a job, work from 8 to 4, smoke hashish in my room from 5 to midnight, get drunk on the weekends, try to get laid, be hungover Sundays, watch porno films or lie in front of the TV, wait for Monday, wait for Tuesday, wait for Wednesday, wait, wait, wait... Or fall in love with a woman, spend the weekends with her, go on excursions, give her little presents, make love in strange places, cheat on her, wait for her to cheat on me, break up and then console her, wipe away her tears, drag out the relationship until one of us found someone else or she got pregnant. I thought of this and almost laughed because, of course, it made me think of my ex-wife. Sometimes I wasn't sure if she was real or if she had just been a demon sent to torment my soul.

After thoughts like these I couldn't fall asleep. I had no hashish and I went through a minor crisis until I found a Valium. Then I swallowed it and turned toward the armrest.

Five days passed. I would get up after Egil and the roommates, shower, shave, and get dressed as if I were on my way out. Then I'd sit on the sofa by the window and look at the street.

Nothing changed outside. The same gray sky, the same wet street, the same intersection, the same hurried silhouettes that strode with big steps toward their destinations. At some point, a little after noon, I would go to the store, buy a newspaper, bread, and a can of mackerel in tomato sauce. Then I'd come home, read the headlines, and chew the fish. In one can of mackerel in tomato sauce is everything a person needs for a day.

When the roommates came home, around five in the afternoon, they would greet me in passing and then go off to make dinner in the kitchen. I'd wait for them to prepare their meals and then I'd go out so that I didn't bother them while they were dining. They ate in the living room, watching television. Egil invited me to join them sometimes, but I'd always thank him politely and decline. On the sixth day of my stay in the apartment, on Saturday, the departing roommate moved out, and I moved in.

II

I brought in my two backpacks and dropped them into the corner. The room was spacious, with a bed, a desk, two chairs, and a wardrobe. The windows looked out on the same street the living room did. I stood and looked at the white walls, which had acquired a dirty yellow sheen. Here and there you could see little holes or torn scraps of wallpaper. I went to the bed and sat down. I thought, well, now something has begun to move.

Now you have your own room and you can furnish it any way you like. You can sit on the bed all day long and watch the street. You no longer need to move out of the way when they come home to have dinner. You needn't go out anymore and climb up to the roof of that building with the sweeping view of Oslo.

From that other building's roof you could see a mosque that had been built several years earlier. In the eastern part of the city there are many immigrants from Muslim countries. The mosque had been built from stone they'd brought all the way from the Middle East. It had two slender minarets, but the Norwegian government didn't allow them to broadcast the call to prayer.

I got up off the bed and went over to my backpacks. I pulled the big backpack over to the wardrobe and began to unpack my clothes and arrange them on the shelves. When I was done, I pulled out my laptop and several books and notebooks from my little backpack and put them on the desk. I turned on the computer, ran a short porno film, and masturbated. After I came, I sat on the bed and stared out the window at the street.

Three months later I moved back to Croatia to start a new cycle. A new story that might have a happier ending.

REBECCA CURTIS is the author of *Twenty Grand and Other Tales of Love and Money*. Her fiction and essays have appeared in the *New Yorker*, *Harper's*, *Harper's Bazaar*, *n+1*, and elsewhere.

BORIS CVJETANOVIĆ is a Croatian photographer and sculptor. Since 1981, there have been more than sixty solo exhibitions of his photography; he has also participated in group exhibitions in Croatia, Japan, and the United States. His photos are in the collections of the Tokyo Metropolitan Museum of Photography, Zagreb's Museum of Contemporary Art and Croatian History Museum, and the Gallery of Fine Arts in Split, as well as in many other venues.

STEPHEN M. DICKEY is an associate professor in the Department of Slavic Languages and Literatures at the University of Kansas. He has translated Bosnian, Croatian, Serbian, and German for the Hague's International Criminal Tribunal for the former Yugoslavia, and has also translated prose and poetry by Meša Selimović, Borislav Pekić, Damir Šodan, and Miljenko Jergović.

ELLEN ELIAS-BURSAĆ has been translating novels and nonfiction by Bosnian, Croatian, and Serbian writers since the 1980s, including work by David Albahari, Neda Miranda Blažević, Slavenka

Drakulić, Daša Drndić, Antun Šoljan, Dubravka Ugrešić, and Karim Zaimović. She received ALTA's National Translation Award for her translation of Albahari's novel *Götz and Meyer* in 2006, and was a fellow at the Banff International Literary Translation Centre in 2011. Along with Ronelle Alexander, she cowrote an award-winning textbook on the study of Bosnian, Croatian, and Serbian.

ZORAN FERIĆ was born in 1961 in Zagreb. His work has received numerous prizes, including the Ksaver Šandor Gjalski Prize in 2000 and the Jutarnji List Award in 2001 and again in 2011. Ferić is the author of three collections of short stories and three novels. His books have been translated into English, German, Slovenian, Polish, Italian, and Hungarian. He lives in Zagreb, where he teaches Croatian literature at a high school.

RACHEL B. GLASER is the author of *Pee on Water*, *MOODS*, and the forthcoming *Paulina & Fran*. She teaches fiction at Flying Object in Hadley, Massachusetts.

GEORGI GOSPODINOV is a Bulgarian poet, writer, and playwright. His book *Natural Novel* has been published in twenty-three languages, and his new novel, *Physics of Sorrow*, is finalist for four international prizes. It will be published in the U.S. by Open Letter Books in April 2015.

DAVID GUMBINER was last seen on the streets of São Paulo, learning every national anthem from roving packs of boisterous men.

KATHERINE HEINY's first book, *Single, Carefree, Mellow*, will be published by Knopf next spring. She lives with her husband and sons in Washington, DC.

From 1971 to 2002, **CELIA HAWKES-WORTH** taught Serbian and Croatian language and literature at the University of London's School of Slavonic and East European Studies. Since retiring, she has worked as a freelance translator. She began translating fiction in the 1960s, and has published some thirty titles to date.

DAMIR KARAKAŠ's first book was a collection of travel writing called *Bosnians Are Good Folks*. That collection was followed by his first novel, *Kombetars*, and a short-story collection, *Kino Lika*. More recently, he has published the novels *How I Entered Europe* and *Perfect Place for Misery*, as well as the short-story collections *Eskimos* and *Colonel Beethoven*. In 2008, a movie based upon *Kino Lika* received numerous awards in Croatia and abroad. Karakaš also writes for the theater; his plays have been performed in Croatia, Serbia, Germany, and Chile. He currently lives in Zagreb.

DAN KEANE served as the AP's last gringo correspondent in Bolivia, publishing stories in the *New York Times*, the *Washington Post*, and many other newspapers. He received an MFA from the University of Michigan. His writing has appeared in *Harper's*, *Zoetrope*, and the *Austin Chronicle*. He lives in Shanghai.

ETGAR KERET is the author of six best-selling story collections, and his writing has been published in *Harper's*, the *New York Times*, the *Paris Review*, and *Zoetrope*. *Jellyfish*, his first movie, which he codirected with his wife, Shira Geffen, won the Camera d'Or prize for best first feature at Cannes in 2007. In 2010, he was named a Chevalier of France's Order of Arts and Letters.

KELLY LINK is the author of the collections *Get in Trouble*, *Stranger Things Happen*, *Magic for Beginners*, and *Pretty Monsters*. She and Gavin J. Grant have coedited a number of anthologies, including multiple volumes of *The Year's Best Fantasy and Horror* and, for young adults, *Monstrous Affections*. She is the co-founder of Small Beer Press. Her short stories have been published in *The Magazine of Fantasy and Science Fiction*, *The Best American Short Stories*, and *Prize Stories: The O. Henry Awards*. She has received a grant from the National Endowment for the Arts. Link was born in Miami, Florida, and currently lives with her husband and daughter in Northampton, Massachusetts.

VALERIA LUISELLI was born in Mexico City and grew up in South Africa. She is the author of the novel *Faces in the Crowd* and the book of essays *Sidewalks*, which have been translated into more than ten languages. Her nonfiction pieces have appeared in the *New York Times*, *Granta*, and *Letras Libres*, and she has worked as a ballet librettist for the New York City Ballet. Her most recent novel, *The Story of My Teeth*, is forthcoming in the U.S. from Coffee House Press. She lives in New York City.

CHRISTINA MacSWEENEY's translations of Valeria Luiselli's *Faces in the Crowd* and *Sidewalks* have been published by Granta and Coffee House Press, respectively. In 2013, her translation of *The Invention of Distance*, a collection of essays by the Paraguayan art critic Ticio Escobar, was published in a bilingual edition by the AICA/Fausto.

JOHN McMANUS is the author of four books of fiction: *Stop Breakin Down*, *Born on a Train*, *Bitter Milk*, and his latest story collection, *Fox Tooth Heart*, forthcoming from Sarabande Books in 2015. He has received a Whiting Writers' Award, a Creative Capital Literature grant, and a Fulbright Scholar grant. His work has appeared in *Ploughshares*, *Tin House*, *American Short Fiction*, the *Oxford American*, the *Literary Review*, and the *Harvard Review*, among other journals and anthologies. He grew up

in Blount County, Tennessee, studied at the James A. Michener Center for Writers at the University of Texas, and lives in Cape Town, South Africa.

JOSIP NOVAKOVICH emigrated from Croatia at the age of twenty and currently lives in Canada. His work has been translated into a dozen languages, and he has won a Whiting Writer's Award and an American Book Award. Last year, he was a finalist for the Man Booker International Prize. He has published ten books in total, the most recent of which is *Shopping for a Better Country*.

GORDAN NUHANOVIĆ grew up in the small town of Vinkovci, Croatia. He currently lives in Zagreb, where he works on Croatian television as a literary critic and editor. He is the author of two short-story collections, three novels, and a collection of travel stories. The winner of multiple national literary awards, Nuhanović has worked as a war reporter and a journalist; his most recent book, *The Jokes Were Left at Home*, chronicles his travels around former Soviet republics. Nuhanović was the lead vocalist in the punk band Short Circuit and founded the Young Croatians Iggy Pop Preservation Group. He continues to serve as the group's honorary president.

TÉA OBREHT is the author of *The Tiger's Wife*. "One, Maybe Two Minutes from Fire" first appeared in the anthology *Tales of Two Cities: The Best and Worst of Times in Today's New York.*

KEATON PATTI is a writer and comedian living in New York City. You may remember him from the previous sentence.

After studying English at the University of Western Australia, **CORAL PETKOVICH** married a Croatian man and lived in the former Yugoslavia for more than twenty years. She has translated a book of poetry by Selvedin Avdić called *Seven Terrors*, as well as a collection of short stories. She is the author of the nonfiction book *Ivan, Adriatic to Pacific*, as well as of several short stories.

ISMET PRCIC is the author of *Shards*, which won the Sue Kaufman Prize for First Fiction and the Los Angeles Times Art Seidenbaum Award for a first novel. In 2014, his feature film *Imperial Dreams*, cowritten with Malik Vitthal, won the Best of Next audience award at the Sundance Film Festival.

ANGELA RODEL earned a B.A. from Yale University and an M.A. from UCLA, both in linguistics. She has translated the work of several authors from Bulgaria, and her translation of Georgi Gospodinov's *Physics of Sorrow* won an NEA grant. Her English translation of Gospodinov's play *The*

Apocalypse Comes at 6 p.m. premiered in the U.S. at Baltimore's Single Carrot Theatre in 2014.

GARY RUDOREN is the coauthor of *Comedy by the Numbers*. He is also the writer of lots of funny words in several plays, including "So, I Killed A Few People," "God In A Box," "A Huge Horrible Failure," and "The Idiotic Death Of Two Fools." He is an architect and the father of twins, so if he falls asleep while talking to you, you'll know why.

OLJA SAVIČEVIĆ is a Croatian poet, writer, and journalist. She was born in Split, Croatia, and won a prize for her first published story as a twelve-year-old girl. Her first collection of poetry was published shortly thereafter, when she was fourteen. Since then, Olja has published several poetry collections: *It Will Be Tremendous When I Grow Up*, *Eternal Kids*, *Female Manuscript*, *Puzzlerojc*, *House Rules*, and *Mamasafari*. She has also published the short-story collection *To Make a Dog Laugh* and a novel, *Adios, Cowboy*, the American edition of which is forthcoming from McSweeney's in May 2015.

BEKIM SEJRANOVIĆ received his master's degree in South Slavic literature from the University of Oslo, where, from 2001 to 2006, he worked as a lecturer. Since 2006, he has published three novels and a short-story collection. He is currently at work on a new novel about life along the river Sava. Sejranović has also translated numerous Norwegian authors into Croatian.

SONDRA SILVERSTON is a native New Yorker who has lived in Israel since 1970. Among her published translations are works by Amos Oz, Etgar Keret, Eshkol Nevo, Savyon Liebrecht, and Aharon Megged.

JULIA SLAVIN wrote *The Woman Who Cut Off Her Leg at the Maidstone Club and Other Stories* and the novel *Carnivore Diet*. She is the winner of a Rona Jaffe Foundation Writers' Award, *GQ*'s Frederick Exley Fiction Competition, and a Pushcart Prize. She is completing *Squatters*, a collection of short stories.

SONNY SMITH is a songwriter and occasional writer of short stories, comics, and plays. He also puts out records as Sonny and the Sunsets.

MATT SUMELL is a graduate of UC Irvine's MFA program. His fiction has appeared in *Esquire*, the *Paris Review*, *Electric Literature*, *One Story*, *NOON*, and elsewhere. He lives in Los Angeles, California.

MIRIAM TOEWS is the author of six novels: *Summer of My Amazing Luck*, *A Boy of Good Breeding*, *A Complicated Kindness* (winner of the 2004 Governor General's Literary Award for Fiction), *The Flying Troutmans* (winner of the Rogers Writers'

Trust Fiction Prize), *Irma Voth*, and *All My Puny Sorrows*. She has also written one work of nonfiction, *Swing Low: A Life*. She lives in Toronto.

TEA TULIĆ was born in Rijeka in 1978. In 2011, she published the fragmentary novel *Kosa posvuda (Hair Everywhere)*. The novel was shortlisted for the Jutarnji List Award and also recognized by the Croatian Ministry of Culture as one of the best prose books of 2011. She was Belgrade's first scholar-in-residence in 2012, and is a member of RiLit, an informal group of Rijeka writers that promotes Rijeka's literary scene.

PAULA WHYMAN's stories have appeared in *Ploughshares*, the *Virginia Quarterly Review*, the *Hudson Review*, and the *Gettysburg Review*, among other places. She has been a resident at the MacDowell Colony and Yaddo, and she was a 2014 Tennessee Williams Scholar in Fiction at the Sewanee Writers' Conference. In 2014, she received a Pushcart Prize Special Mention. "St. E's" is part of a novel-in-stories.

COLIN WINNETTE's latest book is *Coyote* (winner of Les Figues Press's NOS Book Contest). His next novel, *Haints Stay: A Western*, will be released by Two Dollar Radio in 2015. He is an associate editor of *PANK*, and links to everything he has done or is doing can be found at colinwinnette.net.

IN CASE OF EMERGENCY
by Courtney Moreno

"In Case of Emergency is a dark love song, dark as a bruise, for the LA no one seems to see, but it's also a careening, haunted, and hilarious ride." —Susan Straight

What do you do when you can't function? After rookie EMT Piper Gallagher responds to a call outside a Los Angeles shopping mall for a man who can only tell her, "I can't function," the question begins to haunt her. How will Piper continue to function despite the horror she sees in South Central, and despite her own fractured past? And how will the woman Piper loves continue to function as she experiences the aftershocks of her time spent serving in Iraq? Piper's experiences as a rookie break her down and open her up as her genuine urge to help patients confronts the daily realities of life in the back of an ambulance and in a hospital's hallways. This vivid and visceral debut is a rich study in trauma—its causes and effects, its methods and disguises, its power and its pull.

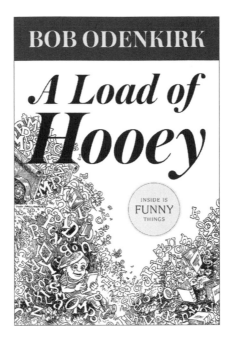

A LOAD OF HOOEY
by Bob Odenkirk

"Whip-smart and laugh-out-loud funny." —Publishers Weekly

Bob Odenkirk has won Emmys and acclaim for his work on *Saturday Night Live*, *Mr. Show with Bob and David*, and many other seminal TV shows. This book, his first, is a spleen-bruisingly funny omnibus that ranges from absurdist monologues ("Martin Luther King Jr.'s Worst Speech Ever") to intentionally bad theater ("Hitler Dinner Party: A Play"); from avant-garde fiction ("Obituary for the Creator of Mad Libs") to free-verse poetry that's funnier and more powerful than the work of Calvin Trillin, Jewel, and Robert Louis Stevenson combined.

Odenkirk's debut resembles nothing so much as a hilarious new sketch comedy show that's exclusively available as a streaming video for your mind. As Odenkirk himself writes in "The Second Coming of Jesus and Lazarus," it is a book "to be read aloud to yourself in the voice of Bob Newhart."

ALL MY PUNY SORROWS
by Miriam Toews

"{A} masterful, original investigation into love, loss and survival." —Kirkus (*starred review*)

Elf and Yoli are sisters. While on the surface Elfrieda's is an enviable life (she's a world-renowned pianist, glamorous, wealthy, and happily married) and Yolandi's a mess (she's divorced and broke, with two teenagers growing up too quickly), they are fiercely close—raised in a Mennonite household and sharing the hardship of Elf's desire to end her own life. After Elf's latest attempt, Yoli must quickly determine how to keep her family from falling apart, how to keep her own heart from breaking, and what it means to love someone who wants to die.

All My Puny Sorrows is the latest novel from Miriam Toews, one of Canada's bestselling and most beloved authors not only because her work is rich with deep human feeling and compassion, but because her observations are knife-sharp and her books wickedly funny. *All My Puny Sorrows* is Toews at her finest: a story that is as much comedy as it is tragedy, a goodbye grin from the friend who taught you how to live.

INFORMATION DOESN'T
WANT TO BE FREE

by Cory Doctorow

"Doctorow throws off cool ideas the way champagne generates bubbles... {he} definitely has the goods."
—San Francisco Chronicle

In sharply argued, fast-moving chapters, bestselling author Cory Doctorow's *Information Doesn't Want to Be Free* takes on the state of copyright and creative success in the digital age.

Information Doesn't Want to Be Free is a book about the pitfalls, and the opportunities, creative industries (and individuals) are confronting today—about how the old models have failed or found new footing, and about what might soon replace them. An essential read for anyone with a stake in the future of the arts, *Information Doesn't Want to Be Free* offers a vivid guide to the ways creativity and the Internet interact today, and to what might be coming next.

READ HARDER

edited by Ed Park and Heidi Julavits

"Nineteen essays, often funny and sometimes poignant, from the journalists, essayists, and novelists long admired by the editors at McSweeney's Believer magazine." —Kirkus

This volume collects the finest essays from the second half of the *Believer*'s decade-long (and counting) run. The *Believer*, five-time nominee for the National Magazine Award, is beloved for tackling everything from pop culture to ancient literature with the same sagacity and wit, and this collection cements that reputation with pieces as wildly diverse as the magazine itself. Featured articles include Nick Hornby on his first job, Rebecca Taylor on her time acting in no-budget horror movies, and Brian T. Edwards on Western pop culture's influence on Iran. *Read Harder* collects some of the finest nonfiction published in America today, from the profound to the absurd, the crushing to the uplifting. As the *Believer* enters its second decade, *Read Harder* serves as both an essential primer for one of the finest, strangest magazines in the country, and an indispensable stand-alone volume.

ALSO AVAILABLE FROM McSWEENEY'S

store.mcsweeneys.net

~

FICTION

POETRY

COLLINS LIBRARY

~

ALL THIS AND MORE

store.mcsweeneys.net

NEXT ISSUE

COVER STORIES

*An entire issue of contemporary authors covering classic stories,
lavishly packaged in a 12" × 12" record case.*

EMILY RABOTEAU *covers* ALICE MUNRO

ANTHONY MARRA *covers* EDGAR ALLAN POE

JESS WALTER *covers* JAMES JOYCE

CHRISTINE SMALLWOOD *covers* FLANNERY O'CONNOR

ROXANE GAY *covers* MARGARET ATWOOD

MEG WOLITZER *covers* J.D. SALINGER

T.C. BOYLE *covers* ITALO CALVINO

CHRIS ABANI *covers* ANTON CHEKHOV

NAMWALI SERPELL *covers* SAMUEL BECKETT

ALICE SOLA KIM *covers* RAY BRADBURY

TOM DRURY *covers* CHARLOTTE PERKINS GILMAN

KIESE LAYMON *covers* ERNEST HEMINGWAY

MEGAN MAYHEW BERGMAN *covers* SHIRLEY JACKSON

LAUREN GROFF *covers* GRACE PALEY

FORTY-Eight